Affirming the Comprehensive Ideal

Affirming the Comprehensive Ideal

Edited by

Richard Pring and Geoffrey Walford

 The Falmer Press

(A member of the Taylor & Francis Group)
London • Washington, D.C.

UK   The Falmer Press, 1 Gunpowder Square, London, EC4A 3DE
USA   The Falmer Press, Taylor & Francis Inc., 1900 Frost Road, Suite 101,
        Bristol, PA 19007

First published in 1997

**A catalogue record for this book is available from the British
Library**

**Library of Congress Cataloging-in-Publication Data are
available on request**

ISBN 0 7507 0619 8 cased
ISBN 0 7507 0620 1 paper

Jacket design by Caroline Archer

Typeset in 10/12 pt Times by
Graphicraft Typesetters Ltd., Hong Kong

*Printed in Great Britain by Biddles Ltd., Guildford and King's Lynn on
paper which has a specified pH value on final paper manufacture of not
less than 7.5 and is therefore 'acid free'.*

*Every effort has been made to contact copyright holders for their
permission to reprint material in this book. The publishers would be
grateful to hear from any copyright holder who is not here
acknowledged and will undertake to rectify any errors or omissions in
future editions of this book.*

Contents

Contents

Preface

The book arises out of a series of fourteen lectures given in 1996 at the University of Oxford, Department of Educational Studies. They arose from a meeting in 1995 between Peter Cornall, formerly Chief Inspector for Cornwall LEA and a headteacher of two comprehensive schools (West Bridgford, Nottinghamshire, and Carisbrooke, Isle of Wight), and Richard Pring, Director of the Oxford University Department. Concern was expressed that, in the politically charged attack which currently prevailed upon the school system attended by 85 per cent of secondary school students, the ideals of that system, its considerable achievements, and the daily success of many teachers were neglected — indeed, denied to the public. It was important, once again, first, to make public the moral and educational ideals which inspired the creation of a system of comprehensive schooling, and, second, in the light of experience, research and criticism, to show how those ideals might be reflected in the organization and practice of schools and colleges in the future.

The lectures, and this book, are an attempt to do that. We hope that the book will be seen for what it is — the basis of serious discussion of the development of education in the future within a system which embodies the ideals of those who saw comprehensive schooling to be the only moral and educational response to the economic, social and personal needs of our society.

In effect fifteen lectures were given, the final one held at Ruskin College, by the Right Honourable John Prescott MP. In all, a total audience of over 1000 people attended the lectures. They were made possible by the generous sponsorship of Basil Blackwell publishers, the Standing Conference for Studies in Education, and the Centre for the Study of Comprehensive Schools, of which Peter Cornall is a Trustee. Thanks are due to the generosity of these sponsors without whom the series would have been impossible.

Particular thanks are due to the Centre for the Study of Comprehensive Schools (CSCS), a charitable trust based at the University of Leicester. Since 1980 it has provided a nationwide focus for the identification and promotion of good practice in comprehensive education and has a current membership of 2000 schools, or half of all the secondary schools in the country. In its work with schools, local education authorities, government departments, industry, further and higher education, and training and enterprise councils, the Centre enjoys significant sponsorship from major industry and the active support of a number of university schools of education. The Centre was a natural partner for the Oxford University Department of Educational Studies in the promotion of the series of lectures.

The Steering Committee for the lectures consisted of, from CSCS, Peter Cornall, Tony Cobb, (Director of CSCS and formerly head of Harwich School, Essex), and

Maggie Pringle, (Associate Director of CSCS and formerly head of Holland Park Comprehensive School), and, from the Oxford University Department of Educational Studies, Geoffrey Walford and Richard Pring. Closely associated with the series too was Fred Jarvis, formerly General Secretary of the National Union of Teachers. Vicki Lloyd managed so very efficiently the organization.

We wish to thank all these for making the series (and, we hope, the subsequent publication) so successful. We are particularly grateful to John Prescott for completing the series and for agreeing to contribute an 'Afterword' to the book. As he says in his final sentence,

> A first class education for all is not just a political slogan. It is a crusade and a crusade which must be won.

That is the comprehensive ideal which the lectures, and the book, reaffirmed. They also indicated how the ideal might be pursued in the future.

Introduction

Geoffrey Walford and Richard Pring

Comprehensive secondary schooling is a political issue — it has always been so. Just over thirty years ago a Labour government published its highly controversial *Circular 10/65*. This Circular formally declared that government's opposition to selection at 11+ and requested all local education authorities to reorganize their secondary schools on comprehensive lines. The Circular was withdrawn in 1970 when the Conservatives returned to power, but the policy was effectively reinstated in 1974 on the return of Labour. However, throughout the entire period — no matter who was in power — the proportion of children attending comprehensive schools rapidly increased. In 1971 only about 40 per cent of children in UK local education authority maintained secondary schools were in comprehensives; by 1981 this had risen to about 90 per cent.

Recent controversies about selection in secondary schooling show that many politicians and educationists have forgotten the reasons why comprehensive schools largely replaced selective systems of schooling during the 1970s and 1980s. As with most major social changes, this movement towards comprehensive education was the result of pressures from an uneasy alliance of groups and individuals with a range of ideologies, interests and visions for the future (Ball, 1984; Benn and Simon, 1972). They responded to a diversity of evidence about the workings of the tripartite system.

The 1944 Education Act introduced 'secondary education for all' which, in most places, meant that a system of grammar, secondary modern and (sometimes) technical schools was established. By the mid-1950s there were many obvious problems. For example, it became clear that there was a considerable social class bias between the intakes to the three types of school in the tripartite system (Floud *et al.*, 1956; Douglas, 1964). The grammar schools were dominated by middle class children, while the secondary modern schools were largely the preserve of the working class. The problem was largely seen to be the IQ tests that were generally used to select children, and arguments centred on the fairness of these tests for children from different backgrounds, the extent to which they were able to discriminate between children according to their abilities or their academic potential, and on the examinations having to be taken at an age when children were still developing at different rates (Yates and Pidgeon, 1957). It was also found that the reliability of the tests was low and that children could be coached into obtaining higher scores in these examinations, even though they were supposed to measure some 'innate' abilities (Ford, 1969). Even accepting a narrow definition of efficiency of selection based on what the IQ tests could measure, it was estimated that about 10 per cent of children were wrongly selected each year — half of these being wrongly selected for grammar schools and half wrongly going to secondary modern schools (Vernon, 1957). By 1970, IQ tests were largely discredited as a means of selection, but most of the problems associated with them also occur in other ways of selecting. As is argued in chapter 4 of this volume, the variety of other selection methods that are creeping into British schooling are likely to be *more* rather than less biased. Headteachers' or teachers' reports, interviews of parents and children, or special selection tests are all likely to be even *less* reliable than IQ tests — as well as favouring children from particular social and economic backgrounds.

But 'accurate' selection was only part of the problem. In the late 1960s a variety of sociological studies of grammar and secondary modern schools also began to raise questions about the desirability of selection at 11 independently of the degree to which selection could be accurately achieved. The classic case studies of grammar and secondary modern schools by Lacey (1970) and Hargreaves (1967) showed the detrimental effects of selection and differentiation between and within schools. Those children at the bottom of a grammar school tended to think of themselves as failures and developed anti-school attitude. Other studies highlighted the cultural conflict experienced by a working class child in a grammar school. Where working class children did manage to enter grammar schools the cultural expectations were in stark contrast to their own (Jackson and Marsden, 1962; Dale and Griffith, 1965).

A further important factor that led to comprehensive schools was an increased demand for a 'grammar school-type' education. This was partly due to rising expectations on the part of parents, but demographic trends also had their effect. The postwar 'bulge' entered secondary education at a time when only a few new grammar schools had been created. As the percentage of children being selected varied markedly between local education authorities, in many areas, middle class parents were finding that their children were not being admitted to the grammar schools which they had themselves attended (Ford, 1969). Instead, their children were being forced to attend secondary moderns which they perceived (often correctly) were funded at a lower level, had poorer paid and poorer qualified teachers, and were only able to enter children for a limited range of public examinations. This individual concern about sons and daughters was largely transmuted to a call for greater educational equality of educational opportunity for all and greater national efficiency. It was believed that both of these would be provided through comprehensive education. This parental demand for a high quality education is certainly no lower now than is was in the 1960s and 1970s. Grammar schools for 20 per cent, or even 40 or 60 per cent would not satisfy the demand. And what would the schools for those not selected be like?

But comprehensive schools also developed because there were many who believed that educating all local children in a single school, where they would have equal physical facilities and equal access to high quality teachers, would raise the aspirations of all children and teachers, bring about greater equity within the schools and lead to greater opportunities outside in the world of work. It was hoped that mixing children from different social class backgrounds in the same school would lead to a lowering of barriers between classes and a reduction in class antagonism and class differences. This reason for comprehensive schools is far stronger now than it has ever been. But it challenges the dominant principle on which the British system of schooling has been historically based, and to which the Conservative government wishes to return — selection of children for unequal provision. Throughout British history, social class and gender have been the major determinants of the quality of schooling that children received. While there has been some decrease in gender inequalities, we now live in a multicultural society that is increasingly harshly divided by class and ethnicity. Social mixing gives at least some possibility for mutual understanding and greater equity.

A group of commentators on the political Right has long argued that social mixing was achieved at the expense of academic success (Cox and Dyson, 1973; Cox and Boyson, 1975 and 1977). They have claimed that a selective system of grammar, technical and secondary modern schools is better able to meet the needs of a diverse range of children than a comprehensive system. They claim that comparisons between comprehensive systems and selective systems show that selection produces better overall examination results, and that the 'comprehensive experiment' has been a great mistake that should be rectified.

At first sight it would seem to be a relatively simple exercise to compare the academic results of children in local educational authorities which retain selective systems with those which only have comprehensive schools. As has been shown elsewhere (Walford, 1994), in practice, any such comparisons are frustrated by innumerable difficulties, and all the studies that have been conducted have serious shortcomings.

Three very different studies which attempted to compare examination performance of children were published in 1983. One compared the public examination results of local education authorities with selective and comprehensive systems (Marks *et al.*, 1983), the second examined the performances of members of a national sample of children born in one week in March 1958 (Steedman, 1983), and the third analyzed questionnaire responses from a Scottish national sample of school leavers (Gray *et al.*, 1983). Each drew upon data which had not been collected with this comparison in mind, which meant that each had significant omissions. While some of these problems are accepted by the various authors and their findings have appropriate caveats, there ensued a considerable academic debate (Heath, 1984), and vitriolic political controversy (Cox and Marks, 1988; Steedman, 1987).

Of necessity, all three studies looked at examination performance in a diverse and changing national system, so none compared like with like. There are difficulties of definition of type of school, of limitations in the data available, and in methods of taking account of social factors. In all cases the comprehensives were less well established than the selective schools, and the presence of the private sector further confounded any comparisons, as the introduction of comprehensive schools in particular areas encouraged a distinct group of parents to opt for the private sector (Fox, 1985; Johnson, 1987). The group using the maintained sector thus differed according to whether the LEA system was selective or not.

The first study by Marks *et al.* (1983) claimed that 'substantially higher "O" level, CSE and "A" level examination results are to be expected in a fully selective system than in a fully comprehensive system'. The second (by Steedman) found no clear overall advantage or disadvantage to selective or comprehensive schooling, and the third (by Gray *et al.*, 1983) suggested that

> comprehensive education had a levelling effect on attainment, raising fewer pupils to the highest levels of attainment, but helping more of them to progress beyond the minimum. It appears to have raised average attainment.

In all three cases, once background factors had been taken into account, the overall differences were small.

Some more recent studies have attempted to add to these three. Two of the authors of the first report (Marks and Pomian-Srzednicki, 1985) again used local education examination results from a slightly better sample and largely substantiated the earlier results. Some account was taken of the criticisms of the earlier study, but this second study still has major difficulties (Fogelman, 1984; Clifford and Heath, 1984). In particular, it still used data relating to the whole local education authority rather than examining individual schools — as have some other similar studies using DES statistics (DES, 1984; Gray *et al.*, 1984; Gray, 1990). Follow-up research to the Scottish study has also been published (McPherson and Willms, 1987), and here the data sources and analysis are of a higher quality. The authors show that once the comprehensives in Scotland had become established, they contributed to a rise in examination attainment and to a decrease in social class differences in attainment. By looking at national representative samples of pupils who left school in 1976, 1980 and 1984, the authors also demonstrate that the decreasing gap in attainment between middle class and working class children was due to small but significant levelling-up of working class attainment and not levelling-down of middle class attainment.

The need to take account of the time taken for schools to become established is also indicated in a study of a South Wales community by David Reynolds and Michael Sullivan (1987). The area partially reorganized secondary education in the mid-1970s such that a third of pupils remained in a selective system or grammar and secondary modern schools, while the majority went to new comprehensives. This study found that high ability children were catered for nearly as well in both systems, but that these comprehensives were failing the middle and lower ability children academically and socially. The authors argued that the comprehensives were failing some pupils because they had not become established comprehensives and had not adjusted to their new clientele. They described a range of internal organizational aspects (such as poor management, lack of pupil involvement and inadequate pastoral care provision) which made these schools less effective. Compared with these factors, whether the system was selective or not was unimportant.

Since the time of these studies there has been increasingly sophisticated research on how 'value-added' can and ought to be measured, but the number of selective school systems has declined to a level where further meaningful comparisons between systems are impossible. While there are still those on the political Right who still advocate a return to selective schooling (for example, Marks, 1991), the limited evidence on which they draw is now highly dated and, as has just been shown, the group of studies is unsatisfactory in various ways and gives partially contradictory results.

The most reasonable conclusion to be drawn from these early studies is that any differences between the overall examination effectiveness of the two systems were small but, once comprehensives had become established, they appeared to slightly reduce social-class differences in attainment. A return to selection on measured ability or aptitude at 11 would initiate a further long period of instability and would probably reduce overall attainment. More significantly, all of the studies found that there were far larger differences between the examination successes of different schools of the same type than between the average examination results of different systems, even after such factors as social class had been taken into account. The most important finding from these studies is that individual schools differed greatly in their effectiveness.

But, in spite of the evidence generally in favour of comprehensives, during the early 1980s there were several attempts by Conservative controlled local education authorities to try to reintroduce selection by academic ability. All these attempts failed. In Solihull and Richmond-upon-Thames, for example, local parents campaigned against the proposed changes and won their demands for the retention of existing comprehensive schools.

The all-out frontal attack on comprehensives did not work, so a more gradual approach was adopted. Since the election of Margaret Thatcher's first government in 1979 a series of separate, yet interlinked, policies has been introduced to support and encourage the selection of particular children for unequally funded schools. First came the Assisted Places Scheme of 1980 where poor but 'academically able' children were to be 'plucked like embers from the ashes' of the state system to enter private schools of high academic reputation. In practice, those families sufficiently knowledgeable about the procedures, and able to negotiate the choice and selection processes inherent in the scheme have been rewarded with more costly staffing and facilities than in the state sector. Further support for selection occurred in 1986, when central government announced that it intended to establish a network of twenty city technology colleges. These were intended to provide free technology-enhanced education to selected children within particular inner city areas. Selection of specific children for inequitable provision was a central feature of the plan. In this case selection was not to be on academic criteria, but on 'deservingness'. The 1988 Education Reform Act introduced further anti-comprehensive ideas. At first comprehensive grant-maintained schools were not officially allowed to select children by ability, but many demanded a high degree of commitment from parents and children, a separate application, an 'informative' interview and sometimes a test. They found that, if the barriers to entry were set high enough, self-selection can operate as an effective way of ensuring that 'deserving' families are selected.

There were several aspects of the 1993 Education Act that re-emphasized the government's attack on comprehensive education. The most important change was that all secondary schools were given the right to 'specialize' in one or more curriculum areas and select on the basis of particular aptitudes or abilities in music, drama, sport, art, technology or foreign languages. What is crucial is that the introduction of a 'specialism' did not necessitate an official 'change of character' as long as only up to 10 per cent of the intake were selected according to criteria related to the specialism. The results of such a changes were not unexpected. The recent and impressive research by Gewirtz, Ball and Bowe (1995) indicates that, where curriculum specialisms are being introduced by schools, they are acting as selection mechanisms for high academic ability and middle class children. In particular, the development of specialisms such as dance or music indirectly discriminates against working class children, and allows schools a greater chance to select 'appropriate' children.

Most recently the government's White Paper *Self-Government for Schools* (DFEE, 1996) makes several more proposals that challenge comprehensive schools. The Paper proposes that all grant-maintained schools should be able to select up to 50 per cent of their pupils by general ability, or by ability or aptitude in particular subjects, without needing central approval. LEA technology and language colleges are to be allowed to select up to 30 per cent of their pupils according to abilities or aptitudes in their specialist subject, and all LEA schools are to be given the right to select up to 20 per cent of their intakes. The Specialist School Programme is to be expanded to include sports colleges and arts colleges as well as technology and language colleges. Finally, and at last openly, the White Paper explicitly states that the government wishes to encourage the establishment of new grammar schools. It will encourage promoters to establish new grant-maintained grammar schools. It will encourage schools to become selective. It will allow the Funding Agency for Schools to bid against LEAs and put forward proposals that 'extend the diversity' of schools.

The comprehensive ideal affirms that children's education should not be disadvantaged by their backgrounds, and that the state should provide free, high quality education for all in comprehensive schools. Selection of specific children for differentially funded and supported schools clearly violates this principle, and encourages a move back to a discredited system. The result has been greater fragmentation into different types of school, greater selection according to a range of different criteria and greater inequity in what schools offer. Market forces (under the guise of choice and diversity) reflect and promote a different set of values; growing inequalities between schools militate against social equity. Much of the present government's educational policy will increase injustice and inequity. It will lead to a system of unequally funded schools which will provide very different educational experiences for children of different abilities, social classes and ethnic groups. It will fail to raise educational standards for all.

This is thus the appropriate time to address and affirm the principles that inspired comprehensive schools thirty years ago. What principles lay behind the comprehensive ideal? What has been gained — and, indeed, what has been lost? How should schools be organized such that all young people are provided with an appropriate education and training irrespective of ability, aptitude, social class, gender, sexuality, ethnicity or religion?

This book gathers together chapters that have been developed from a series of lectures that was held in early 1996 at the University of Oxford, Department of Educational Studies. There were fourteen lectures in all that aimed to assess the achievements of comprehensive schools and reaffirm a commitment to the ideals of comprehensive education. The following chapters survey the ideals and history of the comprehensive movement, describe the current context and the effects of recent legislation, and offer possible ways forward. It is recognized by all that there can be no simple turning back the clock. There is a need to safeguard the ideals on which the comprehensives were built but to construct a new, appropriate education system in the light of what we have learnt from the past. The contributors to the series of lectures have presented their ideas in this book in a variety of different styles. While some have chosen to transform their lectures into tightly argued and fully referenced chapters, others have preferred to retain a style more representative of their lecture presentations. In whatever form the chapters are presented, the contributors draw upon their recent research and experience and explore the continued relevance of those original comprehensive ideals in a sympathetic, yet not uncritical, way.

Following this introductory chapter, the book opens with Brian Simon's and Peter Cornall's analyses of the ideals and history behind the comprehensive movement. This is followed by critical discussions of recent fragmentation into different types of school, privatization and selection by David Halpin and Geoffrey Walford. Stephen Ball and Richard Pring follow with their commentaries on the social and political philosophies behind markets and competition and the values of personal worth and community inherent in such systems. Denis Lawton and Sally Tomlinson focus on the curriculum and what will be worth learning in the next century, while Caroline Benn and Ted Wragg concentrate on what makes effective comprehensive education and effective teachers. Moving further into examinations of possible futures, Bernard Clarke discusses what comprehensive schools do better, while John Abbott examines how developments in information technology support the comprehensive ideal. Finally, Tim Brighouse and Stewart Ranson put forward their ideas for a local democratic framework that embodies comprehensive values and examine how the comprehensive school fits within the learning society.

While the early chapters take a more historical approach, the chapters show that comprehensive ideals and principles can be reapplied in the very different social and economic circumstances of the next millennium. The future will demand that we take far more seriously the need to develop a range of personal and social abilities. The different forms of intelligence will need to be nurtured; the new opportunities for organizing learning which technology makes possible will need to be exploited. Most of all, however, there will be a need to ensure that every child has access to the highest possible quality schooling and that provision does not depend on privilege and social background.

The demands and opportunities of the new millennium will require modification to the form of comprehensive schools that thrived in the 1970s, but this book seeks to show that the ideals on which they were based are very much worth reexamining and reaffirming.

References

BALL, S.J. (1984) (Ed) *Comprehensive Schooling: A Reader*, London, Falmer Press.

BENN, C. and SIMON, B. (1972) *Half Way There* (*2nd edn*) Harmondsworth, Penguin.

CLIFFORD, P. and HEATH, A. (1984) 'Selection does make a difference', *Oxford Review of Education*, **10**, 1, pp. 85–97.

COX, C.B. and BOYSON, R. (1975) (Eds) *The Fight for Education: Black Paper 1975*, London, Dent.

COX, C.B. and BOYSON, R. (1977) (Eds) *Black Paper 1977*, London, Temple Smith.

COX, C.B. and DYSON, A.E. (1973) (Eds) *The Black Papers on Education 1–3*, London, Davis-Poynter.

COX, C. and MARKS, J. (1988) *The Insolence of Office*, London, Claridge Press.

DALE, R.R. and GRIFFITH, S. (1965) *Down Stream: Failure in the Grammar School*, London, Routledge and Kegan Paul.

DEPARTMENT FOR EDUCATION (DFE) (1992) *Choice and Diversity: A New Framework for Schools*, London, DFE.

DEPARTMENT FOR EDUCATION AND EMPLOYMENT (1996) *Self-Government for Schools*, London, DFEE.

DEPARTMENT OF EDUCATION AND SCIENCE (DES) (1984) *School Standards and Spending: Statistical Analysis: A Further Appreciation*, Statistical Bulletin 13/84, London, DES.

DOUGLAS, J.W.D. (1964) *The Home and the School*, London, MacGibbon & Kee.

FLOUD, J.E., HALSEY, A.H. and MARTIN, F.M. (1956) *Social Class and Educational Opportunity*, London, Heinemann.

FOGELMAN, K. (1984) 'Problems in comparing examination attainment in selective and comprehensive secondary schools', *Oxford Review of Education*, **10**, 1, pp. 33–43.

FORD, J. (1969) *Social Class and the Comprehensive School*, London, Routledge and Kegan Paul.

FOX, I. (1985) *Private Schools and Public Issues*, London, Macmillan.

GEWIRTZ, S., BALL, S.J. and BOWE, R. (1995) *Markets, Choice and Equity in Education*, Milton Keynes, Open University Press.

GRAY, J. (1990) 'Has comprehensive education succeeded? Changes within schools and their effects in Great Britain' in LESCHINSKY, A. and MAYER, K.U. (Eds) *The Comprehensive School Experiment Revisited: Evidence from Western Europe*, Frankfurt am Main, Verlag Peter Lang.

GRAY, J., JESSON, D. and JONES, B. (1984) 'Predicting differences in examination results between local education authorities: Does school organisation matter?', *Oxford Review of Education*, **10**, 1, pp. 45–68.

GRAY, J., MCPHERSON, A.F. and RAFFE, D. (1983) *Reconstructions of Secondary Education: Theory, Myth and Practice Since the War*, London, Routledge and Kegan Paul.

HARGREAVES, D. (1967) *Social Relations in a Secondary School*, London, Routledge and Kegan Paul.

HEATH, A. (1984) (Ed) *Oxford Review of Education*, **10**, 1 (Guest editor A. Heath).

JACKSON, B. and MARSDEN, D. (1962) *Education and the Working Class*, London, Routledge.

JOHNSON, D. (1987) *Private Schools and State Schools*, Milton Keynes, Open University Press.

LACEY, C. (1970) *Hightown Grammar*, Manchester, Manchester University Press.

MCPHERSON, A. and WILLMS, J.D. (1987) 'Equalization and improvement: Some effects of comprehensive reorganisation in Scotland', *Sociology*, **21**, pp. 509–39.

MARKS, J. (1991) *Standards in Schools*, London, Social Market Foundation.

MARKS, J., COX, C. and POMIAN-SRZEDNICKI, M. (1983) *Standards in English Schools: An Analysis of Examination Results of Secondary Schools in England for 1981*, London, National Council for Educational Standards.

MARKS, J. and POMIAN-SRZEDNICKI, M. (1985) *Standards in English Schools: Second Report*, London, National Council for Educational Standards.

REYNOLDS, D. and SULLIVAN, M. with MURGATROYD, S. (1987) *The Comprehensive Experiment: A Comparison of the Selective and Non-selective System of School Organization*, London, Falmer Press.

STEEDMAN, J. (1983) *Examination Results in Selective and Non-selective Schools: Findings of the National Child Development Study*, London, National Children's Bureau.

STEEDMAN, J. (1987) 'Longitudinal survey research into progress in secondary schools, based on the National Child Development Study' in WALFORD, G. (Ed) *Doing Sociology of Education*, London, Falmer Press.

VERNON, P.E. (1957) *Secondary School Selection*, London, Methuen.

WALFORD, G. (1994) 'A return to selection?, *Westminster Studies in Education*, **17**, pp. 19–30.

YATES, A. and PIDGEON, D.A. (1957) *Admission to Grammar Schools*, London, NFER.

Ideals and History of Comprehensive Schooling

1   A Seismic Change:
Process and Interpretation

Brian Simon

Recent events have highlighted the need to enhance understanding of the nature and causation of the swing to comprehensive education after 1965 and to bring out clearly its overall significance. It is increasingly important that we should restate, and rethink, the principles embodied in the practice of these new schools. Therefore I am delighted to contribute to this series. Comprehensive education has been an issue close to my heart and mind over the last fifty years and more — covering the whole of my adult life.

Indeed, in 1954, forty-two years ago, Robin Pedley and I were able to take time out and visit all the comprehensive schools then in existence in England and Wales. There was a total of thirteen, mostly in offshore islands, four in Anglesey, four in the Isle of Man, two in Middlesex, one each in the West Riding, Walsall and Windermere. In addition there were a number of so-called 'interim' comprehensive schools in London which we also visited. We were impressed — both of us wrote about these experiences later. We were already strong supporters of the idea of comprehensive education.

Three or four years later our home county, Leicestershire, under Stewart Mason, introduced its experimental two-tier system, and our students at once inundated these schools which generously welcomed them in large numbers, and indeed we rapidly developed a creative partnership with several of these innovative schools. Nor should we forget the transformation of primary education consequent upon the elimination of the 11+; many of the county's schools seized their new opportunities creatively and here also our primary students benefitted enormously. A general feeling of excitement and commitment pervaded the scene. The school system was being transformed — or so we thought.

I had personally first come into contact with the comprehensive idea nearly twenty years earlier when, as a very junior member of the Labour Party's Education Advisory Committee in 1938–39, I acted as Assistant Secretary to Barbara Drake, the Committee's exemplary Secretary, niece of Beatrice Webb. Barbara was then a leading member of the London County Council which, already in 1936, had committed itself to establish these new-type schools if and when it became legally possible. Within Labour's Advisory Committee, a critical assessment of the Spens Report of December 1938 concluded, in opposition to that Report's recommendations, that support for the multilateral (or multibias) school should be recommended

as policy (Simon, 1994). Coming new to this whole field of public policy forma-
tion, I personally found these arguments convincing. However, as is well known,
the Labour governments of 1945–51 proved unsympathetic. After the war the tripartite system was generally imposed, though there were loopholes, London being
one, and, as we have seen, sparsely populated offshore islands and remote country
areas. But, generally, those supporting comprehensive education had very little to
encourage them in the bleak post-war years.

There had been supporters, even before the war. It is perhaps significant that
the first teacher organization deliberately to support the move had been the Assistant Masters Association, male grammar school teachers who, in 1925, passed unani-
mously a resolution at their annual conference in favour of secondary education for
all — in *one* type of school. 'If secondary schools of various types were set up',
said the mover, 'it would mean that there would be in secondary schools of the
present type (that is, grammar schools) a class which was bound to be looked upon
as something socially superior to the children who would attend the new schools
of the distinct types' (quoted in Rubinstein and Simon, 1973, p. 15).

Several other teacher organizations lent their support in the mid-thirties, articu-
lating their views in evidence to the Spens Committee, then considering the future
pattern of secondary education. There was also support from the Trade Union Congress and other organizations of the Labour movement. Further, the concept of
the single school found prestigious external advocates. In *A Modern Philosophy
of Education*, published in 1929, Godfrey Thomson, a distinguished educationist,
strongly supported the move, based partially on his own experience in the United
States. 'The social solidarity of the whole nation', he wrote, 'is more important
than any of the defects to which a comprehensive high school may be subject'
(p. 274). This, incidentally, was probably the first use in this country of the term
'comprehensive'. However, all this proved insufficient to build up the head of steam
necessary to bring about the crucial change that comprehensive education clearly
involved.

The thirteen schools that Robin Pedley and I visited in 1954 have now bur-
geoned to a total of about 3400. Indeed, they provide the bulk of secondary education in maintained schools in the country as a whole — or, if you prefer it, in
the three countries of England, Wales and Scotland. Outside them of course — and
this is one of the problems — there exist the private or 'independent' schools which
have no connection with the publicly provided system, apart from the siphoning of
public money to many through the Assisted Places Scheme due now, malevolently,
to be expanded. The comprehensive system has been forced to fight for its continued existence and viability in an increasingly harsh climate over the last ten to
fifteen years especially. Governments have been successively unsympathetic, to put
it mildly. While no overt, direct attack has yet been made on the system as a whole,
a series of measures seem to have been motivated by a policy of destabilization.
These include the continuing downgrading of local authorities who, in fact, brought
the system into being, responding to demands by local populations. They include
also the establishment of city technology colleges lacking any connection with
local democratic forms of government; opting out — a means of weakening local

comprehensive systems; the recently covert but now overt reintroduction of selection on a considerable scale (and threats of further such measures), and so on . . . and on. The list could be extended. Nor have I mentioned increasingly tight resource limitations. Beyond all this the system has suffered almost continuous attack and negative criticism by leading politicians, including the Prime Minister.

But the striking thing about all this, it seems to me, is that the system in all its essentials survives — has survived and, I think, will continue to do so. Comprehensive education has shown an extraordinary resilience. Of course there are exceptions but the bulk of the schools, taking the country as a whole, have established deep roots in the local communities they serve and remain extremely popular with parents from whom they derive consistent support. These schools embody ideals and practices which stretch back into the past and which retain their predominance in the minds and hearts of local populations. That is the achievement of their teachers, other school workers, governors, local authorities. This, I suggest is why they have been able to withstand the blows specifically directed against them on the national scene. This is why the comprehensive school system that now exists can, and I am sure, will act as the ground base for the massive advances now increasingly seen as necessary right across the board. This is why any future government that wishes to ensure such advances must begin to find ways of recognizing, and reinforcing, success within this system, rather than focussing on punishing failure, sadly seen as the popular stance at present.

This is not mere rhodomontade. I believe that the experience of 'going comprehensive' had a very profound effect on the thinking and on the ideals of wide sections of the people, and that this we can evaluate as capital in the sense of a stockpile of values now held deeply in the country — values which include holding non–selective education in high repute. I want now to look first at the process of transition as it actually happened. I shall then attempt an interpretation of the seismic change this brought about — how can we account for it? Finally I will refer, very briefly, to some of the problems that emerged that have prevented comprehensive education realizing its full potential. Other lecturers in this series, I am sure, will be dealing with these issues which need solutions.

My aim now is to establish the scope and extent of the change to comprehensive education. This involves reliance on statistics for which I apologize since the human element is excluded. But we will come back to human beings later — since after all this is what comprehensive education is all about. Figure 1.1 is perhaps the most striking. It charts the growth in the number of pupils in comprehensive schools in England and Wales from the early 1950s (when the number was negligible) to 1976 when the total reached three million — the great bulk of secondary school pupils in the two countries, and then to 1980 when it was approaching four million.

There were some among my friends at the time who thought the swing to comprehensive education was too slow. Others, of course, thought it was a great deal too fast. Looking carefully at this graph we see that the movement was slow to get under way. Progress only really began around 1956, but from then until 1964–65 a speeding up took place as Edward Boyle, when Secretary of State, removed some of the brakes on comprehensive education put in place by Conservative

Figure 1.1:   *Comprehensive secondary schools (includes middle schools deemed secondary) in England and Wales 1950–1980: numbers of pupils (thousands)*

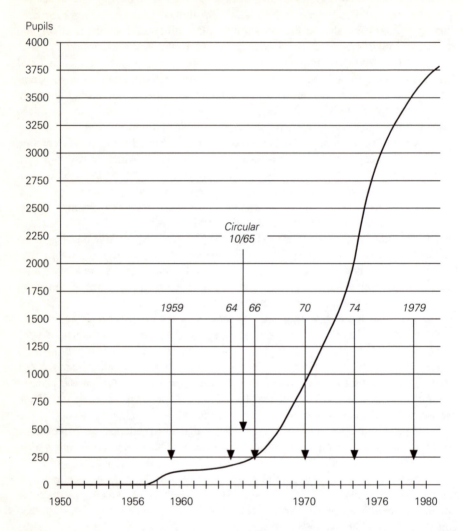

governments in the 1950s. When *Circular 10/65* was issued following the 1964 General Election there were about 250,000 pupils in comprehensive schools. But from then, or, more accurately, a year later (in 1966) the floodgates opened. The fact is that the crucial arguments, which we will return to later, were fundamentally fought out in the late 50s and especially the early 60s. By that time the case had been made. Above all, the country was now determined to get rid of the 11+. As can be seen from the slope of the curve, comprehensive schools now came into being with *increasing* rapidity. The 1970 General Election, which brought back the Conservatives with Margaret Thatcher as Secretary of State, was accompanied, perhaps paradoxically, by an actual *acceleration* of the swing which was continued after the 1974 General Election returned Labour to power. It is a matter of fact, and I think of considerable significance, that the political complexion of succeeding governments appears to have had no effect whatever on the rate of change, even though Thatcher was clearly unsympathetic and attempted, partially successfully, to insert various spanners into the works to slow the rate or reduce its impact. Here was a movement involving radical educational (and perhaps social) change that appears, as it were, autonomous — not to be a direct product of competing party policies. This characteristic of the transition to comprehensive education, I suggest, is unusual and ignored at peril.

In connection with this, one crucial point should be born in mind. *Circular 10/65* did not *require* local authorities to produce development plans embodying comprehensive education, it *requested* them to do so. This had been a matter of hot dispute within the Labour party and continued so within the Cabinet while Michael Stewart was briefly Secretary of State. The Cabinet determined on 'request' for a period (against Stewart's advice incidentally), keeping the option of compulsion in reserve, and Crosland, who brought out the Circular, also took this line. With hindsight I would now say that history has shown this to have been a far-sighted policy. Every single local authority in the country (and Scotland had its own Circular) had to argue the issue out for themselves, and come to *their own decisions*. Their own decisions — that is the important thing. Were they going to accept or reject the request? If they were to accept it, then by what means precisely? I would argue that the decision by the great bulk of the then 169 authorities of whatever political complexion (and many were then Tory-controlled) to go comprehensive was a positive, proactive decision, having big implications. The fact that most of them did in fact take this road, following sometimes years of discussion (which in many cases, for instance in Manchester and Liverpool, preceded *Circular 10/65*), and including also in very many places holding a series of public meetings including parents and local communities generally is, in my view, of overall significance in estimating the impact and nature of the change. Through this process the ideas behind comprehensive education became lodged securely in the hearts and minds of countless local populations and communities.

Figure 1.2 shows the rate of change in England, Wales and Scotland respectively. Various things could be noted here but we shall focus only on essentials. First, that the pattern is similar in all three countries both concerning the rate and extent of change. Wales and Scotland both have a head start over England — with nearly 60 per cent in comprehensive schools by 1970, when in England the figure only reached 35 per cent. But in all three cases the crucial years lie between 1965 and 1975, by which time both Wales and Scotland have reached nearly 90 per cent. After that England catches up a bit but Scotland actually finally by 1985 reaches 100 per cent, Wales 96 per cent and England, lagging behind, 94 per cent. These percentages, of course, refer to pupils in *maintained* schools. So, with some slight reluctance on England's part, comprehensive education finally carried the day in all three countries, the Scots, with their democratic tradition, taking the palm.

Second, with regard to the last of this group of studies (figure 1.3), we can see how the four types of school — grammar, modern, technical and comprehensive

Figure 1.2: Percentage of pupils in comprehensive secondary schools (includes middle schools deemed secondary) in Great Britain, by country

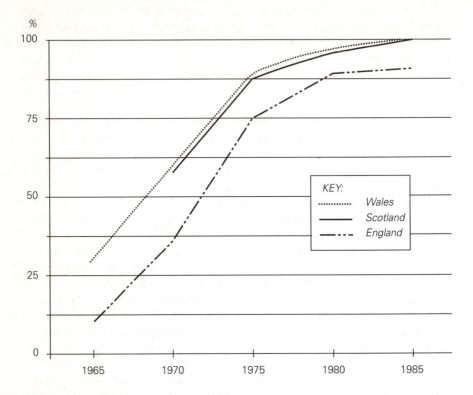

— fared over the thirty-plus years 1946 to 1980. First, let us take the sadly abortive secondary technical schools at the bottom of the graph. These seem never to have been taken seriously nationally or locally. They maximize their intake in 1960 with just over 100,000 pupils but thereafter gradually decline as technical schools were embodied in the new comprehensives whose numbers now begin to rise. Secondary modern schools, products of 1926 (The Hadow Report) reorganization and then the 1944 Act, when they were sold as the great solution to mass education, maximize their intake in 1961 (with nearly 1,700,000 pupils) thereafter suffering first a slow decline and then a rapid plunge almost to extinction. Finally, the grammar schools which, after 1944, provided a free education to selected pupils. These show no serious increase for ten years after 1946, then a slow but steady rise to a maximum in 1964, followed by continuous decline as comprehensive education gets under way to roughly 100,000 pupils (about 150 schools) in 1988 — a position retained to this day.

Finally there is the success story of comprehensive schools. It is the consistent and rapid rise shown here which we saw in detail in the earlier graphs which accounts for the decline of each of the three specific functional types of school. This is self-evident. Here is an epitome of the history of post-war secondary edu-

Figure 1.3:   Total of pupils in different types of maintained secondary school in England and Wales, 1946–1980 (thousands)

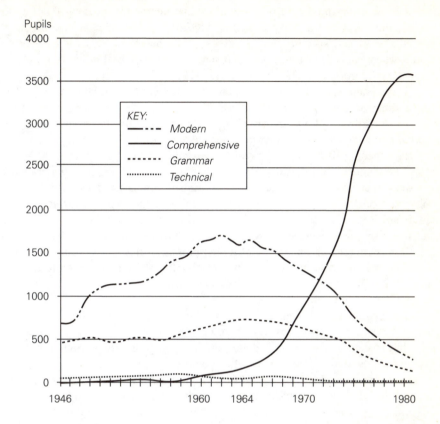

cation. We must remember that this was a period of really massive expansion in that field. In 1946 only 1,270,000 pupils were in schools legally defined as 'secondary'. Thirty-one years later, in 1977, there were over four million — the bulk of them (over three million) in comprehensive schools. This is surely a very significant movement in the field of social history.

Could the move to comprehensive education have been avoided? Were there any alternative policies that might have had a prospect of success? Those who blame all the ills of society on the 'sixties' move to comprehensive education, claiming it basically as a Labour political ploy — as John Major does — need to clarify what their ideal alternative policy might have been, and how they would have implemented it (see Jarvis, 1993, pp. 28–9, for John Major's views on comprehensive education). They have not done so. In my view, however, there *were* two alternative policies which *might* have been pressed. One was deliberately to encourage grammar schools to expand in response to demand — a policy, I understand, adopted in Germany, by the German states that control their own education. Had this been done, it might perhaps have headed off the growing clamour against the 11+. It would, however, have involved a very considerable expansion of these schools. The other alternative might have been again the deliberate building up of the new secondary modern schools as a genuine alternative, opening them up to examinations and so the paths to higher education. An attempt in this direction, with the overt and specific aim of reducing 11+ pressures, was tried partly by Eccles when Minister of Education, and shortly after by Lloyd in his White Paper *Secondary Education for All: A New Drive* (1958).

There is not space here to deal more than summarily with both of these. The first alternative, grammar school expansion, was never tried or ever placed on the agenda. As Edward Boyle makes clear, Ministry officials, far from wanting to *expand* grammar schools, wanted the opposite — to limit places in them and even to reduce them. This had been official Ministry policy for many years after World War Two (Ministry of Education, 1951). The idea of radically *expanding* grammar schools was an absolute non-starter among Ministry officials and also Conservative politicians generally. To have proposed it would have meant political suicide. This is Edward Boyle's assessment (see Kogan, 1971, pp. 114–17). So, this alternative was never seriously considered. Nor do I recall anyone, even among the powerful and then vociferous grammar school lobby, proposing this course. They were too bound up with the concept of the grammar school as an elite institution to harbour such ideas. This Canute-like stance was the cause of the grammar schools' own downfall — as 'grammar' schools.

The upgrading of secondary modern schools as a genuine alternative, in the sense of pouring in resources, re-equipping them, opening up new opportunities including access to exams on a quite new scale, appeared as a viable policy to Eccles and Lloyd in the late 1950s. This would draw the sting of the comprehensivists. This issue is discussed by Edward Boyle (1972) in his very useful assessment of the whole movement. In his own words, this policy failed to take the sting out of the 11+. The only possible means, he says, of preserving the bipartite system (as he calls it) would have been through the encouragement of GCE courses in secondary modern schools 'from the first'. That is, back in the 40s and early 50s. When the policy was taken up and pursued, he says, 'It was too late' (*ibid.*, p. 31). History proved him right.

How then, can we account for the rapidity, and extent, of the change, both of which, I suggest, were unexpected? What everyone underestimated was the degree of frustration that built up in the late 50s and early 60s, as scheme after scheme submitted by local authorities were summarily rejected, to explode when *Circular 10/65* finally burst the dam so determinedly erected. From that moment transformation took place at an accelerating rate.

Analysts frequently, and I think rightly, point to crucial changes in the social structure as underlying this whole movement, leading to raised aspirations right across the board. Such changes were themselves the outcome of scientific and technological change — the introduction and growth of new-type industries embodying science and technology in a new way, including automation, and requiring higher skill and knowledge levels among the population as a whole, as the Crowther Report of 1959 so consistently underlined. Figure 1.4 presents these data (Rubinstein

Figure 1.4: Social classes (males only) England and Wales (in thousands)

Date	I Professional, etc.	II Intermediate	III Skilled	IV Partly Skilled	V Unskilled
1931	336	1,855	6,848	2,552	2,459
1951	494	2,146	8,041	2,433	2,258
1961	591	2,368	7,933	3,237	1,422
Percentage increase					
1931–61	75.9	27.7	15.8	26.4	(−42.2)

and Simon, 1973, p. 53). The striking figure is the huge decline in the number of unskilled workers. All the other categories show an increase over the thirty years up to 1961 — professional occupations show the greatest proportional gains, but intermediate, skilled and partly skilled are all up. We must remember also that, although Britain was already falling behind other advanced industrial countries in its rate of economic growth in the 50s, an average growth rate of 2 per cent a year meant that real incomes *were* generally increasing and this in itself further raised aspirations resulting in a greater demand for education. The post-war period up to the late 60s was also one of full employment. So both from the demand and the supply side pressures for greater opportunities increased through the late 40s and 50s. The immediate result was paradoxical — the existing system rapidly became increasingly competitive. Streaming in primary and secondary schools was enhanced in the attempt to winnow out the successful few. The school population was thrust into a Procrustean bed. It was C.P. Snow who referred to this (in his famous *Two Cultures* lecture in 1959) as a 'rigid and crystallized pattern' from which a breakout was essential. Figures 1.5 and 1.6 are graphic if highly schematic representations of the school system as it had evolved by about 1960 showing the channelling and categorization of children first in primary schools (figure 1.5), and then through the state system as a whole (figure 1.6).

This was the situation that now came under increasingly critical scrutiny. It is possible, I think, to argue that the crucial battles on comprehensive education were fought out in the period 1956 to 1963 by which time in essence they had been won, even if the essential administrative actions came later. I know of no attempt to estimate, statistically or otherwise, the extent of frustration among ordinary people — parents — as the 11+ ruthlessly, year after year, relegated some 75 per cent of the age group to secondary modern schools. Public opinion polls were already clearly indicating that the great bulk of parents (including working class) rejected these for their children, and generally, in spite of heroic efforts by some schools and teachers, they led nowhere. There is no doubt that Chief Education Officers were inundated with complaints and appeals — in the case of Stewart Mason, Leicestershire's Director, it was *this* which caused him to change his mind on the whole issue and energetically to espouse non-selective education (Jones, 1988, pp. 51–5). But everyone knows today something of the agony the 11+ brought into the homes of children up and down the country, and this, of course, was a major

Figure 1.5: *Primary schools: Internal structure*

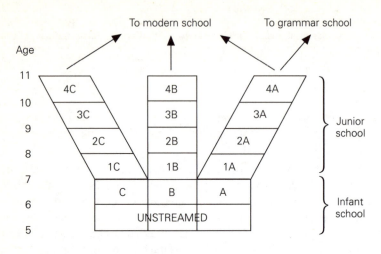

Figure 1.6: *The streamed system of education*

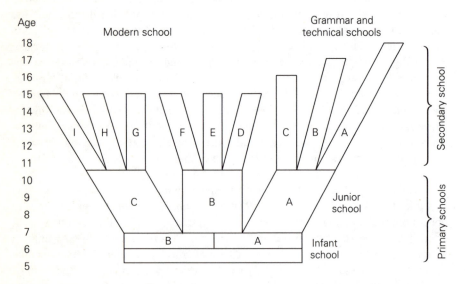

factor which must not be forgotten in any attempt at an historical reconstruction. It was this which lay behind the whole groundswell of popular support for the non-selective, or comprehensive school, and which rendered its achievement a viable proposition.

The tripartite system was, as just mentioned, now coming under scrutiny. 1957 was a key year. Two studies cast serious doubt on the viability of 11+ selection — Yates and Pidgeon's evaluation of the exam for the NFER showed that as many as 60,000 children were annually allocated to the 'wrong' type of school, and further, since there was no serious possibility of further refining selection techniques, comprehensive, multilateral, or some more flexible structure, was desirable (Yates and Pidgeon, 1957). In that year also the British Psychological Society set up a working party of leading psychometricians to consider the criticisms being made of intelligence testing and selection by Alice Heim and others — a step taken since educational psychologists were now themselves increasingly concerned about what many saw as the misuse of their instruments. The report distanced its members from the classic, hard line theory of intelligence propagated for many years by Cyril Burt as a fixed, genetically determined factor of the mind unaffected by education or experience and accurately measurable by a group test. Instead the report, masterminded by P.E. Vernon, now the leading psychometrist, accepted the variability of measured intelligence as a result of interactive life experiences, strongly rejected early streaming and espoused the idea of comprehensive education for all at least till the age of 13 (Vernon, 1957, pp. 35–53). This, you might feel, was a modest recommendation, but the deep significance of the report is that, in rejecting the highly determinist theories of the past, it assisted in opening the way to the much more radical critique of the concept of the limited pool of ability which was to come a few years later — in 1963, with the Robbins Report. From now on, those who insisted on the *educability* of the normal child could claim legitimating support from psychometricians themselves. It was Vernon's own evidence to the Robbins report on this issue that was decisive (Vernon, 1963, pp. 170–8).

These and other factors led to that crucial change in outlook which began now to seize the educational world (and beyond), and that was epitomized in Boyle's (1963) famous interpellation to the foreword of the 1963 Newsom Report. 'The essential point', he wrote, 'is that all children should have an equal opportunity of acquiring intelligence, and of developing their talents and abilities to the full'. I would say that it was this positive evaluation of the potentialities of all for intellectual, as well as other, development which now gained a certain hegemony and which, in a real sense, fuelled the movement for comprehensive education. It embodied a deliberate rejection of the chilling fatalism which had governed education through the inter-war years and beyond.

In the late 1950s, concern about the inadequacies of the school system was expressed in official reports by the then existing Central Advisory Council for Education (England), particularly the 1956 *Early Leaving* Report and more thoroughly in the Crowther Report (*15–18*) which followed in 1959. These were the first such reports to use sophisticated sociological techniques of analysis. Both revealed the massive wastage of ability suffered by pupils passing through the school system, a wastage particularly marked among working class pupils; a situation that was strikingly underlined in the research undertaken for the Robbins Report of 1963. This is not the place to recapitulate these findings, the general drift of which are well known. The Crowther Report, partly to alleviate this, proposed a much more flexible educational structure — but these proposals were never seriously implemented. The times were not quite right, but actually shortly would be. But here also were factors for change.

It could be argued that the final death of the bipartite system was brought about by two books published in 1962 and 1963 respectively — though in fact, like Caesar's its death was the result of a thousand cuts. The two I have singled out are Brian Jackson and Dennis Marsden's (1962) *Education and the Working Class* and William Taylor's (1963) *The Secondary Modern School*. The former, refreshingly using new-type (ethnographic) research techniques, came as a really devastating critique of the traditional boys grammar school, its ethos and procedures, bringing out very clearly the overall alienating effect of this culture on working class pupils and their parents. Bill Taylor's book, an equally devastating critique of the impossible tasks set to secondary modern schools by the circumstances of their establishment, and in spite of the very best efforts of many teachers, was succinctly and rightly described in a contemporary critical bibliography as 'the book to end all books on this subject' (Richmond, 1972). In 1963 the number of pupils in secondary modern schools was already declining; the grammar school decline started a year after the publication of Jackson and Marsden's book. I am not so naive as to suggest there was a direct relationship; but both books fitted the new climate of thinking that underlay the swing to comprehensive education, now approaching the point of take-off.

Right up to 1962/63 the Conservative government maintained a hard line against comprehensive education. Such schools, when proposed, David Eccles told the National Union of Teachers in 1955, would only be approved 'as an experiment' and when 'all the conditions are favourable and no damage is done to any existing school', implying that no grammar or modern school served the area where a comprehensive school was proposed (Simon, 1991, p. 184). This hard line policy was followed by later ministers and found expression in the 1958 White Paper. The result was a growing conflict with a number of local authorities who found their long cherished plans turned down out of hand. Nevertheless, some progress was being made. The Leicestershire two-tier plan, for instance, was allowed to go forward. By 1963 180,000 pupils were in schools in England and Wales categorized as comprehensive by the Ministry, with another 180,000 in schools defined as 'bilateral and multilateral' (and 'other secondary'). The total of thirteen comprehensive schools Robin Pedley and I had visited in 1954 had now, nine years later, reached 175. This covered only about 5 or 6 per cent of all secondary schools — nevertheless there now existed a substantial group.

It was the evident success of these schools, or their leading members, which now emerged as an important factor in the whole situation. Robin Pedley (1963) now published his popular Pelican, *The Comprehensive School*. This emphasized the success of the early comprehensives — in London, the Isle of Man, the Calder Valley and elsewhere. Written in a straightforward, simple and engaging style it appealed particularly to parents. Pedley's book went through nine printings and three revisions up to 1978. Its technique of basing the case for comprehensive education on the evident success of many of the early schools was extremely effective — he managed to bring the experience of these new-type schools into the public domain. At this stage also the press, including the Sunday broadsheets, gave considerable space to reporting developments to which they were, at that time, increasingly sympathetic. The public as well as educationists' growing interest and

Figure 1.7: Books and pamphlets and articles on comprehensive education, 1945–1972

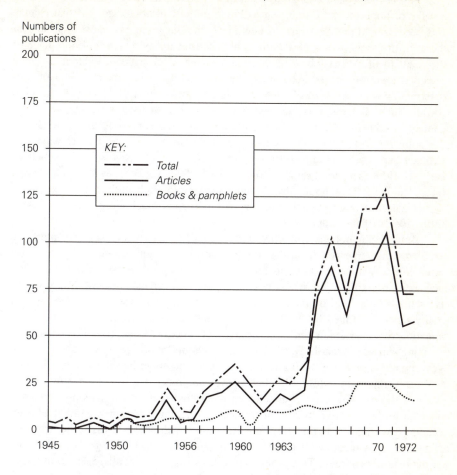

concern with the whole issue is dramatically reflected in figure 1.7, which charts the publication of books and articles on comprehensive education over the period 1945 to 1972 (Laurence, 1973). The totals for 1967 have been rounded. You will see there a spurt in discussion in the period 1956–59, but a genuine take-off from 1963 to maximize six years later (in 1969). It is not surprising that the establishment of a new-type school sparked a massive discussion on crucial issues such as the content of education now appropriate, pedagogy, inner school organization and so on. Everything was now up for discussion — and new solutions. Indeed to be a member of staff of a comprehensive school during these years, and later, was often an education in itself through intensive interstaff discussion. It should be said also that the calibre of the teachers in the early schools was probably above average, since these naturally attracted highly committed teachers — and perhaps the most advanced of students emerging from university education departments and colleges (such, at least, was certainly our experience at Leicester).

I think I have said enough to show that comprehensive education was born on a wave of hope for the future. It was based on structural change, but that change was necessary to realize a host of new ideals in education. The most important of these, in my view, was a new faith in human educability which took the place of the fatalism of the past Instead of rigid systems of classification, streaming and selection there was to be substituted the open road — the postponement of life-determining decisions for as long as possible, the offer of a full, all-round education for all. Such, at least, was the objective, together with the transformation of the content of education as a common curriculum offered equally to all, so reflecting the unification of the system as a whole. This latter objective, by the way, was strongly expressed and argued for by pioneering comprehensive school teachers as early as 1958 (see, for example, Simon, 1957, Part 4). There was also a change in the ethos of the school towards more democratic, collegial procedures, and a humanization of teacher-pupil relations. All these, and much more, were embedded in the ideals of the pioneers.

But all did not go smoothly. Other contributors to this book identify the problems that emerged from the late 60s onwards — this cannot be part of my brief. We may note, however, that although the swing to comprehensive education was extraordinarily rapid, it was not complete — in England at least. Many selective schools outside or on the periphery of the maintained system continued so that many schools, defined by the DES as 'comprehensive', were never really so — a situation reflected chiefly in large urban areas such as London and, for instance, Birmingham and Bristol. The independent schools remained independent and no government summoned the political will to integrate them into the system. Further, and most important, while schools became comprehensive in response to popular demand the examination system, which controlled their inner working, remained adapted to the selective system of the past. No serious attempt was made by succeeding governments to transform this situation in a direction to assist the structural change brought about and to create a new system setting attainable goals for the mass of the nation's children. This problem is still with us. Finally all governments since the issue of *Circular 10/65* have been content to let the whole situation drift — not one even considered establishing a committee of enquiry to investigate and assess the move to comprehensive education and so to chart the future, inviting evidence from schools, teachers, pupils, governors, the local community — everyone. This is English planning at its most symptomatic, and stands in sharp contrast with the way a parallel reform was carried through in Sweden — a transition marked by long years of research and study linked to cooperative planning for the future.

That said, I would like to finish on a positive note. The comprehensive revolution did take place. It was a seismic change. Nothing has been quite the same since — or will be.

The process of change itself was highly educative. It made a deep impact on the thinking of a generation of parents and children. This is a permanent attribution. Not a single attempt by a local authority to turn back the clock and reimpose selection for all has been successful. That is a matter of record. And that is why attempts to destabilize comprehensive education, which are unceasing, use covert or oblique procedures, as at present and over the last ten or fifteen years.

In essence, with all the changes, the system remains in being, firm as a rock. It now forms the basis, or infrastructure, upon which future growth and development, which are inevitable, can be firmly grounded. Those who pioneered the system, twenty or thirty years ago and sometimes more, have nothing to apologize for — on the contrary, much to be proud of. And that goes especially for the teachers on whose skills and commitment everything depends. Their contribution is celebrated in this book, since it is this which was crucial and, especially in the present climate, deserves the fullest recognition from all concerned with the success of the major component of the country's prevailing system of secondary education — the comprehensive school. May I conclude by reminding you of Godfrey Thomson's assessment:

> The social solidarity of the whole nation is more important than any of the defects to which a comprehensive high school may be subject.

This comment is as apt now as it was when he made it, nearly seventy years ago.

References

BOYLE, E. (Lord) (1963) *Foreword to Half Our Future* (The Newsom Report). (Report to the Central Advisory Council for Education [England]), London, HMSO.

BOYLE, E. (Lord) (1972) 'The politics of secondary school reorganisation: some reflections', *Journal of Educational Administration and History*, **4**, 2.

JACKSON, B. and MARSDEN, D. (1962) *Education and the Working Class*, London, Routledge & Kegan Paul.

JARVIS, F. (1993) *Education and Mr Major*, London, Tufnell Press.

JONES, D.K. (1988) *Stewart Mason: The Art of Education*, London, Lawrence and Wishart.

KOGAN, M. (1971) *The Politics of Education: Edward Boyle and Anthony Crosland in Conversation with Maurice Kogan*, Harmondsworth, Penguin.

LAURENCE, D. (1973) *Writings on Comprehensive Education, 1500 References with Index*, London, Campaign for Comprehensive Education.

MINISTRY OF EDUCATION (1951) *The Road to the Sixth Form*, pamphlet No. 19, London, HMSO.

PEDLEY, R. (1963) *The Comprehensive School*, Harmondsworth, Penguin.

RICHMOND, W.K. (1972) *The Literature of Education*, London, Methuen.

RUBINSTEIN, D. and SIMON, B. (1973) *The Evolution of the Comprehensive School, 1926–72*, (2nd edn) London, Routledge & Kegan Paul.

SIMON, B. (1957) (Ed) *New Trends in English Education*, London, McGibbon and Kee.

SIMON, B. (1991) *Education and the Social Order, 1940–1990*, London, Lawrence & Wishart.

SIMON, B. (1994) 'The politics of comprehensive reorganisation: A retrospective analysis' in SIMON, B. *The State and Educational Change: Essays in the History of Education and Pedagogy*, London, Lawrence and Wishart.

SNOW, C.P. (1959) *The Two Cultures and the Scientific Revolution*, Cambridge, Cambridge University Press.

TAYLOR, W. (1963) *The Secondary Modern School*, London, Faber & Faber.

THOMSON, G.H. (1929) *A Modern Philosophy of Education*, London, Allen & Unwin, 2nd impression 1947.

VERNON, P.E. (1957) (Ed) *Secondary School Selection*, London, Methuen.

VERNON, P.E. (1963) *Memorandum, Higher Education, Evidence, Part II* (documentary evidence to Robbins Report).

YATES, A. and PIDGEON, D.A. (1957) *Admission to Grammar Schools*, London, Newnes.

2 'Hopeful Travel on a Long Road'

Peter Cornall

The great hope of the comprehensive movement must be that it will unite the people. We need not pretend that there is not far to go. (Sharp, 1973, p. 116)

There is no way that we identify or refuse to identify with those among whom we live more completely than through the activities and education of our children. (Daunt, 1975, p. 103)

In 1955, when I left Oxford, comprehensive secondary schools were few, and I was possibly the only Diploma student who designedly joined one. From that year until my retirement in 1991, I spent twenty-three years working in these schools, fourteen of them as headteacher, and thirteen years working on their behalf as an LEA officer and inspector. My own papers from these years have been important sources for this chapter, but the context of their writing was common to those who were learning how to develop comprehensive education in the 1950s, 1960s and 1970s.

When I was 10, what we might now term an 'assisted place', privately-funded and competitively-awarded, bore me as on a magic carpet from my elementary school into successively the preparatory and senior sections of a well-known 'public school'. Such a translation was not roses all the way, but the educational and cultural benefits of the experience were undeniable. Looking back in my mid-twenties, I was uneasy; how could a system which made so much available to so few, in return for money, be morally justified? In defence of the contemporary 'scholarship' (later 11+) system for admission to maintained grammar schools, it was argued that places went only to those displaying special promise. Admission to most 'public schools' was not so restricted. At Clifton College there were clever boys, and numerous capable boys very well prepared, but there were many others there, of more modest talent, whose career opportunities were enhanced and lives enriched for one reason only — because their parents could afford to keep them on at school, and at a school which had so much to offer.

In the mid-1950s, segregation-by-testing in the maintained sector, continuing even in parts of Oxfordshire, appeared to parallel the segregation-by-class which was the basis of private education. Exclusiveness was the common feature and crucial tool of both systems, with superior resources, prestige and expectations the reward of the elect. Meanwhile evidence of the fallibility of the 11+ selection process accumulated, and its credit sank. How was this morally unacceptable situation to be resolved? Things might have changed for Chipping Norton, and I might for the moment have preserved my integrity, through my choice of first post, but what was the way forward for the country? A decent society must surely wish to make a rich, extended education available to all its young people, and to encourage them in every way to accept it. So I concluded; and believed that this could and would be done. Rendered increasingly peripheral in the national life, the private sector could be shrunk, both numerically and in influence, to the tolerable and non-damaging levels of other advanced countries. One professional lifetime should be ample time for the job!

Already there were some exciting new schools, planned on the grandest scale, in which to explore further the way of non-selection. I moved from a four-form-entry school in rural Oxfordshire, designated 'bilateral', to a fifteen-form-entry giant in suburban London. In the first school we had begun the progressive reintegration of education in a small community; the second would illustrate how the comprehensive purpose could be hindered — outside the school — by a London-wide pecking order of schools in competition for pupils, and within by a stratified pattern of classes and curricula. The prospectus of Crown Woods School, as late as 1963, said of its students: —

> They have to find out what human society is really like: where they them-
> selves stand in the scheme of things.

The statement makes a point, yet the tone seems closer to 'the rich man in his castle, the poor man at his gate', than to the positive emphasis on human potential which was the higher promise of getting rid of selection. This tone was confirmed by the diverging curricula of the four bands: Alpha, A, B, and C, which as Director of Studies I was called on to administer, and felt obliged to modify where I could.

As Pat Daunt (1975) was to comment in his *Comprehensive Values*, some sixteen years later, there were: —

> two mutually antagonistic ways of conceiving what comprehensive educa-
> tion, and therefore comprehensive schools, are really for. (p. 13)

There were also, as there still are, two very different environments for comprehensive schools — the highly competitive and the one which offers a virtual monopoly. By the age of 30, I had experienced both concepts and both environments, and was beginning to feel my way.

John Sharp's summary in *Open School* matches my state of mind in the early 1960s:

> This is a very exciting time to be teaching. Probably more is happening,
> and at a greater rate, than ever before. It is a genuine Renaissance. Here
> we are at the same moment seeking to abolish selection . . . to move away
> from streaming . . . to deal with the whole child . . . humanely . . . to create
> large schools . . . and yet to make the child feel that a large school is

neither forbidding, incomprehensible nor impervious to the expression of his personal wishes. (Sharp, 1973, p. 102)

While still in London, I had the privilege of a two-month study tour of schools and colleges in the United States, a Gulbenkian grant of £300 taking me more than halfway across the continent! This, together with three years of close contact with both primary and secondary schools as an education officer in Wiltshire — at a period before general advisory services had reached such places — enormously extended my experience and offered time for my views to clarify about what the comprehensive ideal must imply for the curriculum, for teaching method, for pupil support and for the lifestyle of a school. As the only Wiltshire officer with experience of the comprehensive, I had necessarily to become the universal public advocate and private counsellor, just as the county committed itself to reorganize its secondary education. The task of briefing architects for many building conversions, and one newly-built school, forced me to evolve arithmetical formulae for a conjectural common curriculum and pupil deployment; I was soon to need them on my own account!

I took up my first headship in 1967, appointed to amalgamate a prestigious mixed grammar school and an excellent secondary modern school, in South Nottinghamshire. I clearly felt myself ready for anything! The contrast between discarded segregation and new-found integration was excitingly sharp. Henceforward everything was to be subordinated to *the principle of maintaining and promoting opportunity for every pupil, for as long as possible*. That the progress of every individual was of equal importance was quite explicit. *The first consequence had to be a largely common curriculum*. Its delivery must take account of two factors: first the need to minimize timetable-based hindrances to individual advance; secondly, the need to recognize that ability to master the skills and knowledge on offer would vary across a wide range. *In other words, the drive for common educational experiences must be capable of adjusting to different capacities to respond.*

Both in this 11–18 school and later in an Isle of Wight high school with intake at 13, I insisted on a minimum period of mixed-ability teaching across the curriculum, and had some success in encouraging its prolongation in some curricular areas. The obviously attractive idea of a special team of teachers for the earlier secondary years secured no volunteers, principally because it ran entirely counter to the other comprehensive school maxim that every teacher should meet as wide a spread of ages and attainments as possible. Our success with mixed-ability teaching was as patchy then as I suspect it has been patchy everywhere from that day to this. I canvassed as vigorously as I could the only long-term solution — much greater emphasis on individualized learning; although commonplace in every primary school, this seemed a mountain too high to be scaled, except by practical subjects teachers, once children had turned 11. Surely the methodological challenge has been exaggerated? (Brazenly, I had provided generously for much individual — and independent-learning in that first purpose-built comprehensive in Wiltshire; but I never dared to ask, when it was built and I had left, whether or not the staff thought I had done them a service or imposed a gross physical handicap!) The failure within almost all comprehensive schools to achieve an effective third way, to reduce the strain of endless argument for and against mixed-ability classes, has been very disappointing, and one of the two most significant weaknesses in the comprehensive record, the other, of course, being the widespread failure to recognize and wholeheartedly support the surprisingly democratic implications of the original National Curriculum.

There was a radical solution of sorts, to this dilemma. It went on offer at Countesthorpe, Leicestershire, at just about the same time as we were combining schools in the next county. It was associated with changes in school life-style which sounded intimidating to most teachers. (The notoriety of this bold attempt to transform almost everything at once may have hindered progress nationally for mainstream comprehensive education. At the time it was exploited by conservatives in the same way as the activities of the so-called 'Loony Left' councils were later to be used to smear local government as a whole.) Countesthorpe certainly believed in the individualization of both instruction and learning; but it did *not* believe in an imposed, and therefore common, curriculum. *By contrast, people who thought as I did wanted individualized learning methods precisely in order to achieve the introduction of all students to a broad curriculum entitlement.* Choice was to be 'within and not among subject-areas, in the context of compulsory education' (Daunt, 1975, p. 67). This was the radicalism which was needed to resolve the dilemma of maximizing individual progress across the whole of a curriculum designed both for a successful working life and in recognition of common citizenship. At the time, in the 1960s, we naturally speculated about teaching machines, language laboratories, and programmed books: today we have much more promising technological supports, if only we can afford them; yet still it is teachers who must first be persuaded to back the drive for the individualization of learning.

Maintenance of opportunity being the key principle for the comprehensive school, its treatment of new pupils, whether at 11 or later, is crucially important. There is an inescapable problem to be understood, and a contradiction to be lived with. Especially in the 13–18 school, I was regularly criticized by contributory headteachers and by our own senior staff, for talking about new students having a 'fresh start', it being obvious that continuity in curriculum content, in skills acquisition and in confidence is the ideal for each individual boy and girl. Yet the step from one school to another is a very significant one, and every new pupil needs to be met with a cheerful expectation of success. The last thing wanted is the in-house equivalent of the brown envelope which told of 11+ 'failure'. John Sharp (1973), writing of his years at Egremont, seems to associate himself with my view

> . . . the good principle of continuity should not be carried too far, because children change rapidly into different people. (p. 111)

For curricular continuity things may be easier now, with a National Curriculum and testing; but the psychological experience of transfer surely remains the same, and this dilemma of reconciliation should continue to test our sensitivity.

The curriculum, very broadly interpreted as everything the school arranges for the child to experience, is obviously the raison d'être for any school. In a comprehensive school two other features are also vital — a personal support system, often called the 'pastoral' system, and a very purposeful system for educational guidance. The first of these has the general protective and enabling function of helping each student to overcome any circumstance which may stand in the way of successful learning. It is sometimes the fashion of the Right to belittle the importance of such work, and to suggest that it is no part of a school's responsibility or a teacher's duty. Anyone who has any experience of even the most favoured common school knows how mistaken such a view is, while schools serving less advantaged areas have no choice at all; unless staff time is generously found for pastoral work with children, their families and other agencies, the prospect of educational progress for some pupils is very distant indeed. Supportive work of this sort is inextricably linked in most schools to the general maintenance of good order, and thus to a guarantee of proper conditions for learning.

Educational guidance has the optimistic and developmental role of making sure that pupils take full advantage of the opportunities which are being preserved for them through the common curriculum and the chance to find their own level, subject by subject. It encourages realistic self-appraisal, and the capacity to relate ambition to opportunity. Without it, some may lose their way, and perform well below potential.

The allocation of resources poses problems in a comprehensive which were unknown in schools where, for example, the creation of a new 'A' level class never had to be weighed against the need for increased help in special needs — which began neither with Warnock nor with the somewhat overblown Code of Practice issued in 1994. Clearly compromises had to be made, even in the times which in retrospect glow so rosily; on 31 October 1969 I told parents, governors and staff at the first certificate-giving of the new amalgamated school:

> our resources have, unavoidably, to be stretched almost to breaking-point, and (as we are discovering) decisions about priorities are taxing in the extreme: behind them, often enough, lie issues of a quasi-moral nature which confront one in a comprehensive school much more clearly than in 'separated' schools, where more closely prescribed objectives permit a more restricted field of concern. For our part, we cannot allow ourselves to shrink from facing these questions about where scarce human resources should go . . .

In the first weeks of 1996, I found myself as a school governor still facing the problem of human resources; but now it took the harsher form of deciding which of our teachers might no longer be affordable.

During my second headship on the Isle of Wight, I was visited one day by a well-educated and articulate couple, (the son and daughter-in-law of a baron, no less) whose visit came about through their decision to choose another county school for their elder daughter. The discussion began, somewhat oddly, by their expressing to me, as Christians, their appreciation of the great consideration which we were known to extend to pupils with any kind of handicap, especially as this could only limit our ability to develop the more able students. As, by definition, their own children could not benefit from our generous bias, they would be sent elsewhere, where remedial classes were large and 'O' level' classes small — but nevertheless they did respect deeply our choice. Their premise of course was sound enough, but their conclusion totally mistaken. We had no such bias; we simply coped as best we could with the unceasing dilemma. Two satisfactions were later to compensate me for my inability to convince these parents. The first was that they inspired me to write up our encounter in the *New University Quarterly*. The second was that in my very last term, they turned up again at new parents' evening to enrol daughter number two, having had enough of school X, and as it happened I was sitting in for the missing group tutor who was to interview them! The meeting provided an interesting surprise for both of us, and a test of urbanity which I believe we both passed with credit.

And then there is the fascinating question of the *mores* appropriate to a comprehensive school — what we might nowadays understand best as 'life-style'. In *Comprehensive Values* Daunt (1975) draws a parallel with the family, in which all the children are treasured and supported, however different their personalities and needs. This conveys the spirit but hardly the complexities of what common schools must attempt. Some of them have to straddle wide social divisions, and must always be asking themselves whether or not they may, unwittingly, be alienating some students for reasons related to their background. The question should always be posed; its importance and urgency will depend on the social composition of the school. That schools send out messages, through their daily practices, is unavoidable. It may not be a surprise to hear Tim McMullen, founding Principal of Countesthorpe, declare the need to eschew 'unnecessary regulations based on middle-class concepts of taste and discipline', but nor is it at all strange that his creation underwent serious trials at the hands of its community. Many of us addressed the problem, but tried to cull and innovate with greater discrimination, picking a deliberate path among such hazards as school uniform, academic dress, prefect systems, sanctions, the use of first names, ceremonies of respect, speech days and so on. These things mattered, but differently according to place and time. Our general aim, of course, was to achieve open societies, with an emphasis on such features as collegiality, participation, cooperation, consultation, delegation, freedom of expression, gender equality, and self-discipline, and to carry with us our colleagues, students, parents and local communities. I shall never forget that for me the first task of all, at West Bridgford, was to struggle out from the restrictive carapace of divine headship into the freedom, and the vulnerability, of being merely human.

The comprehensive ideal was particularly tested, I sometimes thought, when we had to face the problem posed by the serious offender. On the one side was the school community, and the interests of the many individuals who belonged to it. On the other a young man or woman, one of our own or one seeking admission after trouble elsewhere. How often we resisted the call for exclusion or for 'no asylum', instinctively following the familiar imperative, accepting risks to our institution in the interest of maintaining its inclusiveness! What was always a sound test of a comprehensive school — its readiness to give second chances to outsiders — presents an even more telling moral challenge in these days of deliberately heightened competition. The latest statistics of exclusion suggest, among other factors, a reduced readiness to carry burdens and to take risks. The underlying principle here is simple enough — *that there shall be no worship of the institution for its own sake*, because it has no moral purpose beyond the service of the individuals whom it serves, and its claims to significance must be strictly limited to that obligation.

By definition, the pride felt for an institution open to all-comers cannot be based on any kind of exclusiveness. It is probably unwise to claim superiority for any such institution, and best to limit expressions of satisfaction to the quality of service provided to the individuals in membership, in relation to the particular local challenges. What is more, a system founded on equality must surely be inspired with a concern for universal well-being, and cannot be parochial in its outlook. *Comprehensiveness and competitiveness, as principles for a school system, are inconsistent.* If we seek success — naturally enough — for our own students, we are expressing no more than our local share of concern for the success of all students — a universal hopefulness and a universal, collaborative striving to see all young people done well by. Here the comprehensive spirit conflicts starkly with the private tradition of 'top schools', each affecting superiority, as the school song I once learnt proclaimed with more spirit than sense 'we'll honour yet the school we knew, the best school of all!'. The contrast is equally strong with the spirit of the league table, and with the self-regarding attitudes openly encouraged by the promoters of grant-maintained status.

In our Nottinghamshire suburb there were two comprehensive schools, one newly-founded, the other (of which I was head) with a long history and strong grammar school tradition. In the first summer after reorganization, some senior members of the former grammar staff asked me to continue the grammar school practice of publishing examination results. I was not keen, and asked them why this was desirable. Their disarming reply was that families liked to see the pupils' successes put on record. Taking this at its face value, with the ready cooperation of the other headteacher, a combined list of results was produced, with all the names in alphabetical order without mention of their school; and this was published. The proud grannies and aunties were presumably satisfied, but I strongly suspect that there was some disappointment in corners of the staff room! For a few years at least competitiveness was held at bay in West Bridgford.

How quixotically outmoded those evasive tactics must appear in contrast with the current drive to deride and undermine all sense of fraternity, to have every school either fatuously proclaiming its superiority or resignedly recognizing inferior status, in beleaguered and isolated decline. A feeling of common responsibility for the welfare of the whole is not merely inappropriate for a school, it positively undermines the spirit of the market in education! Meanwhile the fantasy of my salad days — that the private sector would be withering away-has been laughably disproved; almost every feature of today's education scene derides our hope for a system which might in the best sense be egalitarian, fraternal and a proper source of national pride. Our party and electoral systems have offered no opportunity to translate into clear voter opinion the almost invariably favourable views taken by parents of their children's schools. They are splendidly effective at inhibiting the wholehearted adoption of imaginative and generous initiatives. Even in the country's more prosperous days, no party ever measured up to the cost of an education system which aimed to be second to none. Now, as the country steadily drops place after place in the international league-table, in large measure because of our under-investment in education, we are to be driven apart rather than drawn together; mutual responsibility is derided, competition promoted, and devil take the hindmost. Because fair shares would mean some belt-tightening, better forget fair shares! Never have our social divisions and our political system exercised a more malign and potentially fatal influence on our future.

Attributed to GK Chesterton was the contention that the Christian ideal, far from having failed in England, had in fact been found difficult and never tried. In terms of an unequivocal national commitment, the saying applies well to that other moral programme, the comprehensive ideal for secondary education. The Right asserts that it has unquestionably failed, and expects the public to accept this as self-evident, and as the end of the story. The reality is much more complicated, and much more favourable to the comprehensive school. Leaving aside the unchallenged position of the comprehensive school in Scotland and Wales, there are very many areas in England too where these schools are popular, successful and unchallenged; this is where the system has really been tried, in the smaller country towns and the rural areas where (as I saw forty years ago in Chipping Norton) nothing is more natural than that local children should share a common experience of schooling. Even the Tories have nothing worse to propose for such schools — at present — than trying to persuade them to destroy their links with their neighbours.

And there are, of course, many successful and popular comprehensive schools in our cities; but here also there are districts where the schools, however they were to be organized, would be struggling against compounded disadvantages. Neither the tenacious altruism in our society nor its enlightened self-interest should tolerate the state of affairs; something more is needed than the harsh discipline of the shrinking budget, the time-serving scourge that is OFSTED at its worst, the cruel exposure of the league table, the hypocrisy of ministers, the rejection of all arguments for positive discrimination. We must find a better way, and soon.

Writing twenty years ago, when the earliest comprehensive schools had already celebrated their silver jubilees, Pat Daunt (1975) cautioned us: —

> We have not completed a major act of educational reform, but started one, have not even broken the back of a problem but merely set the scene in which the problem may at last begin to be tackled. (p. 7)

How right he was. The twenty years since he wrote have seen unremitting financial constraint, a huge growth in youth unemployment, and a very long period — not yet over — of policy being dominated by persons with no personal stake in ordinary schools and little or no pride in what they stand for. Nevertheless, and paradoxically, these years have probably made good much of the undoubted deficit in the teaching profession's understanding of, and commitment to, the comprehensive ideal. In part this has come about through the growing influence of a new generation of teachers; in part, I suspect, in reaction against a constant atmosphere of central government mistrust and subversion — not the first movement to achieve a deeper allegiance and a clearer self-knowledge when faced by hostility, and by evidence that in some schools adherence to a universal concern for the younger generation has proved to be no more than skin-deep. It was perhaps vain to expect that the private sector would hold back from the temptations of the Assisted Places Scheme; but it was a grave disappointment to see so many maintained and voluntary schools seeking their futures in difference rather than comradeship, in separation rather than solidarity, in moving apart rather than moving together, holding out their hands for bigger slices of cake and the chance to gain the edge over other schools by operating their own version of a comprehensive admission system. Even if I am right in guessing that the increasingly obsessive promotion of the grant-maintained school has done much to consolidate the comprehensive movement, the success it has achieved (however disappointing to its sponsors) has highlighted the unsettled character of our reform nearly half a century after it began.

The lessons of recent years can be stated positively as conditions for the fresh start which is so urgently required. We must achieve a firm political will for a national comprehensive system, consensual if possible for the sake of stability, but certainly strong and unequivocal. We must ensure that there is a fully-argued intellectual basis for this system, with the practical implications of the philosophy thought through and clearly stated. The essentially interdependent features of a comprehensive school's organization must be spelled out. We must recognize that our reform must be truly nationwide, the basic principles of which are to be applied as precisely as the requirements of a National Curriculum or a national system of tests and examinations. We must provide for the thorough exposition of both principles and practice, both as training within the educational world, and as public information for parents, communities and citizens at large. We must commit resources to the development of teaching methods, in particular to individual study techniques. We have had enough of leaving people in schools to find their own way; not everyone can be expected to achieve these things on their own, and there is now ample experience upon which to draw.

The virtues of collaboration and mutual support between schools must be restored to preeminence, and the vice of competitiveness marked down. We must insist that where schools coexist in urban areas, they complement one another within a comprehensive and fairly-resourced pattern of provision. We must acknowledge the fact that schools do not start on equal terms, even in their ability to add value to student performance, let alone by objective standards of economic and social advantage; some will need differential levels of support if their pupils are to be accorded the equal value which is their right. We must refuse to tolerate unjustified disparities in resource, by setting national standards on a basis much more sophisticated than a mere head-count, and therefore more closely related to real needs, school by school.

As to whether under the present electoral system educational resources will ever again match minimum reasonable needs, to say nothing of funding the development of a maintained service which can outshine the private sector as decisively in performance as it certainly exceeds it in moral standing — that is another question! The constant drain of influential parental support away from publicly-provided schools is a huge national handicap, and for as long as it continues at the present level, the maintained system will never be allowed to meet its obligations. The economic arguments are utterly compelling, the world will not wait for us to sort ourselves out; and yet the malign effects of educational segregation, and the attitude which finds it natural, still confuse the vision of the governing class, still block the essential decisions. Are there any politicians within earshot who are willing to disregard the private sector, to act as if it were not there, and to acknowledge that it is upon the public provision of education that the future quality of life in this country utterly depends?

References

DAUNT, P.E. (1975) *Comprehensive Values*, London, Heinemann.
SHARP, J. (1973) *Open School: The Experience of 1964–1970 at Wyndham School, Egremont, Cumberland*, London, Dent.

Context

3   Fragmentation into Different Types of School: Diversifying in the Past?

David Halpin

Introduction

This chapter looks critically at what is presently happening within some comprehensive schools as a consequence of the increased diversification and marketization of secondary education initiated by the Education Reform Act (1988). In particular, it argues that the creation of a grant-maintained schools sector, coupled with the encouragement of open competition between schools, is helping to foster a resurgence of traditional forms of education that are inimical to the demands of a modern society which is increasingly post-traditional in character. The chapter concludes by outlining some policy ideas to help remodernize comprehensive schooling and thus enable it to escape the limitations of traditionalism.

Diversity and the Comprehensive Ideal

While it is important to have as our starting point the shifts in education policy that have taken place since 1988, we need to rid ourselves immediately of the view that the present government has been the sole, even chief, architect of the diversification of secondary education in England. Instead, it is more accurate to say it exacerbated existing divisions within the state secondary sector, the systemic characteristics of which were authorized from the very outset of the comprehensive school reform.

As every history of the reform routinely points up, the early development of comprehensive education was based on the six, in effect four, different schemes or patterns of provision set down in *Circular 10/65* (DES, 1965): the single-tier school for pupils aged 11 to 18; a two-tier or 'end-on' system in which all pupils transferred automatically at 13 or 14 to the same upper or high school; a two-tier system comprising schools for the 11–16 age range and sixth form colleges for those aged 16 to 18; and a two-tier system comprising a 'middle school' for pupils aged 8 to 12 (or 9 to 13) followed by an upper or high school for the age range up to 18. These alternative models of comprehensive school provision were recommended in the light of the variety of arrangements which some LEAs at the time had already developed or were developing to end 11+ selection. To that extent, *Circular 10/65* deferred to, rather than led, local opinion. The consequence was the introduction in different parts of the country of a large number of assorted ways of providing for comprehensive schooling, which Benn and Chitty (1996, p. 90) estimate to be in excess of twenty by the end of the 1960s. Admittedly, the situation currently is significantly less heterogeneous, with all-through and 16+ transfer schemes commanding the allegiance of most communities. Even so, there remains considerable variety in the way in which comprehensive schooling is interpreted and provided locally. Ironically, then, a movement which had aimed at greater homogeneity in the basic structure of English secondary education was the instrument by which it became more varied from district to district. This variety, as Lowe (1989) stresses, needs today to be set against important demographic trends, notably the continuing suburbanization and economic expansion of the South and South-east, set against the relative stagnation of the North which together further diversify an already highly diversified system.

But there is another aspect to all this, and it is one that goes beyond both structural mechanisms and demographic changes. It concerns the definition of what counts as a comprehensive education which from the outset to this day remains elusive. There has never been, as Benn and Chitty (1996) accurately assert, 'any positive definition about the nature of the system or any positive statement about (its) . . . aims, objectives and practices . . .' (p. 26). Part of the difficulty here is the confused educational pedigree of the comprehensive school. For some of the reform's early advocates, the basic aim of comprehensive education was the promotion of equality of opportunity (the so-called 'meritocratic' ideal) while, for others, equality of outcome (the 'egalitarian' ideal) was the leading leitmotif. However, behind this tension between different ideals for comprehensive schooling went a largely taken-for-granted view that its creation would undermine the middle-class, and therefore minority, monopoly of an academic education and make it available to the majority. Of course, that is a gross simplification of what was a much more complex process. But there is little doubt that what partly held together the wide variety of organizational schemes within which local comprehensive systems developed was the manner and extent to which the comprehensive school curriculum in the early years of the reform continued to reflect in broad outline the basic assumptions of the tripartite system. Thus, while there was considerable curriculum innovation within comprehensive schools from the very beginning (see Moon, 1983; and Fletcher, Caron and Williams, 1985, for details), much of it was constrained by the demands of a public examination system that stressed then, as mostly now, academic achievement. Consequently, many of the early and later comprehensives resorted to forms of internal selection and differentiation among pupils rather than develop a distinctive common curriculum for their more socially-mixed intakes.

Autonomy and Traditionalism

The Tories then did not create a diversified system of secondary education. Nor did they, and for that matter neither did previous Labour governments, feel under any pressure to encourage forms of curriculum innovation which queried the value of an academic education. Rather, both Conservative and Labour education policy for comprehensive schooling built on what was already well established and mostly taken for granted. In the case of the Thatcher and Major administrations, however, it is fair to say they exploited, and chiefly for party political ends, the fault-lines of a loosely held together system of comprehensive education in order to foster further diversification and, concurrently, to diminish the influence of local education authorities (LEAs). Central to this effort has been their attempt to destabilize the local control of comprehensive education through grant-maintained (GM) or 'opted out' status.

At this point, however, there may be those who would argue that a sense of realism is badly needed. After all, at 16 per cent, the proportion of state-funded secondary schools which have become GM is relatively small. That is true. But 16 per cent (or, at the last count, 644 schools) is not a small proportion especially when one considers that it implicates nearly half a million pupils and over 30,000 teachers. Moreover, only a minority of GM secondary schools (less than 10 per cent) are grammar schools. Indeed, even taking into consideration the findings of Bush *et al.* (1993, p. 95), which indicate that roughly one third of the comprehensives to opt out by 1991 were operating some form of selective admissions system, and that, proportionately, more grammar schools have opted out than any other kind of secondary school, the current position is that by far the greater number of secondary schools in the GM sector have mixed-ability intakes and continue to think of themselves as members of the comprehensive school movement. In fact a few of them opted out in order to retain their comprehensive character.

But, more to the point, opting out is part of a general movement — to which each and every one of the main political parties in the United Kingdom is currently committed—whereby all public institutions, not just schools, are enjoined to take increasing responsibility for their own affairs through the mechanism of self-governing status. On this understanding, funding disparities excepted, and the damaging consequences of GM schools for some local systems of educational provision apart, opting out of local authority control can be less pejoratively thought of as an extended form of local management. One might go further and argue that studies of how individual GM secondary comprehensive schools interpret and use their powers of independent action may help us to understand better the workings of education markets and, in particular, the relationship between institutional autonomy and educational change and continuity. In this chapter, as will become evident, such studies also demonstrate what radical educational reformers are up against when self-governance is promoted alongside increased competition between schools.

Before getting to the heart of the analysis, let us for a moment reflect a little on the background to the government's GM schools policy. In common with much recent educational reform, its precise objectives are complex and have shifted over time. Nevertheless, its advocates have consistently argued that enabling schools to break free of their LEAs brings about widespread systemic effects. They identify three benefits in particular: first, they claim the policy helps to diversify local school provision and increase parental choice; second, they claim it encourages competition between schools, including those in the private sector, and thus helps to raise standards; and third, because the policy locates key decision-making at the level of the school rather than the LEA, they claim it fosters greater managerial efficiency and an increased capacity on the part of individual GM schools to recognise and respond to local needs. Implicit in these alleged benefits is the belief that GM schools will use their autonomy to become 'leading edge' institutions or 'beacons of excellence' that make a difference locally by offering something which is both distinctive and exemplary.

Two separate studies of opting out, both independently funded by the Economic and Social Research Council, inform the discussion that follows. The first, which was completed in 1992, monitored its early impact on LEAs and systems of local education provision (see Fitz, Halpin and Power, 1993). That project concluded that GM schools were neither significantly increasing parental choice nor encouraging greater parental and community involvement in the running of their affairs. The second project, completed two years ago, and the one drawn on entirely from here on, shifted focus to concentrate on the changes which opting out had wrought within schools. In particular, it explored how the form of self-governance arising from the GM schools legislation impacts on the organizational features, management structures and educational identities of the schools involved. This investigation entailed intensive fieldwork in three localities and the collection of an enormous amount of comparative data from nine secondary GM schools and seven secondary locally managed LEA schools, many of which had featured in the first study of opting out. These data comprise material derived from two questionnaire surveys of 242 teachers and nearly 600 pupils respectively and transcripts of extended on-the-record interviews with headteachers and governors, as well as much more. Clearly, there is not enough space here to consider all of this material (however, see Halpin, Fitz and Power, 1995, for more detail). What is offered is a summary account of those findings which relate to continuity and change in the management of schools and their curricula.

All of the GM schools investigated appeared to have successfully absorbed the extra responsibilities that self-governing status assumes. However, it is headteachers and senior management teams who seemed to bear most of the brunt of this increased pressure of work, a finding also reflected in research on the headteachers of self-governing LEA-maintained schools (Thomas and Martin, 1996). However, while headteachers were often keen to stress the extra work which self-governance entails, they frequently neglected to mention the enhanced opportunities it afforded them as managers. Indeed, in most cases, there appeared to be a noticeable shift in power upwards to headteachers who were located at the centre of all flows of information, advice and policy directives coming into the school. In this sense, GM heads were well placed to 'manage' (control, if you like) both staff and governors. Certainly, they forced most of the pace and shaped most of the key decisions. Moreover, for all the GM schools studied, autonomy had not as yet been translated into a different, more extended, notion of teacher professionalism and empowerment. There was no evidence, for example, to suggest that the advent of GM status had resulted in classroom teachers having a greater material control or influence over the direction of whole school policy, although an increased number of middle managers [mostly subject heads of department] were significant budget-holders in their own right and thus more involved in financial decision-making. Although other work (for example, Maychell, 1994) suggests that similar processes are taking place in LEA schools operating under the local management of schools policy, the data here suggested that the concentration of power within the hands of headteachers was more attenuated in schools which had opted out. Pronouncing judgment on the significance of outcomes of this sort is notoriously difficult. For while Hargreaves (1994) has argued that a stricter division of labour between those who largely manage and those that mostly teach may be a more efficient and more effective way of running schools, other analyses, such as those emanating from the school effectiveness movement, would suggest differently. Either way, there can be little doubt that the autonomy afforded by opting out has no inevitable implications for the development of innovative management practices. To be sure, GM schools are more likely to have additional administrative posts and more teacher support than their locally managed neighbours. But these developments in staffing are not associated with an organizational structure that departs from that found in most other schools. On the contrary, the data here pointed up that the management structures found in GM schools were likely to be more hierarchical and traditional than those found in many LEA maintained schools.

But what about innovations in curriculum content and delivery? Curricular change within the GM schools studied, it has to be said, was limited, though not unknown. For instance, one mixed GM comprehensive school serving a largely Asian community worked hard to reflect aspects of its catchment area within its curriculum. In another case, a single-sex girls' comprehensive emphasized and invested in its science and technology curriculum in order to provide its pupils with educational opportunities hitherto monopolized by boys. But these innovations were exceptional. While the picture was somewhat obscured by the introduction of the National Curriculum, few of the schools had embarked on significant, mould-breaking, curriculum reform. Most of the changes mentioned by GM heads in interview represented either glosses on the National Curriculum (notable in technology) or revivals of academic selectivity and other traditional modes of education. Even where there were attempts to modernize the curriculum, these were surrounded by a proliferation of traditional values and symbols. For instance, the mixed GM school just mentioned also emphasized the traditionalism of the English academic curriculum (for a mainly Asian intake remember) where 'old standards are cherished and upheld'. The girls' GM school, despite its high tech image, required its pupils to use fountain rather than ball-point pens! Another boys' GM comprehensive school represented the most extreme case of opting into the past. It was busy delineating behaviours and installing props to augment its grammar school legacy. For instance, £10,000 was being raised to provide a pipe organ for assemblies. In addition, the canteen had been redesignated the 'dining hall' and a strict dress code reintroduced. And, again, while one would not want to argue that trends like these are unique to GM schools, the extra money and flexibility they enjoy just means they can take it further than other maintained schools.

Traditionalism and the Uncertainties of the Education Market Place

How can we best understand the various ways in which these schools appear to have opted into the past? Some explanations might focus on the political complexion of the present government and its agencies, the public pronouncements of which (witness the Chair of SCAA, Nicholas Tate, criticisms of the moral inadequacy of school curricula and the Senior Chief Inspector, Chris Woodhead's, periodic condemnations of progressive teaching methods) are underlain by preference for old-fashioned values. However, no matter what the government's implicit and often explicit perception is of what counts as 'real' and 'good' schooling, there is nothing within the terms of the GM legislation which prevents opted-out schools from being innovative, even leading-edge. The same, but differently, applies, to locally managed schools operating under LMS, which also seem prone to traditionalism. Maybe, then, what we have here is a version of that well known phenomena whereby the conservatism found in both GM and LMS schools simply reflects an English context in which educational innovation persistently fails when it diverges too sharply from the academic model (Edwards and Whitty, 1992, p. 113). Looked at this way, the traditionalism of all the GM and most of the LMS schools represents the latest manifestation of 'a constant tendency to revert to a bipartite or tripartite division across very different formal structures' (Johnson, 1989, p. 98).

While there is some merit in this sort of analysis, the reinvigorated traditionalism manifest in the workings of these schools, it will now be argued, represents something more than continuity. For what, at first sight, appears to be an anachronistic legacy is in fact recently manufactured. The boys' GM school's reinvented traditionalism, for example, is more thoroughgoing than any it experienced as a grammar school. True, the school draws on this powerful legacy, but its pipe organ and renamed dining room are newer than its computer suite. All of which leads one to speculate differently about what is going on here, in particular to ask if the managerial orthodoxies and curriculum conservatism to which reference has been made represent an effort on the part of the schools concerned to reembed certain educational traditions so as to provide a form of protection against the unpredictableness of the education market place.

Giddens' (1994a) notion of 'manufactured uncertainty' is helpful in taking this line of analysis further forward. Giddens characterises 'manufactured uncertainties' as 'globalized forms of risk', the damage resulting from which is impossible to compensate for because 'their long-term consequences are unknown and cannot be properly evaluated . . .'. He identifies four 'global bads' that provide the main contexts in which manufactured uncertainty is experienced: the negative impact of modern social development on the world's ecosystems; the polarizing effect that global capitalist markets exert on worldwide distributions of wealth and income; the widespread existence of weapons of mass destruction; and the large-scale repression of democratic rights (*ibid.* pp. 97–100).

To suggest that such profound forms of globalized risk connect straightforwardly with the potentially unsettling consequences of the education market place lays one open to the charge of overstretching, even trivializing, Giddens' analysis. But this may be a gamble worth taking if it is assumed that the education market place is a distributive mechanism premised on capitalistic economic principles. As such, it could be said therefore to create its own set of uncertainties which, like Giddens' 'global bads', willy-nilly interpenetrate the lives of teachers, parents and children, whose experience of the education service takes on a greater degree of indeterminacy than hitherto. What they previously regarded as a relatively stable and enduring service is now experienced as fallible and obdurately imperfectable. Thus headteachers can no longer assume a steady and ready supply of pupils to fill their schools; teachers no longer feel that permanency is written into their informal working conditions and they have a strong sense of being undermined professionally; parents can no longer be confident they will get the school of their choice or the education they want for their children; and pupils, faced with uncertain futures of their own, no longer accord schools the moral legitimacy which in a previous age could mostly be taken for granted. Thus 'manufactured uncertainties' do not impact simply through the means by which education is distributed — they are likely to threaten the legitimacy of the entire enterprise.

Confronted by this wave of uncertainty, schools can respond, broadly speaking, in either one of two ways: they can imitate a particular version of the past in order to protect against chronic contingency, or they can engage with and anticipate change through innovation and risk-taking. In the schools reported on here, it is the former rather than the latter strategy which has proved more attractive. Comfort has been sought in reproducing the past, an approach justified in terms that take for granted its 'traditional' qualities. 'Traditionalism' in education actually becomes in these cases a sort of a priori 'good', which is used to celebrate an unchangeable past and to defend the status quo. However, what is drawn on in this process is assumed rather argued for. This gives rise to a form of educational 'fundamentalism' (*ibid*. pp. 84–6) in which certain rules, routines and rituals are reinvented and defended in a traditional way. Defending tradition in the traditional way means asserting its 'formulaic truth without regard to consequences' (Giddens, 1994b, p. 100). This entails a disengagement from the requirement to justify one's position using reasons. In the schools reported on here, the assertion of formulaic truth amounted to an unargued for reconsolidation of educational values which prioritizes academic achievement and assumes an unproblematic interpretation of the role of authority. Through assemblies, systems of rewards and punishments and rigorously enforced dress codes, the schools reproduced without argument a 'traditional' education based on conventionally understood notions of rigour and discipline. In their literature — prospectuses, mission statements, etc. — they reiterated the self-evident 'truth' that a 'traditional' education is by definition a 'good' and therefore better education.

This is profoundly paradoxical given that young people (quite apart from the rest of us) live today in a modern, industrial and post-traditional society in which it is no longer possible to assert with absolute confidence that there is any one way of doing anything. In this post-traditional society we are all routinely caught up in 'everyday experiments' (Giddens, 1994a, p. 93; and Giddens, 1994b, pp. 59–60)

47

involving 'a multiplicity of changes and adaptations in daily life' ('deciding "how to be" in respect of the body . . . what one's "sexuality" is, as well as grasp what "relationships" are and how they might best be constructed' [Giddens, 1994a, pp. 82–83]), and which therefore require us 'to choose among alternatives'. Put another way, the modern social order is one characterized by constant mobility and change, but with no clear direction or development. Within a host of key sites of social practice everyday life has taken on fresh and, in some cases, potentially unsettling directions. Within the site of economic production, for example, the speeding up of turnover time arising out of new modes of capital accumulation has been accompanied by parallel accelerations in exchange and consumption which have accentuated volatility and ephemerality of fashions, products and production techniques, not to mention damage on a massive scale to the earth's environment and natural resources. Within the family, and intimate relations generally, the emergence of 'pure' or 'convenience relationships' (Giddens, 1991, pp. 87–98) which are 'sought only for what (they) . . . can bring to the partners involved' and a form of decentred sexuality freed 'from the needs of reproduction' (Giddens, 1992, pp. 2 and 27) have placed new demands on people who, in a previous age, looked to religion or conventional morality (tradition, in other words) for guidance.

Now it could be said that the current trend towards traditionalism in schools is nothing more than superficial gloss or a cynical marketing ploy designed to create associations between 'good' education and high status models of schooling with the aim of attracting gullible or frightened middle class parents. But this account does not explain adequately why traditionalism in education is presently so appealing across the board, nor, relatedly, why alternative value systems are so universally unreassuring and therefore unattractive. We need an analysis which connects present-day swings towards traditionalism in education with wider social transformations. Giddens' theorems certainly help here, but only up to a point. For while they enable us to appreciate better the links between traditionalism in education and fundamentalism generally, they do not explain the current salience of this phenomenon. Stuart Hall's (1988) discussion of the nature of the emergence of what he terms 'authoritarian populism', on the other hand, does (pp. 138–47).

Briefly, Hall argues that the power of the political Right in recent times to redefine significant fields of public discourse — around popular morality, 'law and order' and 'welfare' — derives in large part from its capacity to exploit successfully particular fissures in modern British society. The chief among these is the diminished capacity and influence of social democratic ideals and a growing disenchantment with most forms of welfarism. The context here then is a crisis of political representation in which old allegiances and visions appear to be breaking down (witness the emergence of New Labour and the abandonment by both socialists and Tories of class politics in favour of appeals to 'middle Englanders') and the growing recognition that the state is no longer capable, if it ever was, of providing efficient public services. Traditionalism successfully fills this vacuum through its wide appeal and its 'common touch'; that is, through its ability to condense moral, philosophical and social themes; and its capacity to make reaction both radical and true. On this understanding, the current fashion for traditionalism in education (and traditionalism in discourses around the family, law and order and elsewhere) links with conditions of radical social upheaval that (after Giddens) create sets of new uncertainties. What it does, at a time when people are chronically unsure of which way to turn, is produce a new, but familiar, kind of common sense which makes the conditions of their lives intelligible because it addresses what is perceived by them to be 'real problems, real and lived experiences, (and) real contradictions' (*ibid.* p. 56). Apple (1993), tellingly, makes and develops the same point:

> What has been accomplished has been a successful translation of an economic doctrine into the language of experience, moral imperative and common sense. The free-market ethic has been combined with a populist politics. This has meant the blending together of a 'rich mix' of themes that have had a long history — nation, family, duty, authority, standards and traditionalism — with other thematic elements that have also struck a resonant chord during a time of crisis. Such themes include self-interest, competitive individualism . . . and anti-statism. In this way, a reactionary common sense is partly created. (p. 101)

Populist in form and content, Rightist discourse therefore appeals to all manner of people and circumstances. In the education sphere it connects with the experience of individual parents right across the social divide, many of whom, irrespective of class origin, share the same concern about their children's future in a society they perceive to be increasingly characterized by structural forms of unemployment, lawlessness, and the breakdown of moral and other forms of authority. No wonder sitting children in rows, whole class instruction, the teaching of 'right' from 'wrong' and academic knowledge seem so relevant to our times when the latter are characterized in such pathological terms.

Three Policy Ideas for the Next Millennium

But the point is that a traditional, mostly academic, education, is an unreliable and unhelpful response to the contemporary condition, least of all the requirements of the next millennium, and for three reasons in particular. First, it tends to assume and reproduce artificial distinctions between subject domains at a time when exactly the opposite is happening in the real world of knowledge creation. Second, and crucially, many of the very subject domains which have the potential to enable us to deal systematically with the experimental nature of everyday life have currently either low or no status within the academic curriculum of most schools — subjects and subject areas like politics, sociology, anthropology, cultural studies, psychology and philosophy. But, third, the very institutional structures that a traditional education gives rise to — steep management hierarchies, the concentration of power in a few individuals and the disempowerment of subordinates — are antithetical to a society made up people who, paradoxically, today rely less on tradition to guide their actions and more on their own judgment.

Also, a traditional education tends to create a boundary between education in school and education elsewhere. In particular, it overlooks the extent to which the application of modern media technologies are currently altering conceptions of what it means to be a teacher and a learner and therefore what it means to 'go to school'. Such technology can deliver lessons, assignments simulations and the world's libraries to anyone with a laptop and modem — it can also empower learners to select and manipulate data and interact with experts and sources of knowledge from around the world. Virtual seminars and intellectual dialogue already flourish in the university sector via open specialist mailing lists, which means that learners need not be constrained by membership of any one institution. Clearly, learning at a distance using recent developments of this sort will take some time to make a full impact in schools. But the gap between 'techno-hype' and the way we think of schooling and being educated is likely to be much shorter than is commonly appreciated given the pace and ubiquitousness of change in the modern era.

In any event, we will need in the next century to get seriously away from age-specific educational categories. This is not, by the way, a version of 'accelerated learning'. Rather, what is being pointed up is the importance of taking seriously the need to foster ever increasing opportunities for recurrent and continuous education as a necessary condition for creating what Stewart Ranson elsewhere in this book refers to as a 'learning society'. A pole apart from this requirement is the idea of a uniform system of comprehensive education. But, then, comprehensive schooling has never been seriously in favour of one. On the contrary, as was observed earlier, it has promoted diversification in one form or another throughout its history. Now maybe is the time for it to embrace diversity as an aim — rather than as an expedient — and to create the necessary conditions that help to provide an education for all the generations of the next millennium — one that provides 'really useful knowledge' that enables people to make sense of, and make their way in, an uncertain world.

Let us now reflect on the merits of three policies which would help this process along — one concerned with enabling structures, a second with new forms of democratic control, and the last with the teaching profession. The structural idea has already been tried, but only selectively, and always in an under-funded way. It is the idea of the community college. Although in the past it has taken a variety of forms and stressed different aspects of the educational process (see Martin, 1987), the philosophy of community education upon which it is based is grounded in a fundamental commitment to public sector provision and to the principles of comprehensive and continuing education. Community education in practice, it has to be acknowledged, has not always lived up to these high ideals (see Wallis and Mee, 1983; Cowburn, 1986). There have been, for example, problems with shared use of facilities, the democratization of provision and access to educational opportunity. Despite these difficulties, four aspects of the philosophy of community education are enduring and warrant consideration by all those anxious to affirm the comprehensive school ideal. First, policies for community education embrace the best features of self-governing status — whether in the form of a grant maintained school or a locally managed one — because they are designed to redirect educational priorities and practice in ways that bring education and community into a closer and more equal relationship. Second, they offer a basis and rationale for developing positive, coherent and user-friendly responses to the educational needs of all people in a locality. Third, they encourage the idea that education should work towards the harmonization of intellectual and practical study and their integration with the pursuit of leisure. And, fourth, they signal that education should be regarded as a continuous process from which people may take a break but never leave off entirely.

But embracing diversity as an aim will require networks of community colleges to be managed locally in such a way that the rights of the educationally vulnerable and disadvantaged are met and protected and the quality of provision properly monitored and its providers made fully accountable for their actions. A new type of local education body will need to be created to effect this. Brighouse (1996), Birmingham's Director of Education, and another contributor to this book, has persuasively outlined one model for the regeneration of local democratic control of education. It envisages an elected 'education council' which, besides having a key role in leading the drive for school improvement, acts as an honest broker to ensure the fair distribution of resources and places. As Brighouse concludes: 'It is not ownership that is the issue, rather access. Access to publicly provided facilities should . . . be locally accountable through the democratic process, especially when that process paid for the facilities to be provided in the first place' (p. 14).

The effective implementation of the sort of diversified comprehensive continuing education service which is being argued for here will also require a new generation of teachers committed to exploring and working on the margins of knowledge; who are happy to embrace a form of professional cosmopolitanism that pours scorn on all forms of educational fundamentalism; and who have a vocation to work with the most disadvantaged. We have to be find ways of attracting back into teaching, and teaching in the inner city, our most able young men and women. This might include (after Barber, 1996) offering them short-term contracts with performance related pay, or sabbaticals and other opportunities for refreshment and personal renewal. Whatever is decided eventually, something urgently needs to be done to ensure that there are the right kinds of teachers teaching in the worst kinds of settings.

At this point, it might be argued that what is being proposed here are inspiring visions for radical reform at the expense of being realistic about the possibilities for change. Such a conclusion would not be a fair one. The idea of the community college is neither fundamentally radical nor new, although there is a sense in which its central organizing principles resonate better with the conditions of the moment than the ones for which they were first created as a response. The idea about democratic control already has successful embodiments as evidenced in the manner in which many LEAs — not just Brighouse's — have adjusted significantly the manner in which they work today with local schools. The idea about the teaching profession, if anything, is fairly commonplace. Taken together, they could provide ground for some optimism for the future of comprehensive education.

Acknowledgment

The research reported in this chapter, as well as the analysis concerning the nature of traditionalism in education, is the product of work jointly undertaken by Professor David Halpin (Goldsmiths College, University of London), Dr Sally Power (University of Bristol) and Dr John Fitz (School of Education, University of Wales Cardiff), all of whom were funded on two occasions between 1990 and 1994 by the Economic and Social Research Council to conduct investigations of the grant-maintained schools policy.

References

APPLE, M. (1993) 'Rebuilding hegemony: Education, equality and the New Right' in DROWN, D.L. and ROMAN, L.G. [Eds] *Views Beyond the Border Country: Raymond William's and Cultural Politics*, New York & London, Routledge.

BARBER, M. (1996) 'The eye of the storm', *Guardian*, 30 January.

BENN, C. and CHITTY, C. (1996) *Thirty Years On: Is Comprehensive Education Alive and Well or Struggling to Survive?*, London, David Fulton.

BRIGHOUSE, T. (1996) *A Question of Standards: The Need for a Local Democratic Voice*, London, Politeia.

BUSH, T., COLEMAN, M. and GLOVER, D. (1993) *Managing Antonomous Schools*, London, Paul Chapman.

COWBURN, W. (1986) *Class, Ideology and Community Education*, London, Croom Helm.

DEPARTMENT OF EDUCATION and SCIENCE (DES) (1965) *The Organisation of Secondary Education* (Circular 10/65), London, HMSO.

EDWARDS, T. and WHITTY, G. (1992) 'Parental choice and educational reform in Britain and the United States', *British Journal of Educational Studies*, **40** 2, pp. 101–17.

FITZ, J., HALPIN, D. and POWER, S. (1993) *Grant Maintained Schools: Education in the Market Place*, London, Kogan Page.

FLETCHER, C., CARON, M. and WILLIAMS, W. (1985) *Schools on Trial: The Trials of Democratic Comprehensives*, Milton Keynes, Open University Press.

GIDDENS, A (1991) *Modernity and Self-Identity: Self and Society in the Late Modern Age*, Cambridge, Polity Press.

GIDDENS, A (1992) *The Transformation of Intimacy: Sexuality: Love and Eroticism in Modern Societies*, Cambridge, Polity Press.

GIDDENS, A. (1994a) *Beyond Left and Right: The Future of Radical Politics*, Cambridge, Polity Press.

GIDDENS, A. (1994b) 'Living in a post-traditional society' in BECK, U., GIDDENS, A. and LASH, S. (Eds) *Reflexive Modernization: Politics, Tradition and Aesthetics in the Modern Social Order*, Cambridge, Polity Press.

HALL, S. (1988) *The Hard Road to Renewal: Thatcherism and the Crisis of the Left*, London, Verso.

HALPIN, D., FITZ, J. and POWER, S (1995) 'Self-governance, grant-maintained schools and educational identities', end of award report, Project No. R00023391501, Swindon, Economic and Social Research Council.

HARGREAVES, D. (1994) *The Mosaic of Learning: Schools and Teachers for the Next Century*, Cambridge, Demos.

Johnson, R. (1989) 'Thatcherism and English education: Breaking the mould or confirming a pattern?', *History of Education*, **18** 2, pp. 91–121.

Lowe, R. (1989) 'Secondary education since the Second World War' in Lowe, R. (Ed) *The Changing Secondary School*, London & Washington DC, Falmer Press.

Martin, I. (1987) 'Community education: Towards a theoretical analysis' in Allen, G., Bastiani, J., Martin, I. and Richards, K. (Eds) *Community Education: An Agenda for Educational Reform*, Milton Keynes, Open University Press.

Maychell, K. (1994) *Counting the Cost: The Impact of LMS on Schools' Patterns of Spending*, Windsor, NFER.

Moon, B. (1983) (Ed) *Comprehensive Schools: Challenge and Change*, Windsor, NFER-Nelson.

Thomas, H. and Martin, J. (1996) *Managing Resources for School Improvement: Creating a Cost-Effective School*, London, Routledge.

Wallis, J. and Mee, G. (1983) *Community Schools: Claims and Performances*, Nottingham, Department of Adult Education, University of Nottingham.

4   Privatization and Selection

Geoffrey Walford

Introduction

This chapter examines two broad ideological movements within recent educational policy that have attacked the comprehensive ideal. These are privatization and selection, and it will be shown how these two policy thrusts have been interwoven in many government initiatives since 1979. Some of the results and dangers of such policies will be indicated, and one possible way in which comprehensive ideals within British education can be strengthened will be suggested.

Before doing so, however, it is necessary to provide an outline of the historical context, and to examine briefly some of the pressures that led to the development of comprehensive schools. Doing so will illustrate some of the problems that comprehensive schools sought to overcome, and show that those problems are being intensified by recent increases in privatization and selection.

The 1944 Education Act introduced 'secondary education for all' which, in most places, meant that a system of grammar, secondary modern and (sometimes) technical schools was established. By the mid-1950s there were many obvious problems. Fundamentally, it became clear that there was a considerable social class bias between the intakes to the different types of school in the selective system. The grammar schools were dominated by middle-class children, while the secondary moderns were largely the preserve of the working class (Floud *et al.*, 1956; Douglas, 1964). At that time, concern largely focused on the IQ tests that were generally used to select children. Arguments centred on the fairness of these tests for children from different backgrounds, the extent to which they were able to discriminate between children according to their abilities or their academic potential, and on the examinations having to be taken at an age when children were still developing at different rates (Yates and Pidgeon, 1957). It was also found that the reliability of the tests was low and that children could be coached into obtaining higher scores in these examinations, even though they were supposed to measure some 'innate' abilities (Ford, 1969). Even accepting a narrow definition of efficiency of selection based on what the IQ tests could measure, it was estimated that about 10 per cent of children were wrongly selected each year — half of these being wrongly selected for grammar schools and half wrongly going to secondary modern schools (Vernon, 1957). By 1970, IQ tests were largely discredited as a means of selection, but most of the problems associated with them also occur in other ways of selecting, Indeed, it might be argued that other methods are likely to be more rather than less biased. Headteachers' or teachers' reports, interviews of parents and children, or special selection tests are all likely to be even less reliable than IQ tests — as well as favouring children from particular social and economic backgrounds.

But 'accurate' selection was only part of the perceived problem. In the late 1960s a variety of sociological studies of grammar and secondary modern schools also began to raise questions about the desirability of selection at 11 independently of the degree to which selection could be accurately achieved. The classic socio-logical case studies of grammar and secondary modern schools by Hargreaves (1967) and Lacey (1970) showed the detrimental effects of selection and differen-tiation between and within schools. Those children at the bottom of a grammar school tended to think of themselves as failures and developed anti-school attitude. Other studies highlighted the cultural conflict experienced by a working class child in a grammar school. Where working class children did manage to enter grammar schools the cultural expectations were in stark contrast to their own (Dale and Griffith, 1965; Jackson and Marsden, 1962). There is little evidence to suggest that any of this will have changed if we return to more selective education. A further important factor that led to comprehensive schools was an increased demand for a 'grammar school-type' education. This was partly due to rising expectations on the part of parents, itself a partial result of changes to the social class structure as Brian Simon's chapter indicates, but pure demographic trends also had their effect. The postwar 'bulge' entered secondary education at a time when only a few new gram-mar schools had been created. In many areas, middle-class parents were finding that their children were not being admitted to the grammar schools which they had themselves attended. Instead, their children were being forced to attend second-ary moderns which they perceived (often correctly) were funded at a lower level, had poorer-paid and poorer-qualified teachers, and were only able to enter children for a limited range of public examinations. This individual concern about sons and daughters was largely transmuted to a call for greater educational equality of educational opportunity for all and greater national efficiency. It was believed that both of these would be provided through comprehensive education. This parental demand for a 'grammar school type' education is certainly no lower now than is was in the 1960s and 1970s. Grammar schools for 20 per cent, or even 40 or 60 per cent would not satisfy the demand. And what would the schools for those not selected be like?

But comprehensive schools also developed because there were many who believed that it was highly desirable to educate all local children in a single school. The 'social engineers' believed that schools where all children would have equal physical facilities and equal access to high quality teachers, would raise the aspira-tions and achievements of all children and teachers, bring about greater equity within the schools and lead to greater opportunities outside in the world of work. Additionally, it was hoped that mixing children from different social class back-grounds in the same school would lead to a lowering of barriers between classes and a reduction in class antagonism and class differences.

It must never be forgotten that the introduction of comprehensive schools began to challenge the dominant principle on which the British system of schooling has historically been based — selection of particular children for unequal provision. Throughout British history, social class and gender have been the major determinants of the quality of schooling that children received. While there has been some decrease in gender inequalities, we now live in a multicultural society that is increasingly harshly divided by class and ethnicity. Inequalities are increasing and, sadly, many of the educational policies of the last one and a half decades appear to have been designed to increase these inequalities. These policies can be examined through the interwoven ideologies of privatization and selection.

Privatization

Privatization has been one of the major policy priorities of successive Conservative governments since 1979. But it is not an easy term to define — for the concept has come to be applied to a number of apparently disparate government policies. Most obviously, it refers to the sale of government owned monopolies and trading companies to shareholders, but the range of areas where privatization can be said to have occurred includes residential homes for the elderly, bus deregulation, the sale of council houses, and changes to pensions, health and social services. In all of these cases there has been a shift away from state provision (although not necessarily state subsidy), and a corresponding encouragement of the private sector. Writing in a pamphlet published by the right-wing Adam Smith Institute, Madsen Pirie (1985) described privatization as a general approach with can generate and focus policy ideas. He illustrated this diversity through a list of about twenty different methods by which privatization has been introduced. These include selling the whole or the part, charging for services, contracting out, buying out existing interest groups, encouraging private institutions, encouraging exit from state institutions, and divestment.

Within education privatization has similarly taken many different forms. Richard Pring (1987) discussed these in terms of the government's two main thrusts of supporting and encouraging the private sector whilst gradually decreasing its support for the state maintained sector. Thus, while the state maintained sector has seen, for example, contracting out of services, increasingly inadequate funding, and a growing need to beg for support from industry, parents and the local community, government has given positive encouragement to alternative private institutions through its ideological and financial support, and has encouraged exit from state institutions.

Selection

Selection is somewhat easier to define, but still not straightforward. What is important to recognize is that, while most British children now attend comprehensive schools, selection of children for unequal provision has been the dominant principle on which the system of schooling has been historically based. Throughout British history, social class and gender have been the major determinants of the quality of schooling that children received. The move to comprehensive schools began to make a difference and to interrupt this pattern. But Britain has never had a truly comprehensive system. Even in Scotland, where all state maintained schools are comprehensive, there still remains a small private sector of about 3 per cent. In England and Wales the proportion of children going to private schools is larger. On average some 7 or 8 per cent attend private schools, but this rises to over 20 per cent of secondary pupils in some areas of the South East. In this situation, comprehensive schools are comprehensive in name only.

Moreover, within the so-called comprehensive system, selection by mortgage (Clarke, 1991) has remained. Concerned, affluent parents have always been able to buy a home near to a school which they perceive to be of acceptable quality. Children from families without the necessary financial and cultural resources have had to accept whatever is on offer locally.

The grammar school scholarships prior to 1944, and the tripartite system that followed, were both concerned with selection by academic abilities, potentials or sometimes 'aptitudes'. There was a myth of 'parity of esteem' that some politicians of the time trumpeted. But it was widely recognized that the various types of school were differentially funded and that some had far better facilities than others. Further, these differences were legitimized through the idea of selection of appropriate children on 'fair' tests. The selected few were seen as 'deserving' better schooling. We now know, of course, that these tests were not 'fair', and this recognition was one of the main factors that led to the demise of the tripartite system. But, the idea that unequal provision was unjust, as such, was not a primary target of the campaign for comprehensives. The lack of focus on the injustice of unequal provision is one of the reasons why it has been possible for the government to so easily reintroduce selection into schooling without great controversy — the idea that 'the chosen' deserve better provision remains largely unchallenged.

Comprehensive schools went some small way towards increasing equity, and offered greater opportunities to all children. But the return of selection for unequal provision is beginning to reverse the trend and to reinforce social class and ethnic differences once again (Walford, 1994a). But selection now comes in several different forms. While selection on academic ability is increasing, most new forms of selection are based upon particular specialisms such as music, drama or technology. The evidence indicates that these specialisms act to separate according to class, gender and ethnicity as firmly and surely (perhaps more firmly and surely) than the old 11+ examinations.

Some Examples

Since the election of Margaret Thatcher's first government in 1979 a series of separate, yet interlinked, policies have been introduced to support and encourage the private sector of education while gradually decreasing the support given to the state maintained sector. There has been a gradual blurring of the boundaries between the two forms of education provision and a growth in market competition between schools. At the same time, the selection of particular children for unequally funded schools has been encouraged. Selection and privatization have been interwoven features of many policy changes. It is worth considering a few of the most significant examples.

The first Conservative legislation to encourage the idea that some children (other than those with special educational needs) 'deserved' to be singled out for greater expenditure came with the Assisted Places Scheme of 1980. This scheme was originally justified in terms of giving 'certain children a greater opportunity to pursue a particular form of academic education that was regrettably not otherwise, particularly in the cities, available to them' (quoted in Griggs, 1985, p. 89). Children from 'modest backgrounds' were to be 'plucked like embers from the ashes' of the state system to enter private schools of high academic reputation (Whitty and Edwards, 1984, p. 164). Edwards, Fitz and Whitty (1989) have shown that a large proportion of the children benefiting from the scheme have been from families able to 'play the system'. Those families sufficiently knowledgeable about the procedures, and able to negotiate the choice and selection processes inherent in the scheme have been rewarded with more costly staffing and facilities than in the state sector. The scheme acts as a direct financial support for selected high status private schools at a time when funding for state education is under heavy pressure. But, perhaps more important, it also gives ideological support to the whole private sector. For the implication of the scheme is that private schools are 'better' than the state sector and that the government has little faith that its own schools are the right place for aspiring parents to send their children.

Stuart Sexton (1987), one of the main architects of the Assisted Places Scheme, and educational advisor to two Secretaries of State for Education and Science, has made it clear that a fully 'privatized' education service was his long-term aim. According to him, the Assisted Places Scheme can be seen as the first step in a gradual plan towards the 'eventual introduction of a "market system" truly based upon the supremacy of parental choice, the supremacy of purchasing power'. This scheme has been extended several times since its inception, and the most recent changes will lead to a near doubling of the scale of the scheme and, from 1996, includes some children below the age of 11 in the preparatory departments of some major schools.

A very different example of the mixing of privatization and selection can be seen in the Technical and Vocational Education Initiative (TVEI). While far from being a simple privatization scheme, the advent of TVEI marked the next attempt to legitimize differential funding on criteria not directly associated with pupil needs. In this case local education authorities and particular schools within them were asked to bid for extra funding to provide for specific schemes. The bidding system and forms of contractual organization were derived from private enterprise and were introduced outside the local education authority framework. Competition and self-interest were encouraged rather than LEA and nationwide planning. The original idea was that, even within the same school, some pupils were to be selected to be 'TVEI pupils' and benefit from enhanced facilities and tuition, while others were to be prohibited from profiting from the TVEI funding. This idea quickly broke down as teachers found ways of ensuring that all children in TVEI schools benefitted, but there were still major differences between the schools taking part in TVEI and those not doing so within the same LEA. What is also of note here is that, in general, TVEI money went to schools that already had well developed plans in technology, or were able to generate sufficiently convincing plans for new projects. Here, schools showing themselves to be 'deserving' were rewarded, whilst others (actually needing more help) were denied funding. By giving more help to those schools which were already advantaged, TVEI money was designed to widen the differences between schools.

The third, and most clearly significant, development of privatization and selection occurred in 1986, when the government announced that it intended to work with sponsors to establish a network of twenty city technology colleges. These were intended to provide free technology-enhanced education to selected children within particular inner-city areas. They were to be private schools, run by independent charitable trusts, with the sponsors having a major influence on the way in which the colleges were managed. These sponsors were also intended to provide substantial financial and material support. A key element of the CTCs is that they were established as private schools and the expectation was that the CTCs would be funded at a higher level than other schools through contributions from both the state and private sponsors. Selection of specific children for inequitable provision was a central feature of the plan. Private school status also allowed the colleges considerable flexibility in staffing, curriculum and management issues (Walford, 1991).

As is well known, there were considerable difficulties in attracting sufficient sponsorship and in finding appropriate sites for the CTCs (Walford and Miller, 1991; Whitty, Edwards and Gewirtz, 1993). The programme stopped at fifteen CTCs with about 20 per cent of capital funding having been provided by sponsors and the bulk of the capital expenditure and practically all of the current expenditure being provided direct by central government. In this case selection of children is not based on academic ability — a spread of abilities is required by law. But the method of selection still closely resembles that for the Assisted Places Scheme. Families need to know about the colleges and be able and prepared to negotiate the entrance procedures (which usually include a test and interview). The children have to agree to work a longer school day and longer terms and intend to stay on at school until 18. Thus, the CTCs are designed to benefit children from 'deserving' working class families. In short, those families who can show themselves to be 'deserving' are far more likely to gain a place than others. Those children from families with little interest in education are ignored.

The 1986 announcement of the CTCs thus marked a break with the traditional pattern that all state-funded schools should be financed and managed through the local education authorities. The 1988 Education Reform Act's introduction of grant-maintained schools made the break decisive. Officially, grant-maintained schools are only allowed to select if they were selective prior to opting-out or if they have been granted a 'change of character' following a full consultation process. In practice,

Bush and his colleagues (Bush *et al.*, 1993) found that several nominally comprehensive grant-maintained schools were unofficially selecting by ability. But, even where they were not, the high degree of commitment demanded from parents and children (which may include a separate application, an 'informative' interview and sometimes a test [Fitz *et al.*, 1993]) introduces another form of selection. Many of these schools have found that, if the barriers to entry are set high enough, self-selection can operate as an effective way of ensuring that 'deserving' families are selected.

The development of grant-maintained schools can be seen to be closely linked to privatization. While the government has given strong financial and ideological support to such schools, the local authority maintained sector has been at the receiving end of various negative elements of privatization. In particular, spending on education overall has not kept up with the necessary demands made on it. A succession of HMI reports throughout the 1980s and 1990s have catalogued the neglect of physical bricks and mortar, and it has become commonplace for parents to paint and decorate classrooms in order to ensure an appropriate environment for their children. Many parents now pay for what were once regarded as the essential of education (Pring, 1987), and their donations have become increasingly important in maintaining the quality of service and facilities. In addition to providing funds for school trips, new computers, decoration of premises and new equipment, many schools now rely on parents to fund actual staff. It is now common for some teachers and additional auxiliary staff to be dependent on voluntary donations for their salaries. Payment has become a ubiquitous necessity for those parents who demand high standards — the problem is that not all parents are able or willing to contribute, leading to inadequate funding in some schools.

There has been a blurring of the line between fee-paying and non-fee-paying schools. Since the early 1980s, state-maintained schools have become more like private schools in the way they tout for financial support from sponsors. Seeking private industrial or commercial funding has become an important part of many headteachers' jobs. In some schools companies now pay to have advertisements sited within the buildings, while other companies can be persuaded to sponsor particular cultural or artistic events if their name is given prominence on advertising. When supermarkets such as Tescos and Sainsbury's offer computers or other equipment to schools if parents shop at their stores, many schools act to encourage parents to do so. The problem, of course, is that some parents are more able or willing to donate than others, and some schools have better links with industry than their neighbours. Schools that serve children from poor homes are unlikely to be able to generate much additional funding from either parents or sponsors, while schools serving more affluent families may do well from both. Consequently the inequalities between schools gradually increase, and some schools become oversubscribed. Schools begin to selectively encourage 'deserving', 'generous', 'supportive' parents. Not even the National Lottery distributes its bounty fairly, for schools have to find 35 per cent of the cost of any project before it will be considered. Schools already having significant support have the chance of even greater, while those unable to raise the 35 per cent have no chance at all.

Recent Growth in Privatization and Selection

There are several aspects of the 1993 Education Act and subsequent government announcements that reemphasized the government's commitment to privatization and selection. The most important change is that all secondary schools have been given the right to 'specialize' in one or more curriculum areas such as science, music, technology or modern languages. What is crucial is that the introduction of a 'specialism' does not necessitate an official 'change of character' and as long as only up to 10 per cent of the intake is selected according to criteria related to the specialism. The results of such a changes are not unexpected. The recent and impressive research by Gewirtz, Ball and Bowe (1995) indicates that, where curriculum specialisms are being introduced by schools, they are acting as selection mechanisms for high academic ability and middle class children. In particular, the development of specialisms such as dance or music indirectly discriminates against working class families, and allows schools a greater chance to select 'appropriate' children. The recent consultation Government Circular is set to increase the proportion to 15 per cent and allow selection on 'general ability' as well as ability in specific subjects.

Further privatization and selection are evident in the idea of technology colleges. The 1993 Education Act allowed voluntary-aided and grant-maintained schools to apply to the Secretary of State for Education for a change to their governing Instruments and Articles to include sponsor governors and become technology colleges. This was later extended to local authority schools. Schools that already have a strong and planned commitment to technology, science and mathematics are expected to be able to find sponsorship from industry in return for these seats on the governing body. The expectation is that there is a 'significant financial commitment' from the sponsors (which has been interpreted as being in the region of £100,000 per school), as well as close involvement by the sponsors in the life of the school. Once this support has been obtained three extra sources of funding are available: an initial capital grant, for furniture, equipment and associated building work; an enhanced annual capital formula allocation intended to contribute towards replacement and upgrading of enhanced equipment; and additional revenue funding above their normal funding designed to 'assist with the extra costs of operating an enhanced, technology-rich curriculum' (DFE, 1993, p. 10). The intention is explicitly that these colleges are funded (both initially and continually) at a higher level than other schools. They are predicated on the idea that some children should be selected to benefit from schools funded at a higher level, while other children are left in schools which, presumably, are not be funded at a level sufficient to provide an adequate, up-to-date technological experience.

The 1993 Education Act also encouraged diversification of schools through the establishment of new grant-maintained schools which support particular religious or philosophical beliefs. These may be schools that aim to foster, for example, Islamic, Buddhist, or evangelical Christian beliefs or which wish to promote particular educational philosophies. Existing faith-based private schools are able to apply to become reestablished as grant-maintained schools. At first sight this aspect of policy would appear to be the very opposite of privatization, for existing private schools are taken into the state sector. In practice, the way the policy is being implemented is closer to a new form of privatization than nationalization.

The important difference between these new sponsored grant-maintained schools and existing grant-maintained schools is that sponsors have to pay for at least 15 per cent of costs relating to the provision of a site for the school and school buildings. The Funding Agency for Schools' booklet *Guidance for Promoters* makes it clear that this 15 per cent is a minimum, and that potential sponsors should not assume that the Agency will fund 85 per cent of the project.

> A major factor for the Agency is whether the proposals represent value for money. If you are able to contribute a higher proportion of the capital costs of a project, any capital grant we pay will represent better value for money for the public and we will therefore be better placed to give overall support for the proposal. (FAS, 1995)

The legislation came into operation in April 1994. So far, only two existing private schools in England have become grant-maintained. Both of these are Roman Catholic grammar schools — one for boys and the other for girls — in Birkenhead, which retains a selective system. In both cases, the existing private schools were already heavily supported by the state through assisted places and through places bought by the local education authority for Roman Catholic children who passed the 11+ examinations. In practice, the state has been able to expand state-funded provision at very low cost, for each school has leased their extensive buildings and grounds for ninety-nine years for a peppercorn rent. While only 15 per cent of capital costs are actually required to be provided by the sponsors, in these two cases the contribution is far higher — in effect, 100 per cent of capital costs (although there is a need for some new building in one case). In contrast, the one application from a group of evangelical Christians who wished to open a new school in Bristol, was rejected by the Secretary of State after over a year's deliberations. While the case was complex, it is notable that the 15 per cent was the very upper limit of what they could afford.

Thus, this new policy on sponsored grant-maintained schools looks to be close to the CTC pattern where sponsors were expected to provide substantial private capital. It also may not be accidental that the first two schools to make the transition are grammar schools. These new sponsored schools bring a further form of selection of children. Once the schools are oversubscribed, they will be forced to select, and those families where education is already valued will probably have an advantage over those where education is of less interest.

Conclusion

Privatization and selection have been important ideological motivations for many Conservative policies in education since 1979. The Assisted Places Scheme and city technology colleges were early examples that had only a limited impact on the system as a whole, but more recent policies have accelerated the push for greater selection of children for unequal provision. These twin ideologies are in sharp conflict with the comprehensive ideal. This ideal is encapsulated by Gewirtz, Ball and Bowe (1995) in the following way:

> The comprehensive system of educational provision is based upon the principles that it is socially and educationally advantageous for all children, whatever their ability, class or ethnic background, to be educated together in a 'common school', and in mixed-ability groups, and that all children should have access to a learning environment which enables them to realize their potential. (p. 187)

This comprehensive ideal affirms that children's education should not be disadvantaged by their backgrounds, and that the state should provide free, high quality education for all in comprehensive schools.

Selection of specific children for differentially funded and supported schools clearly violates this principle, and the increase in various forms of privatization merely encourages greater differences between schools. Much of the present government's educational policy attacks the comprehensive ideal and will increase injustice and inequity. It will lead to a system of unequally funded schools which will provide very different educational experiences for children of different abilities, social classes and ethnic groups. As schools become more different, selection is likely to become more important and disadvantaged children are likely to lose out.

The problem is, of course, 'what is to be done?' It is a right and, I believe, a duty of all parents to seek to do the best they can for their children. In addition, it is the duty of the state to ensure that some parents' individualistic strivings do not damage the chances of children from other families. There are no easy answers to such a balance, but a way needs to be found of harnessing the legitimate desires of those parents who are concerned about the schooling of their own children, such that they demand high quality education for all children and not just their own.

I have suggested elsewhere the elements of one possible system (Walford, 1994b). Any truly comprehensive system demands that individual schools should not have the right to control their own admissions. Selection on abilities, specialisms, interests, aptitudes, or any other anti-comprehensive criteria must be banned. We know that these criteria are all closely linked to social class and ethnicity, and they can be used as surrogates in any selection process. While these specialisms are advertised as leading to a diversity of schools, the truth is that they will form a hierarchy of differentially funded schools that will offer diversity in the quality of the experience on offer more than any other form of diversity (Walford, 1996). We do not have genuine diversity of schools, and we are unlikely to ever have true diversity of schools while the private sector retains its dominant position and emphasis on the academic curriculum. What we have is a hierarchy of schools closely linked to the single dimension of selection by social background.

However, it is undesirable to return to the pre-1979 or even the pre-1944 education system. We need to retain some degree of choice for families. At the same time we need to accept that it is inevitable that some schools will be more popular than others, and that there will be insufficient places in some popular schools for all who apply. The problem is reduced if ways are found to minimise the differences in popularity between schools, and to ensure that some children are not disadvantages in the choice-making process. We need to clarify the choice-making process and introducing clear, simple and unbiased procedures for selecting children for oversubscribed schools.

This is best done if no child is allocated to any school. Instead, all families should be required to select three or four schools in order of preference. Funding should be made available for travel and other incidental costs to ensure that reasonable choices are not restricted by family income. Independent information centres and advisors should be established to encourage and help all families with this decision-making process.

Where there are fewer applications than places available the first preference would be automatically granted. Schools would have no right to reject a child, and the power to exclude or expel a child would be removed from the schools and given to the local authority. Where schools are oversubscribed, successful applicants should be selected randomly from those who apply. Random selection is essential for it guarantees that some parents are not able to ensure the success of their own children by purchasing a home near to the school they aspire to use, or by being able to present themselves as more committed and concerned at interview. To my mind, exceptions to the principle of random selection should be at an absolute minimum, and might include children with specific physical disabilities. Random selection introduces uncertainty, so it becomes necessary for concerned parents to work for high quality schools for all children rather than devoting their efforts entirely towards the schooling of their own children.

Requiring all families to make a choice will broaden and deepen concern for education. More uncertainty in selection will ensure that high quality schooling for all children will become a political imperative. Somewhat paradoxically, requiring all families to make a choice, where there is uncertainty of that choice being granted, will reduce the importance of that choice. An extended hierachy of schools is less likely to develop and schools will be given the chance to ensure that they give the highest possible quality education to all children.

References

BUSH, T., COLEMAN, M. and GLOVER, D. (1993) *Managing Autonomous Schools: The Grant-Maintained Experience*, London, Paul Chapman.

CLARKE, K. (1991) 'Kenneth Clarke in interview with Richard Davison', *The ISIS Magazine*, autumn, p. 9.

DALE, R.R. and GRIFFITH, S. (1965) *Down Stream. Failure in the Grammar School*, London, Routledge & Kegan Paul.

DEPARTMENT FOR EDUCATION (DFE) (1992) *Choice and Diversity. A New Framework for Schools*, London, DFE.

DEPARTMENT FOR EDUCATION (DFE) (1993) *Technology Colleges: Schools for the Future*, London, DFE.

DOUGLAS, J.W.D. (1964) *The Home and the School*, London, MacGibbon & Kee.

EDWARDS, T., FITZ, J. and WHITTY, G. (1989) *The State and Private Education: An Evaluation of the Assisted Places Scheme*, London, Falmer Press.

FITZ, J., HALPIN, D. and POWER, S. (1993) *Grant Maintained Schools: Education in the Market Place*, London, Kogan Page.

FLOUD, J.E., HALSEY, A.H. and MARTIN, F.M. (1956) *Social Class and Educational Opportunity*, London, Heinemann.

FORD, J. (1969) *Social Class and the Comprehensive School*, London, Routledge & Kegan Paul.

FUNDING AGENCY FOR SCHOOLS (1995) *Guidance for Promoters*, York, Funding Agency for Schools.

GEWIRTZ, S., BALL, S.J. and BOWE, R. (1995) *Markets, Choice and Equity in Education*, Buckingham, Open University Press.

GRIGGS, C. (1985) *Private Education in Britain*, London, Falmer Press.

HARGREAVES, D.H. (1967) *Social Relations in a Secondary School*, London, Routledge & Kegan Paul.

JACKSON, B. and MARSDEN, D. (1962) *Education and the Working Class*, London, Routledge.

LACEY, C. (1970) *Hightown Grammar*, Manchester, Manchester University Press.

PIRIE, M. (1985) *Privatization*, London, Adam Smith Institute.

PRING, R. (1987) 'Privatization in education' in ROGERS, R. (Ed) *Education and Social Class*, London, Falmer Press.

SEXTON, S. (1987) *Our Schools. A Radical Policy*, London, Institute of Economic Affairs.

VERNON, P.E. (1957) *Secondary School Selection*, London, Methuen.

WALFORD, G. (1990) *Privatization and Privilege in Education*, London, Routledge.

WALFORD, G. (1991) 'City technology colleges: A private magnetism', in WALFORD, G. (Ed) *Private Schooling: Tradition, Change and Diversity*, London, Paul Chapman.

WALFORD, G. (1994a) *Choice and Equity in Education*, London, Cassell.

WALFORD, G. (1994b) 'A return to selection?', *Westminster Studies in Education*, **17**, pp. 19–30.

WALFORD, G. (1995) *Educational Politics: Pressure Groups and Faith-based Schools*, Aldershot, Avebury Press.

WALFORD, G. (1996) 'Diversity and choice in school education: An alternative view', *Oxford Review of Education*, **22**, 2, pp. 143–54.

WALFORD, G. and MILLER, H. (1991) *City Technology College*, Milton Keynes, Open University Press.

WHITTY, G. and EDWARDS, T. (1984) 'Evaluating policy change: The assisted places scheme', in WALFORD, G. (Ed) *British Public Schools: Policy and Practice*, London, Falmer Press.

WHITTY, G., EDWARDS, T. and GEWIRTZ, S. (1993) *Specialisation and Choice in Urban Education: The City Technology College Experiment*, London, Routledge.

YATES, A. and PIDGEON, D.A. (1957) *Admission to Grammar Schools*, London, NFER.

Social and Political Philosophy

5   Markets, Equity and Values in Education

Stephen J. Ball

Introduction

One of the main arguments mounted against comprehensive education by Right-wing critics of educational reform in the 1960s and 1970s was that it was a form of social engineering. And indeed the comprehensive school was seen by some of its advocates, Benn and Simon and Anthony Crosland in particular, as a means of achieving greater social intergration. For them a major aim of comprehensive education was 'improved qualities of citizenship and the achievement of a tolerant or socially conscious society' (Ball, 1981, pp. 7–8). Benn and Simon (1972) wrote:

> In a society with class and race differences, a school that reflects all sections of a local community will often reflect these differences in the school. The comprehensive school does not offer pupils a chance to hide from society, but the opportunity to learn in the conditions of social reality that prevail in the wider community. Where there are tensions, the opportunity to come to terms with them or to effect improvements through them, (is) just as likely to be realistic, and in the end, lasting, when approached in years to come by men and women who have had a comprehensive, rather than a segregated education. (p. 8)

I do not intend to claim that comprehensive schooling in practice systematically or comprehensively produced such effects or even that comprehensive schools consistently strived to realize this ideal. Leaving aside the question as to whether or not we ever had a fully-fledged system of comprehensive education in England, many so-called comprehensive schools clearly had embedded in their practice the aims, values and assumptions of what Benn and Simon call 'segregated education'. The almost total absence of any political commitment from central government to comprehensive values made inertia a perfectly valid and rational response in those LEAs or schools which also had no local political commitment to serious comprehensive reform.

Nonetheless, I want to suggest that the social values of, and in, education policies are important. That even in half-realized, distorted or indirect ways they do have effects, often very profound effects, on the meaning and processes of education, on social relationships and on the structure and meaning of social experience. My main concern here is with the values which have supplanted those of comprehensivism, that is, with the current experiment in social engineering being undertaken through the policies of the market and choice in education. These policies, in complex interrelationship with such concepts as excellence, quality, effectiveness and the methods of entrepreneurial managerialism, are part of a political crusade and transformational process intended to create a new moral environment, a new kind of citizenship and a 'new cultural hero' (sic), the entrepreneur. As Margaret Thatcher argued, as early as 1975, 'serious as the economic challenge is, the political and moral challenge is just as grave, and perhaps more so, because economic problems never start with economics' (quoted in Hall, 1988, p. 85). Current education reforms are part of a broad programme of political and moral change.

The Education Market

One of the difficulties that arise within policy discussions about social markets in fields of public service like education is that advocates and critics alike confuse the 'market-in-theory', the perfect market, with the 'market-in-practice', the real or realizable market. As Fossey (1994) puts it:

> Too often family-choice advocates have proceeded as if every manifestation of school choice will improve the quality of education, with little regard for how particular programs are designed. (p. 332)

As a sociologist I am interested in these markets-in-practice and their actual effects in the here and now, as represented in research evidence, not in some unrealizable market utopia. It is also important to register here that the market solution is at work not just in education but in virtually every other area of public policy and public service from health, housing and community services to prisons and the Civil Service. In each area the design of the market form differs and the social costs and benefits vary. Significantly, the particular market form in play in 5–16 education is one of those which comes closest to a 'real' market, in that the consumers can make their own choices directly and those choices carry with them a direct transfer of funds to the producer. However, it must be noted that there is an important and increasing practical difference in the education market between making a choice and getting a choice. Some choices carry with them a higher value in the UK education market and thus have a higher chance of being realized than do others.

We are now getting to the stage with the market experiment in the UK and elsewhere where it is possible to identify a variety of pieces of research evidence which directly address the arguments made in favour of markets by politicians and proselytizers and made against them by critics. I want to refer to some of that research as I proceed. My overall concern here is to put the education market and the idea of parental choice back into context — to move beyond abstract rhetoric and develop a social analysis of choice and the market which recognizes both the specificity of local contexts within which market forces are enacted and remains aware of the broader political context which frames and structures the workings of the market (see below). Social markets are practical *and* political, pure market perfections exist only in the vivid imaginations of zealous and unworldly political theorists.

I proceed by taking up two of the issues signalled in my initial discussion of comprehensivism and education markets. That is I will be concerned primarily with the values in, and of, education but will begin with the question of segregation and equity in the education market (for more discussion see Ball, 1995b). More generally I want to turn around the 'accusation' of social engineering and apply the same criticism to the political and educational project of the UK Conservative government.

Arbitrary Exclusions

Choice is not, by definition, available to all. It never can be. While many advocates note, in passing, the practical and other limitations on choice, politicians typically 'sell' choice as a universal right and universal panacea. However, by virtue of geography, cost, school availability and producer power, among other factors, some families have no choice in so called choice systems. Furthermore, families opposed to or who do not value choice have choice thrust upon them (*ibid*). Now the argument is sometimes made that because market forces are 'unintentional', and all markets are imperfect, we should not see arbitrary exclusions in the education market as a problem — that the market is a 'best lousy theory' (Crump, 1994). But the 'unintentional' and imperfect defence is difficult to sustain. The UK market in education, as I shall go on to illustrate, is neither unfettered nor unplanned. It is a highly structured and ordered political market. Social markets are in practice neither natural nor neutral and it is increasingly evident from research studies that their imperfections and exclusions replicate and ramify established social patterns and divisions. Furthermore, the political interventions into the English education market have been selective and partisan. They are not used to equalize access and opportunity — quite the reverse.

However, 'lived' markets function in very different ways according to 'local' idiosyncrasies (Menter *et al.*, 1994; Lauder *et al.*, 1994; Hershkoff and Cohen, 1992). There is no national education market but a constellation of local competitive arenas with varying patterns of opportunity, advantage and disadvantage. The operation of these local, 'lived' markets is complex and often relatively invisible. Devolution, deregulation and open choice produce patterns of access and opportunity which are increasingly difficult to monitor and analyze. And the more deregulation and devolution the more scope for social networking by articulate parents and 'insider trading' in high 'value' students.

In other words, the UK education market is both highly imperfect and highly diverse. General and abstract claims about choice or market effects must be carefully grounded in research evidence. The universalism typically attached to market claims, as in first version of *The Parent's Charter* (DES, 1991), 'You have a duty to ensure that your child gets an education — and you can choose the school that you would like your child to go to' — significantly the latter phrase does not appear in *The Updated Parent's Charter* (1994) — distorts and obscures the fragmentation, differentiation and hierarchy which are evident from research as the major outcomes of choice and the market (I am not suggesting here that the pre-market system was equal and just, but that existing inequalities and social divisions in education are becoming more marked, under the market regime of access, funding and parenting [Gewirtz, 1996; Echols, 1990].). Where most of the most successful economies around the world are committed to mass, inclusive systems of education, in the UK we are going backwards towards division, elitism, and exclusion.

The Equity Fallacies

Chubb and Moe (1990), two very influential prosletizers of the market in education, make, in passing it has to be said, two crucially important points about market imperfections. First, that 'the unequal distribution of income in society may bias certain markets in favour of the rich and against the poor' (p. 31) and second, that 'to the extent that these, and other imperfections are serious, markets are less likely to generate the diversity, quality and levels of service that consumers want' (p. 32). It seems to me that research evidence is telling us that these features of the education market far from being untoward imperfections are actually inherent qualities of such markets. Education markets are organized and animated by inequality, exclusivity and exclusion. Thus, for example, my own research on metropolitan secondary schools (with Sharon Gewirtz and Richard Bowe [see Ball, Bowe and Gewirtz, 1996]) and that of others (like Willms and Echols in Scotland, Hugh Lauder and his New Zealand team (Lauder *et al.*, 1994), Fitz, Halpin and Power in the grant-maintained schools research (Halpin, Power and Fitz, 1991) suggests that choice is driven by intake differentials (for example, Echols and Willms, 1993). That is to say, parental choice is strongly motivated by social closure — class and racial segregation. As schools respond to these parental 'needs' and concerns they become implicated in formal and informal procedures for manipulating intakes (Moore and Davenport, 1990). (Such manipulation is given further impetus in the UK through the effects of government-imposed performance indicators.) All of this produces a further slippage between making and getting a choice. In many localities families are in competition for school places. Certain choices are unavailable to certain families because their children do not possess the qualities required by particular schools. This is hardly the 'common life, rich in choice-worthy options' (p. 110) that Gray (1993) takes as the objective of the social market economy.

Furthermore, only some families have both high inclination and high capacity to participate in the market (Gewirtz, Ball and Bowe, 1993a). Choice and the market mode are familiar and acceptable to such families. They are able to use existing skills, and cultural and social capital to obtain maximum advantage through choice (Ball, Bowe and Gewirtz, 1996). Thus, elsewhere I have argued that choice and the market form is a new cultural arbitrary (Bourdieu, 1990) and as such it produces exclusion and disqualification through a language of empowerment (Ball, 1993). All this highlights the question Pat White addresses to educational choice, that is: 'Can one be a good parent and a bad citizen?' (White, 1994).

In various ways the incentives and disciplines of a market system, and certainly those at work in the UK education market, tend to ramify existing social inequalities. For example, in the UK children with learning difficulties and those presenting behavioural problems, whose presence is seen as a threat to both the reputation and performance of certain schools, are increasingly concentrated in those schools unable to exercise 'discretion' over entry (Gewirtz, Ball and Bowe, 1995). And often these latter are under-subscribed schools with fewer resources than those who are able to manipulate their intakes. Thus, we can begin to see alongside the processes of social differentiation a concomitant movement of funding, from previous arrangements, whereby those students with most social and educational difficulty get fewer resources and those with least difficulty get more. Fossey's (1994) research in Massachusetts identifies such an effect. The possibility of choice in that state, taken up almost exclusively by middle class families, resulted in the movement of middle-class students out of low SES districts and into high SES districts, taking their attached funding with them. Fossey comments that:

> depending on the severity of the penalties for districts that lose students, open enrolment plans may be more than ineffective; they may actually hinder districts that lose students from improving their educational programs. By taking money away from districts that lose students — often districts with fewer resources and lower socioeconomic levels than receiving towns — such programs could make it more difficult for districts that are already handicapped to obtain higher levels of performance. (*ibid.*, p. 332)

Several other studies in the USA have also drawn attention to the deleterious effects of choice and competition, both where 'choice' produces movement between public and private school systems and where there are forms of school specialization in the public system. Hershkoff and Cohen (1992) demonstrate how in Choctaw County, Alabama state subsidies for private school 'choices' have diminished financial support for public schools, produced racial and economic segregation and stigmatized the public school system and its students. 'Parental choice has led to the creation of a dual system that has had a devastating impact on the public schools and the children left behind in them' (p. 3). Here choice is a 'sorting mechanism' that separates children along racial and class lines. In very different settings (magnet school programmes in New York, Chicago, Boston and Philadelphia) Moore and Davenport (1990) reported a very similar pattern of sorting based on race and class. In part the 'sorting' effect is again a reflection of the 'inclination to choice' among high income groups. However, in these programmes the discretion of the selecting schools and the complexities of the admissions procedures also contributed significantly to the segregation effects.

Given the discretion exercised in recruitment, screening, and selection, there was an overwhelming bias toward establishing procedures and standards at each step in the admissions process that screened out 'problem' students and admitted the 'best' students, with 'best' being defined as students with good academic records, good attendance, good behaviour, a mastery of English, and no special learning problems. (p. 201)

Chenoweth (1987) found similar processes at work in San Francisco's magnet programme (see also Blank, 1990). And Goldring and Shapira (1993), reporting on four elementary 'schools of choice' in Tel Aviv, Israel, also note the unrepresentatively high SES composition of the schools of choice. Moore and Davenport (1990) go on to conclude from their study that:

Public school choice is a reform strategy whose advocates have thus far failed to prove that it can bring about the widespread school improvement that is essential in the nation's big cities. School choice has proven risks and unproven benefits for students at risk, and has typically represented a new and more subtle form of discriminatory sorting. . . . (p. 221)

And Hershkoff and Cohen (1992) warn that 'any educational improvement that a market approach might bring comes at a price: the creation of an underclass of disfavoured and underfunded schools' (p. 25)

All of this points towards another sense in which it is important to place the education market in social context. As noted earlier, education is not the only arena of public policy in which the market solution is being experimented with. Educational differentiation and segregation is typically related to, and embedded in, other social divisions and inequalities — for example in cities in the US school choice programmes can be seen as part of what Darden, Dunleep and Glaster (1992) call the 'web of urban racism'. Thus, Margonis and Parker (1996) conclude their review of race issues in US school choice research by stating starkly that 'market driven choice plans serve to ossify and reinforce already established social divisions based on wealth and race' (p. 2) and they see such plans as part of 'the politics of urban racial containment' and as related to 'the political galvanization of white self interest around the issue of race' (p. 10).

This brings us directly to one of the perversities of Conservative government education policy. That is the reinvention of selection. The increasing emphasis upon, and support being given to, 'selection' in effect gives back to schools the discretion and power which choice and market forces, according to many of its advocates, were supposed to remove. The more able schools are to select, the more parental choices are rendered redundant. What use is choice if your choice is rejected by the producer. Schools that are oversubscribed can and do screen out or exclude students who are more demanding, or difficult or expensive to teach, and thus make teaching easier and relatively high levels of performance in public examinations more easily obtainable.

As more schools succumb to the logic and incentives of the education market in this way other changes are effected. Schools are increasingly dislocated from their 'natural' social community. They may be *in* but are no longer *of* their community. Indeed by virtue of changes in school governance schools are no longer accountable to or have responsibilities towards their local community, but rather to their immediate clients. Institutional survival rather than social responsibility is the primary concern. This is one example among many of the 'creative destruction' of market forces and paradoxically these destructive effects may be seen as contributing to the breakdown in moral order and social authority which so preoccupies Conservative social commentators. The neo-liberal Conservative project undermining the neo-conservative one (Ball, 1995a).

The Education Market Experiment as Social and Ideological Engineering

The market is not simply a value-free, mechanistic alternative to partisan planning, as some advocates and choice-politicians suggest. It is a transformational force which carries and disseminates its own values. Choice and market systems re-interpolate key actors — families, children and teachers; re-position schools; and rework and revalue the meaning of education (Gewirtz, Ball and Bowe, 1993a; and Ball, Bowe and Gewirtz, 1994). Families are reinterpolated as consumers of education (Hughes *et al.*, 1994, pp. 66–70). The education market resocializes and desocializes; encouraging competitive individualism and instrumentality. Individual children are positioned differently and evaluated differently in the education market, moreover the child is commodified. In systems where recruitment is directly related to funding then the educational and reputational 'costs' of the child become part of the 'producers' response to choosers. This also occurs where exclusivity is a key aspect of a school's market position. Further, in a whole variety of ways education itself is reworked as a commodity. And finally the dynamics of choice and education markets produces a new 'hidden curriculum'. School students are located within, and subjects of, a new educational and moral environment — they are exposed to, and educated within, a new values set. The sense of what education is and is for, the nature of the social relationships of schooling, teacher-student, teacher-parent and student-student relationships, are potentially all changed by the forces and micropractices of the market and their realization in specific localities and institutional settings. Now some commentators would see this transformation as no bad thing. Robert Lane, American political scientist, argues that the market has a crucial role to play in the political education of young people. He suggests that in fostering the mental qualities of curiosity, creativity or divergent thinking, and cognitive complexity, 'the market has something to teach the schools' (Lane, 1983, p. 57). He goes on:

> But the market incentive system teaches other things. Compared to government, the market is more voluntaristic, relies more on motivation and incentives than upon authoritative coercion, permits, even requires 'shopping

around' and, in that sense and others, maximizes choice; it encourages 'self-reliance' the belief in the autonomous determination of one's own fate, prudent regard for the future, initiative and openness to productive new ideas. (p. 52)

All well and good. But Lane also enters a telling caveat.

the negative ethics of the marketplace . . . and the child's interpretation of commercial lying — all combine to make the school's task of transmitting ethical values harder. What saves the school are its powers of resistance, as culture carrier of a culture of its own, as community, even as bureau- cracy, but most of all, as an institution guided by professionals whose profession embraces the transmission of non-market ethical values. And this transmission, as we know, will not be accomplished by teaching ethics, but by practising ethics: it is the total environment that changes values and cognition. . . . (p. 57)

The point is that the English education market is exactly intended to reduce the influence of the teaching profession, and concomitantly enhance that of 'profes- sional' managers and in doing so change the organizational culture of schools. Those things which Lane sees as bulwarks of resistance to the market are being swept away. Our research indicates a steady shift in schools from what we have called comprehensive values to the values of the market (Gewirtz, Ball and Bowe, 1993b). Non-market values are being devalued and displaced by the need to 'sell' schools in the marketplace. The incentives of the education market encourage commercial responses and marginalise the professional ethics of teachers.

I now want to give some substance to the contrast, at the level of practice, between comprehensive and market values. The two sets of values, as summarized in table 5.1, represent two largely oppositional conceptions of the nature and pur- poses of schooling — but they also relate to more general visions of the nature of society and citizenship. In real terms the pure forms of these values sets are prob- ably hard, but not impossible, to find. Schools occupy positions at different points between the extremes. But our research indicates a process, we call 'value drift', at work across schools. That is a discursive shift from left to right (Gewirtz, Ball and Bowe, 1995); although individual schools have different starting points, and they are moving at different rates. Some embrace the shift with urgent enthusiasm. Others are pushed reluctantly and slowly. It is very difficult to escape entirely from the discursive and financial incentives which drive the movement; although differ- ent local contexts and market configurations do effect the pace of movement. Also there are pockets of concerted resistance and counter-discursive activity.

In some locations the Catholic church is an important buttress against drift and shift. Some groups of schools are attempting to reinvent collaboration and coopera- tion and minimize competition; for example, the Birmingham Catholic Partnership (Mac an Ghaill, 1994); Education 2000 in Letchworth (Monck and Husbands, 1996), and the North Lowestoft Schools Network (Harbour, 1996). There are also

Table 5.1: *Comprehensive and market values*

Comprehensive Values	Market Values
individual need (schools and students)	individual performance (schools and students)
commonality (mixed-ability classes/open access)	differentiation/hierarchy (setting/streaming/selection/exclusion)
serves community needs	attracts 'clients'
emphasis on resource allocation to those with greatest learning difficulties	allocation to more emphasis on resource more able
collectivism (cooperation between schools and students)	competition (between schools and students)
broad assessments of worth based upon varieties of academic and social qualities	narrow assessments of worth based on contributions to performativity
the education of all children is held to intrinsically of equal worth	the education of children is valued in relation to costs and outcomes

ongoing micropolitical struggles over values which take place within schools and the classroom work of many teachers is not tainted directly by the market logic.

A final point about the social effects of the market. In his more recent work Lane (1991) has developed an argument for shifting the criteria by which we assess markets in two respects. His concern is with what he calls 'the market experience'. As one criterion, he argues that satisfaction or happiness and human development are final goods in the market, rather than income, goods and services. Thus: 'I think it is better for people to be happy, more cognitively complex, to think themselves as worthy, and to take responsibility for their own lives where they can influence lives rather than the other way around' (p. 5). However, this raises problems in any evaluation of the education market. Unlike commercial markets, and by definition, as I have argued already, education markets 'value' exclusivity and rejection. For some therefore the market experience is one of damage to their self-worth, loss of effectivity, a diminished sense of influence over events and specific unhappiness (see Maguire, 1996). The work of my colleague Meg Maguire, focussing on children whose parents *make* but do not *get* their choice illustrates the damage and distress experienced by such children for whom the reality of the market *is* rejection. ACE (the Advisory Centre for Education) is recording increasing numbers of cases of rejection of choice many of which, for the children involved, lead to tears, bed wetting and long or short-term school phobia and other social and psychological effects. Concomitantly, the process of choice is itself stressful, and uncertain for many parents (as is evident in our interviews — Gewirtz, Ball and Bowe, 1995), and not infrequently a cause of family tension and disputes over an extended period of time.

I want to conclude now by returning to the politics of the market as the base reality of contemporary education reform. My point is that the market reform essentially has little to do with education *per se* and an awful lot to do with the political problems of governments and parties.

The Politics of Choice

One of the responses made by choice advocates to the sorts of problems and criticisms I have marshalled already is that they are the product of distortions or malfunctions in choice-in-practice, which can be remedied. This, I suggest, is both politically and economically naive. The utopian conditions required for 'full', 'equal' or meaningful choice are unobtainable for a number of reasons.

(i) Some of these malfunctions are probably irremediable at any cost.

(ii) Governments are clearly unwilling or unable to bear the costs of 'fully-funded' choice.

(iii) The politics of choice is founded upon response to the interests of particular constituencies. There is limited political interest on the part of market politicians, or those families who see themselves as having lost their social and economic advantages under systems like comprehensive education *planned* to produce equitable outcomes, in making the market more equitable. In the UK the development of the education market can be seen quite reasonably as an extension of Margaret Thatcher's constituency building policies — the creation of a 'home and share-owning democracy'. Thus, Glennerster and Le Grand (1994) argue that in offering both financial and strategic advantage to the articulate middle classes the market form and its effects are a political means of retaining the commitment of the middle classes to public services (and ensuring vote support and a shoring up of the 'culture of contentment'). 'Universal social services are caught in this dilemma. Respond to the needs of the articulate or lose political support. *That could be what quasi-markets are all about'* (p. 22), [my emphasis]. Mickelson (1990) makes a similar point about the Bush administration school policies in the US (p. 356). Concomitantly, choice is an ideological mechanism for moving resources around the education system to the advantage of certain groups and disadvantage of others, as indicated above. In addition to these barriers to remediation, we should recognize that.

(iv) Choice schemes serve other important political purposes. First, they allow for the displacement of responsibility for educational planning and educational standards. Increasingly it becomes possible to locate the deficiencies of schools or 'planning' mistakes in the 'poor' choices made by families or the inadequate responses of individual schools. The system designer is absolved. Second, agendas of choice, diversity and competition also provide a mechanism for driving down educational expenditures which draws upon a discourse of efficiency and effectively confuses cuts in public expenditure with the procedures of competitive formula funding. Individual institutions are left with the freedom to manage their own contraction. Third, the ideology of the market is introduced by and introduces a common *management mode of regulation* across the private and public sectors based on non-principled self-interest. Again, management here is a 'transformational

force' (Clarke and Newman, 1992) set over and against the values of welfare professionalism and again this transformation has profound implications for institutional
cultures and values. The market, excellence, quality, effectiveness, managerialism
etc. play 'a vital translating role between the government of the enterprise (in this
case the school) and the politico-ethical objectives of neo-liberal government in the
UK' (Du Gay, 1996, p. 85). And fourth, the education market serves to further the
ideological dissemination of the commodity form (Offe, 1984). Education itself is
commodified and the values and practices in which it is embedded are commercial-
ized. Educational provision is increasingly made susceptible to profit and educational
processes play their part in the creation of the enterprise culture and the cultivation
of enterprising subjects. Again the market and new managerialism are central to the
active transformation of the practices and the meaning of education.

Social markets are part of a 'bigger picture' both in terms of class politics,
cultural engineering and government accountability and economics. Thus, it is also
important not to disconnect social markets analytically from related policies and
reforms or broader changes in the nature of social life and social relationships.

This brings me back to the other main point that I am trying to make here, that
the Conservative, neo-liberal reform of education is not simply an ensemble of
structural and financial changes it also involves a major shift in social values. This
is a value change which has its impact *upon* education *and to which* education
contributes. Caught between the state and the market, education may be on the way
to becoming a reflection of and playing its part in reproducing what Kingdom
(1992) calls the 'mastabatory society'; 'offering a solitary view of fulfilment, free
of the complications arising from tiresome moral demands by others' (p. 1). This
is where the twin themes of equity and values come together.

In substantive terms, within the UK education system there is now a struggle
underway over values. On the one side are the values of comprehensivism which
have constituted and provided an incoherent but recognizable language and ethic of
civic virtue in education. These are now being steadily worn down and replaced by
the language and ethics of the market. Comprehensive values (Daunt, 1975) are
essentially an articulation of what Nagel (1991) calls the 'impersonal standpoint'
with its egalitarian and communtarian concerns and this can be contrasted along
several dimensions with the 'culture of self-interest' or 'personal standpoint', rest-
ing upon the personal interests and desires of individuals, as represented in market
values. As a 'moral tradition' Comprehensivism provides a framework for ethical
concerns, it articulates a way of life based upon commutarian principles. It provides
for a 'thick' morality — shared values and common sentiments. I am not saying
that these values and sentiments are realized in practice in any simple or direct
sense. They represent dialogical possibilities. They play their part in what Lowery
et al. (1992) call the 'public sphere', a space in our social world in which issues
are open to debate, reflection and moral argument. On the other side, the market,
by contrast, rests on aggregative principles, the sum of individual goods and choices,
'founded on individual and property rights that enable citizens to address problems
of interdependence via exchange' (*ibid.*). This value regime discourages debate.
Moral argument and conflict are privatized, obscured or trivialized. It provides for

a 'thin' morality, 'oblivious to that essential human interdependency that underlies all political life' (Barber, 1994, p. 25), and generates hierarchy and division based upon competitive individualism. It is oriented to financial incentives, presentational manipulation and expedience. As I have tried to make clear at the outset I am not suggesting that comprehensive values translate unproblematically into practice, nor indeed do the values of the market, although the latter are supported by powerful incentives and legal requirements which the former never had. The ideals and ethics that are embodied in these values systems animate, organize and steer educational provision and practice in fundamentally different ways. They represent very different visions or definitions of what it means to be educated. They define what education is and is for very differently. They contribute to very different visions of future society. For myself, I know which one of these I would prefer to live in.

References

BALL, S.J. (1981) *Beachside Comprehensive*, Cambridge, Cambridge University Press.

BALL, S.J. (1993) 'Education markets, choice and social class: The market as a class strategy in the UK and the USA', *British Journal of Sociology of Education*, **14**, 1, pp. 3–20.

BALL, S.J. (1995a) 'The ideology and politics of school choice: Demythologising the education market', paper presented at the annual meeting of the American Educational Research Association, San Francisco, April.

BALL, S.J. (1995b) 'Parents, schools and markets: The repositioning of youth in United Kingdom Schools', *Young: Nordic Journal of Youth Research*, **3**, 3, pp. 68–79.

BALL, S.J., BOWE, R. and GEWIRTZ, S. (1994) 'Competitive schooling: Values, ethics and cultural engineering', *Journal of Curriculum and Supervision*, **9**, 4, pp. 350–67.

BALL, S.J., BOWE, R. and GEWIRTZ, S. (1995) 'Circuits of schooling: A sociological exploration of parental choice of school in social class contexts', *Sociological Review*, **43**, 1.

BALL, S.J., BOWE, R. and GEWIRTZ, S. (1996) 'School choice, social class and distinction: The realisation of social advantage in education', *Journal of Education Policy*, **11**, 1, pp. 89–112.

BARBER, B. (1994) *Strong Democracy*, Berkeley, CA, University of California Press.

BENN, C. and SIMON, B. (1972) *Half Way There*, (2nd edition), Harmondsworth, Penguin.

BLANK, R. (1990) 'Educational effects of magnet high schools' in CLUNE, W. and WITTE, J. (Eds) *Choice and Control in American Education Vol 2: The Practice of Choice, Decentralization and School Restructuring*, London and Washington, DC, Falmer Press.

BOURDIEU, P. and PASSERON, J-C. (1990) *Reproduction*, London, Sage.

BOWE, R., BALL, S.J. and GERWIRTZ, S. (1994) 'Captured by the discourse? Issues and concerns in researching "Parental Choice"', *British Journal of Sociology of Education*, **15**, 1, pp. 63–78.

CHENOWETH, T. (1987) 'Unanticipated consequences of schools of choice: some thoughts on the case of San Francisco', *Equality and Choice*, **5**, 7.

CHUBB, J. and MOE, T. (1990) *Politics, Markets and America's Schools*, Washington, DC, The Brookings Institution.

CLARKE, J. and NEWMAN, J. (1992) *The Right to Manage: A Second Managerial Revolution*, Milton Keynes, Open University Press.

CRUMP, S.J. (1994) *Public School Choice: A Pragmatist Perspective*, Sydney, Dept of Social and Policy Studies in Education, University of Sydney.

DARDEN, J.T., DUNLEEP, H.O. and GLASTER, G.C. (1992) 'Civils rights in metropolitan America', *Journal of Urban Affairs*, **14**, pp. 469–96.

DAUNT, P. (1975) *Comprehensive Values*, London, Heinemann.

DEEM, R., BREHONY, K. and HEATH, S. (1994) 'Governers, schools and the miasma of the market', *British Education Research Journal*, **20**, 4, pp. 535–50.

DES (1991) *The Parent's Charter*, London, Department of Education and Science.

DU GAY, P. (1996) *Consumption and Identity at Work*, London, Sage.

ECHOLS, F.H. and WILLMS, J.D. (1993) *Scottish Parents and Reasons for School Choice*, Vancouver, Dept of Social and Educational Studies, University of British Columbia.

ESPINOLA, V. (1992) *Decentralization of the Education System and the Introduction of Market Rules in the Regulation of Schooling: The Case of Chile*, Santiago, Centro de Investigacion y desarrollo de la educacion.

FINN, C.A., JR. (1989) 'The choice backlash', *National Review*, 10 November, pp. 30–2.

FOSSEY, R. (1994) 'Open enrollment in Massachusetts: Why families choose', *Educational Evaluation and Policy Analysis* **16**, 3, pp. 320–34.

GEWIRTZ, P. (1996) 'Choice in the transition: School desegregation and the corective ideal', *Columbia Law Review*, May, pp. 729–99.

GEWIRTZ, S. and BALL, S.J. (1996) *From 'Welfarism' to 'New Managerialism': Shifting Discourse of School Leadership in the Education Quasi-market*, 4th ESRC Quasi-Markets Research Seminar, SPS, University of Bristol.

GEWIRTZ, S., BALL, S. and BOWE, R. (1993a) 'Parents, privilege and the education market', *Research Papers in Education*, **9**, 1, pp. 3–29.

GEWIRTZ, S., BALL, S.J. and BOWE, R. (1993b) 'Values and ethics in the marketplace: The case of Northwark Park', *International Journal of Studies in Education*, **3**, 2, pp. 233–53.

GEWIRTZ, S., BALL, S.J. and BOWE, R. (1995) *Markets and Equity in Education*, Milton Keynes, Open University Press.

GLENN, C.L. (1994) 'Balancing roles: Families, schools and government', *New Schools, New Communities*, **11**, 1, pp. 46–50.

GLENNERSTER, H. and LE GRAND, J. (1994) *The Development of Quasi-markets in Welfare Provision: Comparing Social Welfare Systems in Europe*, Missions Interministerielle Recherche Experimentation, Ministere des Affaires Sociales and the Main Francaise d'Oxford.

GOLDRING, E.B. and SHAPIRA, R. (1993) 'Choice, empowerment and involvement: What satisfies parents?', *Educational Evaluation and Policy Analysis*, **15**, 4, pp. 396–409.

GRAY, J. (1993) *Beyond the New Right: Markets, Government and the Common Environment*, London, Routledge.

HALL, S. (1988) *The Hard Road to Renewal*, London, Verso.

HALPIN, D., POWER, S. and FITZ, J. (1991) 'Grant-maintained schools: Making a difference without being different', *British Journal of Educational Studies*, **39**, 4, pp. 409–24.

HARBOUR, M. (1996) 'The North Lowestoft schools network' in BRIDGES, D. and HUSBANDS, C. (Eds) *Consorting and Collaborating in the Education Marketplace*, London, Falmer Press.

HARDMAN, J. and LEVAČIĆ, R. (1994) 'The impact of competition on secondary schools', paper presented at the annual meeting of the British Educational Research Association, Oxford, September.

HENIG, J.R. (1994) *Rethinking School Choice: Limits of the Market Metaphor*, Princeton, NJ, University of Princeton Press.

Stephen J. Ball

HERSHKOFF, H. and COHEN, A.S. (1992) 'School choice and the lessons of Choctaw county', *Yale Law and Policy Review*, **10**, 1, pp. 1–29.

HUGHES, M., WIKELEY, F. and NASH, T. (1994) *Parents and their Children's Schools*, Oxford, Basil Blackwell.

KINGDOM, J. (1992) *No Such Thing as Society? Individualism and Community*, Buckingham, Open University Press.

LANE, R.E. (1983) 'Political education in a market society', *Micropolitics*, **3**, 1, pp. 39–65.

LANE, R.E. (1991) *The Market Experience*, Cambridge, Cambridge University Press.

LAUDER, H., HUGHES, D., WASLANDER, S., THRUPP, M., McGLINN, J., NEWTON, S. and DUPLUIS, A. (1994) *The Creation of Market Competition for Education In New Zealand: The Smithfield Project Phase One*, First Report to the Ministry of Education.

LOWERY, D., DE HOOG, R. and LYONS, W.E. (1992) 'Citizenship in the empowered locality', *Urban Affairs Quarterly*, **28**, 1, pp. 69–103.

MAC AN GHAILL, M. (1994) 'Public service in the market: The Birmingam Catholic partnership' in MAC AND GHAILL, M. and LAWN, M. (Eds) *Cooperating in the Education Marketplace*, Birmingham, Educational Review Publications.

MAGUIRE, M. (1996) 'Choice and rejection in the education market', CES, King's College, London, ongoing research.

MARGONIS, P. and PARKER, M. (1996) 'School choice in the US urban context: Racism and policies of containment', *Journal of Education Policy* (forthcoming).

MENTER, I. and MUSCHUMP, Y. with NICHOLLS, P., OZGA, J. and POLLARD, A. (1994) '*The impact of market ideology on small scale service providers*', paper presented at the annual meeting of the British Educational Research Association, Oxford, September.

MICKELSON, R.A. (1990) 'Markets, values and the business vision of school reform', *Humanity and Society*, **14**, 4, pp. 345–72.

MONCK, L. and HUSBANDS, C. (1996) 'Education 2000 Letchworth' in BRIDGES, D. and HUSBANDS, C. (Eds) *Consorting and Collaborating in the Education Marketplace*, London, Falmer Press.

MOORE, D. and DAVENPORT, S. (1990) 'Choice: The new improved sorting machine', *Choice in Education: Potential and Problems*. Berkeley, CA., McCutcheon.

NAGEL, T. (1991) *Equality and Partiality*, Oxford, Oxford University Press.

OFFE, C. (1984) *Contradictions of the Welfare State*, London, Hutchinson.

WHITE, P. (1994) 'Parental choice and education for citizenship' in HALSTEAD, M. (Ed) *Parental Choice and Education: Principles, Policy and Practice*, London, Kogan Page.

6   Educating Persons

Richard Pring

Introduction

In the Foreword to a collection of essays entitled Authority, Education and Emancipation Lawrence Stenhouse (1967) wrote:

> As a pupil at Manchester Grammar School I had been fortunate in my sixth form experience to meet three teachers . . . who had opened ideas to me in a way that emancipated me by enhancing my sense of my own powers. When I came to teach I discovered that, though the school system valued achievement narrowly defined, it did not for the most part value the emancipation of pupils through knowledge. Nor could I satisfactorily do within the system what had been done for me.

I start with the quotation from Stenhouse for three reasons. First, the comprehensive ideal is that all young people — irrespective of social class, economic circumstance, ethnic origin, intellectual power, geographic location — should be 'emancipated' by the enhancement of their own powers. Second, Stenhouse, through his innovative work within the humanities curriculum and under the aegis of the Schools Council, illustrated in a concrete way the kind of knowledge through which those powers might be enhanced and emancipation achieved. Third, there was in these and similar innovations an idea of the educated person which challenged the view that a liberating education is possible only for some — those who have a certain level of intelligence or come from a culturally privileged background.

I shall attempt to spell out that ideal. Comprehensive education must be about more than a common school which embraces pupils from a range of social classes and ability. It must, too, have built into it an idea of the educated person which accommodates, on the one hand, the best in that liberal tradition (which is often seen as the preserve of a privileged few), and, on the other, the quite different starting points and aspirations of young people.

In doing this I shall make the following points.

- First, I say something very generally about education.
- Second, I indicate how the idea of education has evolved in the pursuit of equality and community through a comprehensive system.
- Third, I return to the theme 'emancipation through knowledge', in particular

the respect for that which is worth knowing and for the learner who is transformed through it.

- Fourth, I focus upon one aspect of such learning, namely, the achievement of 'moral seriousness' — the search, irrespective of class or religion or measured intelligence, for authenticity in a very complex social world.
- Finally, I return to the links between this and the community through which learning and sense of authenticity are to be achieved — an educated community of teachers and learners which I believe can be achieved only within a comprehensive system.

Education

'Emancipation' is a useful metaphor, for education is to be contrasted with the kind of enslavement associated with ignorance and with the lack of those mental powers, without which one is so easily duped and deceived. To be educated, therefore, is at least this — to be in possession of those understandings, knowledge, skills and dispositions whereby one makes sense of the world around one: the physical world to be understood through the sciences and mathematics, the social and political world within which one's life is too often shaped by others, the moral world of ideals and responsibilities, and the aesthetic world of beauty and style through which one finds pleasure and delight. But entry into those different worlds is more than a *making sense of* that which is inherited from others. It gives access to the ideas, and thus the tools, through which the learner's own distinctive personal development might actively take place.

This then is the main theme of my contribution — and the most important challenge for the comprehensive ideal: how might links be made between, on the one hand, the public meanings we have inherited (and which are embodied within the subjects of physics, mathematics, history and literature) and, on the other, the personal strivings of each and everyone to make sense of experience and to find his/her own identity within it? Put in other words, how might one render personally significant to each that which comes in an *impersonal form to all* — the inheritance of previous generations, refined by previous argument, scholarship and criticism, and to be found in textbooks and artefacts of various kinds? How can *all* young people — not just those who are privileged with superior intelligence (howsoever measured) or a culturally favourable background — find value in a culture which so often has been accessible to only the few?

Too much emphasis upon the first — the body of publicly acknowledged meanings as they are embodied in the various subjects — created that earlier comprehensive ideal, namely, a 'grammar school education for all', which, inappropriate for many, resulted in so much alienation from formal education. On the other hand, too much emphasis upon relevance for the intellectually less able, or the culturally deprived, results in the two-track system envisaged by Crowther Report (1957), and endorsed by the Dearing Report (1996), namely, an academic education for some and a more useful, practical and vocational preparation for others — and, thus, selection between schools which specialize in either academic or vocational studies, or within school. Education, as Peters (1965) argued, is the initiation of young people into those worthwhile forms of knowledge which, when *not* narrowly conceived, illuminate experience in its different manifestations and forms. And that is relevant to all young people, not just a selected few.

The comprehensive ideal, therefore, is to extend to all young people the opportunity to participate seriously in the dialogue between the subjective concerns of each and the objective world of meanings which are accessible to all, albeit in different ways and no doubt at different levels, and which at their best illuminate those concerns. It is to recognize the importance in such a dialogue, not simply of the logical structure of the subject matter to be learnt, but also of the variety of experience to be shared and made sense of. And to educate is to enable those young people to enter into that dialogue irrespective of measured intelligence or social background.

Equality and the Evolution of the Comprehensive Ideal

The pursuit of equality in the opportunity to engage in that dialogue has been the hallmark of comprehensive education over the last forty or so years. But egalitarians seem presently in retreat as equality is seen to be antithetical to freedom of choice and to the enhancement of the individual's powers which Stenhouse referred to.

We need, however, to think carefully about what is meant by equality. Certainly it should not be identified with strict egalitarianism — the treatment of every one in exactly the same way irrespective of individual or cultural differences. The struggle against inequality has rarely been motivated by a desire to treat everyone the same. Rather has it been directed, negatively, against specific injustices, and positively towards the common interests of individuals, not what keeps them apart. Let me deal with each of these in turn.

Negative Principle of Equality

The principle might be expressed thus in the words of one influential book of the 1960s:

> What we really demand, when we say that all men are equal is that none shall be held to have a claim to better treatment than another, in advance of good grounds being produced. (Benn and Peters, 1959)

Differences of treatment there might justifiably be, but the onus of proof lies with those who insist upon the differences. The early developments of the comprehensive system aimed at the removal of those differences of provision and treatment which could not be justified — which arose from factors unrelated to the educational purposes of schooling, such as wealth or class or status. It was the application of the same principle which, a generation earlier, had been the moral basis for a differentiated educational system. The achievement of secondary education for all, following the 1944 Education Act and the scholarship system, whereby anyone of ability could achieve a grammar school education, were steps in the direction of a more equal society in this sense. The appeal to equality was really an attempt to remove those discriminations that denied to deserving individuals access to an appropriate education. Intelligence, not wealth or social class, was the relevant base for educational opportunities, and thus measures of intelligence became the appropriate criteria for discriminating between children.

However, the very concerns for equality of opportunity, which gave rise to these social reforms, came to be directed at the reforms themselves — namely, the discrimination against individuals on grounds which became increasingly questionable. In making distinctions, two types of question need be asked. First, are these distinctions the relevant ones, given the overall purpose of the activity? Second, given that they are the right ones, are the measuring instruments, by which they are made, valid and reliable? If the distinctions are not relevant — if the distinction between two classes of learners, the intelligent and the unintelligent, or if the ways of selecting the learners for each category, are flawed — then there is unjust discrimination. People are not being treated equally. And, indeed, with a broader range of educational aims (concerned with more than abstract and theoretical pursuits), and with a more generous notion of intelligence as something (in the words of Sir Edward Boyle in the Preface to the Plowden Report, 1967) to be acquired through learning, distinctions made on the basis of fixed and inherited intelligence (rather than, say, on motivation or need or want) came to be questioned. Furthermore, evidence was accumulating as Professor Simon demonstrated on pages 22–23 in this book, against the validity and reliability of intelligence tests. Therefore, what previously were regarded as relevant grounds for dividing children were now, because of changing views of education and of intelligence, no longer acceptable. In that way the comprehensive school was a response to a particular kind of appeal to equality — not treating people differently in matters that profoundly affect their life chances, unless good reasons can be given for doing so. The onus of proof lies on the shoulders of those who wish to discriminate and make different provision.

Such a principle of equality is procedural. It advances no positive reasons for the comprehensive school, only negative ones. It is saying that given the many different aims of education and given the margin of error exhibited in any attempt to select, then one has no grounds to make different provision.

Positive Principle of Equality

The more positive meaning of equality was referred to by Daunt (1975), at the onset of comprehensive education, in his book *Comprehensive Values*, namely, 'equality of respect'. That is, whatever the differences in intelligence or aptitude or social class, each learner should be *respected* equally. Each is, and thus should be treated as, equally important.

Hence, the argument went, the respect given to individuals reflects the respect given to the groups to which they belong — and thus the respect given to the institutions which particular groups attend. Therefore, it was most important that the three types of school to which children were sent at 11+ should, as the Norwood Report (1943) argued, have 'parity of esteem' — otherwise those attending them would not receive equality of respect. However, it was shown by Banks and others that no such parity of esteem was achieved. And this inequality of esteem for different institutions was reflected in the inequality of respect for persons in them (to be a grammar school boy was more respectable than to be a secondary modern boy) and the consequent lowering of self-respect amongst those who attended the less respectable institutions. It was as though 'their common humanity' was accorded less importance in ascription of respect than the quality of intelligence that divided them.

It is in this sense that Professor Halsey, in his 1978 Reith lectures, addressed himself to the neglected 'social principle of fraternity' as a solution to growing social conflict. Fraternity does not entail intimate and loving feelings for others. The relevant attitude is that of respect based upon the recognition, firstly, of one's partial dependence on others and, secondly, of others as persons. Such respect would be fostered by an increased awareness of what was shared by way of human feelings, needs, aspirations, and by the gradual extension of those areas of agreed understanding. A schooling, which divided people physically, would militate against the ideal of fraternity, prevent the face-to-face contact that is a necessary condition of mutual respect, remove the common learning experience that would be a basis for shared understanding.

Three things should be noted about society as it is depicted here. First, it is rooted in an idea of mutual respect and cooperation. Second, it sees a necessary, though by no means a sufficient, condition of this to be the development of face-to-face relationships. Third, it is increased by an increase of the area of shared understandings and experience.

This aspiration is referred to by Professor Halsey (1978) in his sixth lecture as follows:

> We have still to provide a common experience of citizenship in childhood and old age, in work and play, and in health and sickness. We have still in short to develop a common culture to replace the divided culture of class and status.

In this he echoed the words of Tawney in his 1931 book, *Equality*, so influential in the comprehensive movement, that, in addition to getting rid of gross inequalities of wealth,

> What a community requires, as the word itself suggests, is a common culture, because, without it, it is not a community at all.

Learning

There is an obvious objection to what has been said so far. It is argued that the pursuit of equality in schools has caused a decline in standards in the work of the more able pupils — especially in mathematics and the sciences, but also in literacy and the modern languages. There are many international comparisons which seem to demonstrate that the products of the comprehensive system do not do as well as their counterparts in the more selective systems elsewhere. One pursues equality at the expense of individual quality.

These criticisms should not be dismissed lightly. But they require closer examination of what we mean by standards and how they are to be defined. Standards are bench marks; they are the criteria whereby one assesses or evaluates the quality of a particular activity or process. Strictly speaking there are as many standards as there are activities and there are as many activities as there are intentions and values which drive people on. There are standards peculiar to mathematics, to philosophical argument, to writing sonnets, to giving lectures, to formulating research proposals. Moreover, just as our values and purposes change, so do standards whereby we assess those activities. As mathematics educators reflect on the nature and educational value of mathematical education (practical problem solving rather than theoretical insight) or as modern linguists agree that the importance of studying languages is to converse with the natives rather than to read their literature, so do the standards whereby we judge mathematical or language performance change. It is performance against standards which goes up or down; standards simply change — because of what we think to be important changes.

This provides a key to understanding events which have happened in the last few years. The Technical and Vocational Education Initiative, or TVEI, was important, not, as is often supposed, in providing a different and more relevant curriculum for the less able, but in challenging the standards by which young people should be judged. It was a challenge to our educational aims and values. In assessing the cooperative contribution of students to group or team activities, or in promoting social and economic awareness, or in encouraging technological problem-solving, or in respecting community service sensitively engaged in, so it implicitly declared that standards previously dominant are not as relevant as often supposed to what ought to be valued educationally. Hence, the quite angry discussions at the time with examining boards which wished to apply traditional standards to non-traditional activities.

That is important, because the comprehensive system must be judged against the standards within the comprehensive ideal. And these might be different in important respects from what had prevailed before. But there are limits to how far one might innovate or change the standards according to which educational activities might be judged. Mathematical problem solving or scientific enquiry or historical investigation takes place within a particular discipline of thinking which has a logical structure with its own distinctive concepts or ideas, its own distinctive way of testing the truth of what is said, its own distinctive way of explaining things or finding things out. Such logical structures of that which is to be learnt may evolve over time — there are, for instance, radical changes in the disciplines of social and psychological sciences as new theories evolve and supersede each other, but such innovations tend to emerge from within the community of scholars and researchers, albeit with reference to the wider social purposes.

This respect for the logical structure of the separate disciplines of knowledge has frequently been seen as an argument for a differentiated schooling — one kind for those who can understand the logical structures of the subject matter, and another for those who require a more practical curriculum. However, this, as Jerome Bruner (1960) so effectively demonstrated, shows a complete misunderstanding of the connection between the theoretical and the practical, and between the logical structure of that which is to be learnt and the structure of thinking which the young people bring with them to school. The curriculum should do two things: first, identify those key ideas — those principles and concepts without which (to use Stenhouse's words) one cannot be emancipated through knowledge; and, second, represent those to the learner in a manner which is comprehensible. Such a manner — such a mode of representation as Bruner calls it — may often be a very practical understanding, as when the young child implicitly grasps the principles of mechanics through successful manipulation of the see-saw or implicitly grasps certain theological understandings through practical participation in a worshipping community. The curriculum should be a constant return to these central ideas whether expressed practically or through images or through the symbolic system of more theoretical studies.

Central to one's personal development through education must be a grasp of those key ideas through which is made possible an understanding of what it is to be human. Therefore, Bruner's course *Man: A Course of Study* focused on three major questions: (i) what is human about man?; (ii) how did he become so?; (iii) how can he become more so? The course was structured around five distinctive ideas of being human — prolonged child-rearing, the use of tools, language acquisition and use, social organization and myth-making. These key ideas could be explored at different levels of understanding, drawing upon both personal experience, systematic enquiry and theoretical studies in anthropology and other academic disciplines. In keeping with the importance of active enquiry and shared exploration, the course devised a series of games, simulation exercises and activities, so that the young learners — from diverse backgrounds and measured intelligence — could work together and make their separate contributions to an ever tentative understanding of what it was that made them human (see Bruner, 1966).

It was within a similar vein that Lawrence Stenhouse sought, within the terms of the Schools Council Working Paper Number 2 (1967), to tackle the problems arising from the raising of the school-leaving age. Remember that, in raising the age of compulsory schooling to 16, there was much fear of what the consequences would be — a large number of disillusioned young people, resistant to learning, incapable of the literary and scientific studies with which education was associated, alienated from the educational purposes of the school system.

The problem to be addressed was this. How can we address the aspiration of secondary education for all, irrespective of age, ability and aptitude, where we are deeply rooted in a tradition of liberal education which seems accessible only to an academic few? How could literature, the arts, history, science, be seen to be relevant to those who, often alienated young people, were to be satisfied only with doing and making rather than with thinking, with vocational preparation rather than with the disinterested pursuit of the truth, with the practical rather than with the academic?

However, the Working Paper referred to, whose main author was that visionary Civil Servant, Derek Morrell, far from seeing the solution to these anxieties to lie in a vocational alternative, stated not just the central importance of the humanities to the education of all, but also the essential nature of an education in the humanities — contrasting that essence not only with the narrowness of vocational training but with the too often narrow and impoverished treatment of the humanities within an academic tradition.

The humanities, to quote that Working Paper, was the area of the curriculum in which teachers emphasized their common humanity with the pupils and their common uncertainty in the face of significant and personal problems. But they did so in the light of what others had said through dance, art, literature, poetry, myth or history. And they examined these together — the objective grounds for intersubjective exploration leading to personal resolution. The humanities — the poetry, the novels, the dance, the media presentation, the arts, the historical accounts, the social interpretation, the theological analysis — were, as it were, the text or the objects around and through which emerged the transaction between teacher and learner, and between the different learners from different backgrounds, as they explored those issues of supreme personal and subjective importance: sexual relations, social justice, use of violence, respect for authority, racism, and so on. The humanities could and should be seen as the public recordings of the best of conversations about those very matters which concern all young people and thus the resources upon which the learner might draw. In that way the curriculum was a making personal to each and everyone that which comes, and is too often transmitted, in an impersonal form.

There is not the opportunity here to enter into the details of these attempts to render into programmes of learning the moral principles which lay at the basis of the comprehensive ideal. But they might be summarized as follows:

(i)   they involve the exploration of values in the concrete situation of practical living;

(ii)   they require a shift from a dependence upon the authority of the teacher to a dependence upon the authority of evidence and reason;

(iii)   they therefore require the promotion of certain procedural values which enhance the capacity to reason, reflect and deliberate;

(iv)   they respect the experiences each learner brings to the exploration of these human situations — the value of which experiences relates more to the diversity of backgrounds and seriousness of reflection than it does to measured intelligence;

(v)   they attach importance to the dynamics of the group through which the exploration takes place, wider experience revealed, evidence pointed to, ideas tested out, further enquiries sponsored;

(vi)   they define the role of the teacher to be that of promoting the procedural skills and virtues and that of mediating the various cultural resources upon which that exploration should draw, as the learners come to understand themselves and the social situation in which they live;

(vii) such moral principles, therefore, insist upon academic integrity by referring personal enquiry to the key ideas drawn from recognized intellectual disciplines within the humanities and social sciences.

I have for some years been interested in the curriculum practice of certain American schools which are part of the Coalition of Essential Schools — in particular one in New York. Recently I spent three days in the school observing and working with teachers and students alike. Let me describe what I saw.

The school building is vast, indeed built in 1927 to house 2500 girls. In the 1960s it went mixed, and in recent years it was seen as a 'failing school', the solution to which was to phase it out, all pupils being transferred elsewhere.

The building has now been split into six high schools, each independent of the other — together with an infant and toddler club and a health clinic. None of the six schools must have more than 300 students. The school I visited is one of these with 110 students aged 14 to 20 and nine teachers. There is no differentiation in terms of ability or age or background. The school functions as a community with group exploration and individual enquiry at the heart of the learning process. Progress is closely monitored, written assignments frequent and structured, personal guidance abundant. As a result of school-based research into a general apathy towards reading, each day now starts with mixed reading groups which include the teachers as together they come to understand and discuss a range of novels carefully selected — Sallinger, Marquez, Austen, Bellow, Updike, Morris, Lawrence. Each semester begins with a school project — this semester on 'Children Growing Up', in which the school divides itself into various task-oriented groups enquiring into parenting, street crime, employment possibilities, etc. Systematic enquiry, written assignments, reports of personal experience, reference to published evidence, cross examination of expert witnesses — all enter into the small group (and then larger group) deliberations which ensue. Links with external agencies and institutions — for example, with the local university — ensure that particular talent (in mathematics, say, or in the sciences) is never neglected as credit is obtained elsewhere and transferred.

What one observed was a community — embracing every conceivable ethnic and social class, religious grouping and measured intelligence — working together with a level of 'moral seriousness' that is rarely seen. Straightforward performance indicators, such as a 90 per cent attendance rate up to the achievement of High School Diploma, a decline in teenage pregnancies, the successful removal of electronic screening devices from the entrance, regular course work completed, would point to the success. And the secret would seem to be the fostering of a community, in which the continuum of experience between home and society, on the one hand, and formal learning, on the other, is promoted, respect for diversity of background and experience is cherished rather than regretted, enquiry is preferred (but not exclusively) to instruction, and the social life of the group (carefully nurtured) becomes the focus of each person's striving 'to make sense of' that which is thought important — for, as Stenhouse (1967) argued,

> the fundamental process of learning by taking our part in the social life of groups remains the most potent influence in our lives.

Moral Seriousness

Several ideas are, I hope, coming together as we seek to make sense of the comprehensive ideal without in any way sacrificing the very important concern for academic standards. Those ideas relate to the essentially moral purpose of education — helping each one to become more fully a person and to realize what is essentially human about themselves and others, the inseparable link between such personal development and membership of a community which respects each person, respect for the continuum of experiences between home and formal schooling, attaching central importance to social interaction between student and student, and student and teacher, drawing upon the intellectual resources of the academic disciplines (the public meanings), and the recognition of each person's own authentic response to those explorations.

Central, therefore, to the qualities which such a schooling is intending to foster is what one might call 'moral seriousness'.

I am not talking about anything esoteric. I am talking about the young person who stops to think about how he should live his life, who commits him/herself to certain people or causes, who refuses to treat others as mere pawns in his/her game, who takes seriously any criticism of standards in behaviour or work, who finds challenging the exploration of what is right or worthwhile in literature or art or science, who cares about the environment and other social and political issues, who does not run away from the deeper questions of meaning and value and purpose. Such a moral perspective is not confined to the most able or the most privileged. And it must not be confused with cleverness in argument. It is a matter of *seriousness* in thinking about what is worth living for, what is worth pursuing in the arts or the leisure time, what relationships are worth entering into, what kinds of activities should be avoided, what obligations are to be considered sacred. What is distinctive of being a person is this capacity for being serious about life, a capacity requiring the application of intelligence, of moral judgement, of reflection and of sensitivity, which is often fostered by teachers even when much in the commercial environment militates against it.

Such an emphasis is not foreign to teachers. As I have shown, there have been, apart from the individual efforts of teachers, the exciting innovations in geography, history, social studies and the humanities where teachers attempted to mediate the best within these different humane and intellectual traditions to the real and important questions that young people were asking.

They did so in the light of what others had said through dance, art, literature, poetry, myth or history. The humanities above all, when properly taught, provide the objective base for the transaction between teacher and learner, and between the different learners, as they explore those issues of supreme personal importance: sexual relations, social justice, the use of violence, racism, and so on.

Education is this constant interchange between what Charles Taylor (1989) refers to as the 'horizons of significance' of the learner, on the one hand, and the public meanings which are mediated by the teacher, on the other. And the comprehensive ideal is where that interaction is recognized and the seriousness of young people itself taken seriously. And such serious deliberation is not confined to the academically able.

Community

The comprehensive ideal has too often been associated with schools identified as comprehensive because they are not selective — either in ability or in social class. The hope was that a system of such schools would break down social barriers and open up educational opportunities to those who would otherwise have been denied them. The worry has remained that, however laudable, these aims have not been achieved — greater equality (however defined) has not been attained and many, far from grabbing the opportunities opened up to them, have become alienated from what for many became a grammar school for all.

Far, however, from abandoning the ideal, I believe that we should look a little more deeply at the moral purposes which lay behind it and the educational aims which it embodied. In this concluding section I want to complete the picture by reference to the sort of community within which the educational purposes and practices should be carried out.

I pointed out at the very beginning how the ideal of equality merged gradually with that of 'fraternity' or community, in which the equal respect for everyone required, too, a respect for what they are and for the social or religious or ethnic group from which they come — a point more recently developed by Charles Taylor in what he refers to as 'the politics of recognition'.

> Such a community will be manifest at different levels — at the level of the classroom, where the group reflects upon the variety of experience of its members as each is encouraged to explore and to find value in what is worthwhile; at the level of the school, where teachers and students work together for common goals; and at the level of the political community, which recognises that no one (certainly not politicians or executives from SCAA) has the infallible expertise to say what is the life worth living. (Taylor, 1994)

I want briefly to say something of these last two levels — those of the school and of the wider political community.

The difficulty lies in recognizing, at one and the same time, education as an initiation into worthwhile activity whilst acknowledging the lack of consensus over what is of most worth. There is not, nor ever will there be, consensus over what literature is most worth reading or what period (and location) of history is most worth studying or which subjects most worth struggling with. But although consensus will never be achieved, argument is worth pursuing; teachers are as concerned with deliberating about the ends of education as they are about the means — indeed, 'means' and 'ends' are logically, not just contingently, related. Furthermore, such disputed questions of value cannot be hidden from the students — as they seriously (and using the skills fostered by the schools) contend with the views of the teachers or with each other over the exercise of authority, the use of violence to pursue worthwhile ends, the control of the environment, the nurturing of parenting skills, the censorship of literature, or the promotion of certain art. In the absence of moral expertise, the exploration of what it is to be human is to be shared not only between student and student but also between student and teacher — at least if each student, in his/her exploration of value, is to be taken seriously.

For that reason, the staff workroom of the New York school was also the walk through room of the students — the symbol of a community seriously engaged in the same enterprise.

The political level, too, has to recognize the joint responsibility for ensuring a system of education which includes everyone, and respects everyone, in the exploration of the values which enter into the ever evolving educational ideal — for no one can say they know the answer for certain.

Indeed, it was for that reason that, in the 1960s, the Schools Council was established, bringing together teachers and dons, politicians and parents, civil servants and business people to find ways forward against a background of uncertainty. Morrell, who, you will remember, was the author of the Working Paper *Raising the School Leaving Age* and chief architect of the Council, pointed to the massive changes — economic, social and moral — which create a crisis of values. Old assumptions are challenged about the kind of knowledge which is worth teaching, the literature worth reading, the values worth pursuing.

And thus, he states,

> Our educational crisis is fundamentally part of a general crisis of values. If education, and by implication the curriculum, is not thought of as contributing to a solution of this crisis of values, it can all too easily become an agent of the worst sort of conservatism. (Morrell, 1966)

His answer lay in what he described as a 'cooperative attack' on the problems to be solved.

> Jointly, we need to define the characteristics of change . . . Jointly, we need to sponsor the research and development work necessary to respond to change. Jointly, we must evaluate the results of such work . . . Jointly, we need to recognise that freedom and order can no longer be reconciled

through implicit acceptance of a broadly ranging and essentially static consensus on educational aims and methods.

To do that the community

must also be locally organised bringing together teachers, dons, administrators and others for the study of common problems, some local and others national in their implications.

It is to that end that this book has been organized, knowing that no certain conclusions will be reached. But that striving for worthwhile goals, which are to be shared with a wider community by reason of our common humanity, and yet which are transformed in the very striving, will always remain the paradox of education and the ideal of comprehensive education.

References

BENN, S. and PETERS, R.S. (1959) *Social Principles and the Democratic State*, London, Allen and Unwin.

BRUNER, J. (1960) *The Process of Education*, Cambridge, MA, Harvard University Press.

BRUNER, J. (1966) *Towards a Theory of Instruction*, Cambridge, MA, Harvard University Press.

CROWTHER REPORT (1957) *15–18*, London, HMSO.

DAUNT, P. (1975) *Comprehensive Values*, London, Heinemann.

DEARING REPORT (1996) *Review of Qualifications for 16–19 Year Olds*, London, SCAA.

HALSEY, A.H. (1978) *Change in British Society*, Oxford, Oxford University Press.

MORRELL, D. (1966) *Education and Change*, (The Annual Joseph Payne Memorial Lectures 1965–66) London, College of Preceptors.

NORWOOD REPORT (1943) *Curriculum and Examinations in the Secondary School*, London, HMSO.

PETERS, R.S. (1965) *Ethics and Education*, London, Allen and Unwin.

PLOWDEN REPORT (1967) *Children and their Primary Schools*, London, HMSO.

SCHOOLS COUNCIL (1967) *The Raising of the School-Leaving Age*, London, HMSO.

STENHOUSE, L. (1967) *Culture and Education*, London, Nelson.

STENHOUSE, L. (1983) *Authority, Education and Emancipation*, London, Heinemanm.

TAWNEY, R.H. (1931) *Equality*, London, Allen and Unwin.

TAYLOR, C. (1989) *Sources of the Self*, Cambridge, Cambridge University Press.

TAYLOR, C. (1994) *Multiculturalism*, Princeton, NJ, Princeton University Press.

The Curriculum

7   What is Worth Learning?

Denis Lawton

Introduction

Coming at this point in the book I am not going to argue in favour of comprehensive schools — I will assume those arguments and also assume that part of the logic is that comprehensive schools must have some kind of common curriculum based on common culture. But a common curriculum must not be a uniform curriculum. We must ask what do all our young people need, but that is the beginning, not the end, of the process.

The title I have been given for this chapter is a variation of a very old problem in curriculum: Herbert Spencer's simple question 'What knowledge is of most worth?' Perhaps it is not all that simple because Spencer (1878) got the answer wrong, and times have changed anyway.

Background

An important aspect of any curriculum is its history: the recent history of the secondary curriculum is a record of inadequate planning, mistakes and missed opportunities.

The 1944 Act

The *1944 Act* established secondary education for all without making any provision for a curriculum for all. Solving that problem was delayed by the non-comprehensive tripartite policy of different schools — and curricula — for different types of children. The result was domination by the traditional grammar school curriculum which was not only narrow and over-academic but also neglected some of the most important aspects of modern life — for example, politics, economics, moral education, health education. Even the GCSE reform starting in 1986, although an improvement in some ways, retained those defects and failed to provide a satisfactory curriculum model for the comprehensive school.

The National Curriculum 1988

This was another missed opportunity. Kenneth Baker asked some of the right questions but he had little chance of providing sensible answers:

> The Cabinet Sub-Committee on Education Reform proceeded in a way
> unlike any other on which I have served. The process would start by

Margaret putting forward various ideas — in addition to the Anson Paper she had the No. 10 Policy Group heavily involved in the subject, and its then head, Brian Griffiths, was engaged in little else at this time — and there would be a general discussion, to which I would contribute my four-pennyworth. At the end of it, Margaret would sum up and give Kenneth his marching orders. He would then return to the next meeting with a worked out proposal which bore little resemblance to what everyone else recalled as having been agreed at the previous meeting, and owed rather more to his officials at the DES. After receiving a metaphorical handbagging for his pains, he would then come back with something that corresponded more closely to her ideas. . . . (Lawson, 1992, pp. 609–10)

Hardly the best basis for a coherent policy.

The Baker National Curriculum was immediately criticized for being little different in structure and thinking from the Secondary Regulations 1904. It was a list of academic subjects concentrating on content to be acquired. For some schools the National Curriculum made them retreat from more enlightened practices to an obsolete subject-based curriculum. The HMI idea of entitlement was good but the National Curriculum that was developed after 1988 did not entitle all pupils to what they really needed.

To counter the criticism that the National Curriculum was inadequate because many important aspects of development and experience were not covered by the Foundation Subjects, the National Curriculum Council produced *NCC Circular No. 6: The National Curriculum* and *Whole Curriculum Planning* (NCC, November 1989). It recommended that every school should plan its whole curriculum bearing in mind cross-curricular dimensions, themes and skills. This document was followed by more specific suggestions. For example, *Curriculum Guidance 8: Education for Citizenship* (NCC, 1990) offered 'guidance on ways in which education for citizenship might be strengthened and ensured in every school'. The other four cross-curricular themes were economic understanding, health education, careers, and the environment: each had its own NCC guidelines. This initiative might have gone some way to correct the limitations of the ten subject approach. But the NCC advice was a non-starter for two reasons: first, it was non-statutory — competing for time against the over-specific, compulsory National Curriculum; and, second, some Education Secretaries, especially Kenneth Clarke, were hostile to what they saw as unnecessary complications, and discouraged the NCC from developing these cross-curricula elements.

In any case, the National Curriculum ran into a variety of problems and in 1993 Ron Dearing had to be called in.

The Dearing Review (1993/94)

The Review did not solve the fundamental curriculum problems but, having listened to teachers, removed some of the detailed requirements. Schools were given a little more space — but not enough — to plan their own coherent curriculum.

Why is it that so many 'reformers' have got the curriculum so wrong? Part of the answer is that they looked backwards rather than forwards — they were imprisoned by traditions which provided only partial solutions. This has been particularly true of Conservative administrations since 1979.

A Curriculum Plan for Comprehensive Schools

If we were to look forward (instead of backwards), I am sure that it would be wrong to *start* with a list of ten subjects. We need an analysis of our society now and how it is changing. What aspects of our culture should all our young people have access to? Any kind of cultural analysis would reveal that one of the major omissions in the National Curriculum is adequate understanding of our modern democratic urban industrial society — a society which is changing so rapidly that the young would find it difficult to comprehend the rules and norms even if they were taught more about it.

This kind of analysis would not result in abandoning all the content in the National Curriculum, but it would have to be

- justified in terms of all individuals living in a changing democratic society;
- derived from clear principles and values (not a narrow list of traditional academic subjects);
- seen not as a stage ending at age 16 or 18, but as part of continuing education in a learning society;
- providing broad guidelines not specific details which should be left for school planning.

Some have been tempted to say that curriculum no longer matters — what matters now is the pedagogy and the enthusiasm of the teachers. This is an oversimplification. A more acceptable view is that it is necessary to see curriculum, pedagogy and assessment as dimensions of the same process. It is clearly true that you can have a marvellous curriculum on paper which simply does not work in the context of a school — either because the curriculum has not taken account of pedagogy and assessment, or because in some schools no change in curriculum, pedagogy and assessment can on its own solve fundamental problems of school culture. Some schools are failure systems rather than learning communities. I am not here indulging in the popular sport of teacher-bashing (we can leave that to the Chief Inspector). I am suggesting that just as for historical reasons reformers have repeatedly got the curriculum wrong, for similar sociocultural reasons many schools have a 'culture' which encourages low expectations. After 1944 most LEAs just did not think comprehensive but planned in terms of 20 per cent academic pupils. After the Lockwood Report (DES, 1964) the discussion moved to 20 per cent academic (GCE 'O' level), 40 per cent below the academic (CSE), a few more capable of tackling one or two CSE subjects, but with the rest still being regarded as unexaminable. Even when most secondary schools became comprehensive, the surface culture of schools might embrace equality and educability, but the deep structure of society retained the traditional minimalist (Lawton, 1992) thinking of education for an academic elite with the others seen as failures or lesser mortals who needed training. Comprehensive schools had to develop in a culture which was antagonistic to many comprehensive ideals.

Bearing all that in mind, let us move on to the curriculum. What is missing? A major omission is that our young grow up not understanding the moral, social, political and economic structure of our society. There are various ways of trying to put that right, and I want to treat the short-term solution (1996–2000 — the five Dearing years) differently from the long-term plan for the twenty-first century.

In the *short-term* schools have to make the revised National Curriculum work. They will need to think in terms of damage limitation which could be based on a revival of the NCC cross-curricular elements. This would not be a perfect plan because the National Curriculum is structurally flawed. The two immediate tasks would be to look at Key Stage 3 and then at Key Stage 4.

Key stage 3

What is missing from the National Curriculum?

(i) *Politics/citizenship*

We know that young people leave school very ignorant of their own society, including its political institutions, David Trainor, HMI, (1995) was surely right when he spoke at an Institute for Citizenship Studies (ICS) Conference and asked:

> How many secondary school pupils, even if they have achieved starred grade 'A' GCSE in their NC subjects will bother to vote at the next election? If they do bother, how much help have they been offered in our schools to understand the issues on which that election may be fought?

Wilkinson and Mulgan (1995) show us an even more disturbing aspect of young people's understanding of society. *Freedom's Children* appears to be opting out of social and political activities. This may not only be a failure of education but a serious threat to democratic society.

> For many young people in Britain today, politics has become something of a dirty word. People under 25 are four times less likely to be registered than any other age group, less likely to vote for or join a political party, and less likely to be politically active. Only 6 per cent of 15–34-year-olds describe themselves as 'very interested in politics'. (p. 98)

It may well be that young people are not interested because they have never learned the basic rules and principles — even the vocabulary — of politics. I get bored watching chess for the same reason — I simply do not understand what is going on. Social and political games are much more complex than chess, and are much more important aspects of our culture. The basic concepts have to be taught; and there are interesting ways of doing it. It is, of course, not just a matter of knowledge and understanding: attitudes, values and behaviour have to be encompassed in ways which will excite the interest of the young. And it is possible that changes in our political institutions will be needed if we want the young to be more committed to them.

(ii) *Economic awareness*

Much the same arguments apply to understanding our economic system — except that there is already considerable interest in this if the right links can be made (see Linda Thomas' work on economic awareness — Hodkinson and Thomas, 1991).

(iii) *Personal and Social Education*

Some schools have attempted to fill the gap — or at least part of it — by allotting some curriculum time for personal and social education (PSE or PSHE) including moral education, sex education and health education. This often includes some of the social skills that many industrialists are worried about. But inspection reports indicate that PSE is probably the worst taught part of the curriculum. We need a more rigorous as well as a more relevant approach. We cannot expect the most important aspects of a curriculum to be adequately taught by teachers untrained in the subject, with too little time, working in an area which is seen as low status but high risk.

Now for the omissions *Key Stage 4 post-Dearing*. I will be very brief about this because I am in danger of straying into Sally Tomlinson's territory. In addition to (i), (ii) and (iii) above, we have young people who may legally be given a curriculum completely lacking in art, music, history and geography. Broad and balanced? At just the time when many of them would be ready to tackle complex issues and be in need of enriching experiences. This cannot be right and many comprehensive schools have refused to impoverish their curriculum in that way. But the short-term problem of fitting everything in remains.

The long-term plan is perhaps more important and certainly more interesting.

I will begin by going back to the very simple question: What are schools for? If we ignore cynical answers about keeping children off the streets, selection, allocation and social reproduction, the educational answer is straightforward: schools should prepare the young for adult life in a democratic society; and they should help to develop or enrich the life of the child as a child (no order of priority intended).

Both of these answers would need to be sub-classified. Adult life might be divided into *preparation for work* (broadly defined); *preparation for citizenship* (very broadly defined) and *development as a person* which would, of course, over-lap considerably with the development of the child as an individual.

All of that is fairly uncontroversial. The arguments begin when we attempt to be more specific.

What does a child need in order to develop as a person? Despite some well-publicized views to the contrary (for example, Nick Tate, 1996), the development of personal self-esteem and personal identity are very important, but they need to be developed side by side with respect for others — an important aspect of moral development which should be seen as a central concern of the school not an optional extra or a fringe activity. What else? Involvement in art, music and literature; understanding the physical world; understanding and participating in the social and political world. And all pupils should have a right to succeed in the curriculum.

All of that common or entitlement curriculum refers to the development of the child as an individual person; preparation for the adult world overlaps considerably — the main addition necessary would be preparation for work — participating in the economic world. I used to believe that this should be left until after compulsory schooling, but that is clearly an oversimplification of the educational process. There is no necessary conflict between vocational education and general education so long as we stress the word education and do not think of vocational as limited job preparation. The world of work is an important part of our culture and one which the young are concerned about (and anxious about). It is foolish to ignore it or delay including it in the curriculum.

Such a programme might involve some of the content of the present national curriculum; but a comprehensive curriculum would be broader and richer and would have a totally different emphasis. Some planners have become obsessed with subjects which are assumed to be the non-problematic means of delivering the curriculum, when subjects are fraught with difficulties. It is important for us to stress that the curriculum should not be thought of as subject-content to be covered.

A Comprehensive Curriculum

I referred earlier to the need to see curriculum, pedagogy and assessment as dimensions of the same process. Both the short-term and the long-term strategies depend on certain principles of curriculum design, and need to reflect important changes in society, knowledge and culture which have not been recognized in the 1988 National Curriculum or in the 1994 Dearing Review. I want to look at five other aspects of curriculum change:

(i) First I want to consider the necessary shift of priority from content to process. For example, the Higginson Report (hardly a revolutionary document) complained that 'A' level students spent too much time memorizing and recalling facts and arguments rather than acquiring fundamental understanding of the knowledge. Similar comments have been made about the curriculum for younger pupils. For example, Bruner (1960) talked about process, structure and the need for children who were learning science to begin to think like scientists. We need to reinforce that attitude across the whole curriculum 11–18.

(ii) That brings us to the second problem to be overcome: the false and sterile opposition of academic and vocational (see Pring, 1995). Many outside education have complained about this characteristic of educational thinking (for example, Reich in the USA). This is by no means an English phenomenon, but we have the problem intensified because our social structure is so dominated by class. Curricula should be designed with a view to eliminating the distinction between academic and vocational: young people need aspects of both traditions, as suggested by the Institute for Public Policy Research (1990), the National Commission on Education (1993) and Richardson *et al.* (1995) Learning for the Future. We need a curriculum which gets beyond thinking in academic and vocational terms: this will not be easy because the two concepts are deeply embedded, and segregated, in our culture.

(iii)   Both (i) and (ii) above are concerned with the need for more experiential learning. TVEI courses made some interesting progress in that direction; and the GNVQ has been deliberately structured to encourage experiential learning (as well as other desirable features such as self-assessment, with students having responsibility for their own learning programmes and for organizing their own portfolios). Many problems have yet to be solved but there are some promising developments. There are some general issues here: how do we devise a curriculum which focuses to a greater extent on learning and skills, not just on teaching and content? The National Curriculum is not a good model.

And why should achievement be so closely attached to age-related goals? The kind of domination of education by IQ testing and the concept of mental age has also left a strong mark on our educational thinking: does it matter if someone takes two years rather than one to learn X? (I failed the driving test first time, but it has not left me permanently scarred — I may even be a better driver now than some who passed the first time. Does it matter?) The TGAT Report (1988) began taking us away from age-linked assessment, but recent National Curriculum testing has returned to it. We need experiential learning in a more flexible structure of assessment. Streaming and banding are crude techniques for dealing with individual differences — we need to exploit far more sophisticated methods of encouraging progression and differentiation.

(iv)   Some of the non-professional announcements about process and memorization (for example, the CBI, 1989) may indeed go too far too quickly in the direction of a content-free curriculum based on generic skills. We need to emphasize balance and coherence. Because we have information technology and the Internet it does not mean that memorizing and recall of *some* kinds of knowledge is completely unnecessary, for example, knowing a few significant dates in history prevents the past from being a mere jumble of events. Some carefully planned memorization can contribute to structure and meaning.

(v)   The task for curriculum planners should now include two requirements:

(a)   The first being more specific about processes and skills ('skill' is not a sufficiently powerful concept for what I mean but I will use it as a shorthand term). Reich (1991) argues that the skill and knowledge demands of occupations are converging. The fastest growing occupational group are 'symbolic analysts'. Reich suggests they will need a curriculum based on generic skills of four kinds: connective skills; conceptual skills; collaborative skills; and risk-taking skills. The Learning for the Future Report (Richardson *et al.*, 1995) suggests that none of Reich's four kinds of skill fits easily into either academic or vocational curricula at present. We need to think of curriculum design more in terms of those capacities.

(b)   On the other hand it is important to make sure that too much cultural heritage is not lost in the reorganization. We do not want a curriculum that is all skills and processes. Nick Tate and the SCAA seem to be acting as self-appointed cultural heritage watch-dogs (Tate, 1996), but they may not have analysed the problem adequately. It is no good just asserting that Jane Austen is superior to *Neighbours* — the case has to be argued out. But it is true that curriculum planners cannot be cultural or moral relativists: they have to make choices about what to include/exclude and say why in terms of value-priorities and quality criteria. It is not just a question of X is better than Z, but why X in a particular sequential programme? Ideally, anything in the curriculum should be justified in three ways:

— intrinsic merit
— as part of the whole curriculum
— and in the right order. (Remember Bruner's shuffle test: if you change the order and it makes no difference, maybe it should.) Sequence is often an important aspect of structure.

Much of what I have been talking about is appropriate for national guidelines, but some of it would be better considered at school level: the trouble with many national curricula, including ours, is that they try to cram in detail rather than concentrating on getting the principles right.

School-based Curriculum Planning

It is not my task to say how those two problems — i.e. the short-term 1996 solution or the long-term plan for the twenty-first century — could be solved in detail. This is a problem for school-based curriculum design. There are no magic solutions, but there is plenty of advice around about how not to attempt curriculum change — for example, Fullan (1991) and many others have written about the problems of implementing new ideas.

Summary

You may think that I have taken a circuitous route to answer what I suggested was a simple question. Perhaps I should summarize the answer to the question 'What is worth learning?'

(i)   Learning how to learn — with a greater (but not total) emphasis on process and skills.

(ii) Acquiring the kind of knowledge that leads to and makes sense of other worthwhile knowledge — retrieval skills, organizing skills, key words and concepts.

(iii) Moral values, attitudes and behaviour (with an emphasis on participating in a democratic society). This will require schools themselves to be more democratic and better models of moral principles.

(iv) Selected features of cultural heritage, but not defined in national terms. For example, in the case of history, we cannot understand England today without knowing something about the Reformation and the puritan revolution, but we also need to understand the Enlightenment, the French Revolution, the rise of fascist regimes in the 1920s, the Second World War and the holocaust. Our cultural heritage is partly local, partly national, partly European, partly universal. It is a mistake to neglect any of those four.

(v)   And there must be room for individual choice. Learning to choose is part of the educational process, too. A comprehensive curriculum is not a uniform curriculum. A comprehensive curriculum must be designed to enable all pupils to succeed in making progress appropriate to their abilities.

References

BRUNER, J. (1960) *The Process of Education*, Cambridge, MA, Harvard University Press.
BRUNER, J. (1962) *On Knowing*, Cambridge, MA, Harvard University Press.
CBI (1989) *Towards a Skills Revolution*, London, Confederation of British Industry.
CORSON, D. (1991) (Ed) *Education for Work*, Clevedon, Multilingual Matters.
CRICK, B. and PORTER, A. (1978) *Political Education and Political Literacy*, London, Longman.
DEPARTMENT OF EDUCATION and SCIENCE (1964) *Report of Working Party on Schools Curricula and Examinations* (Lockwood Report), London, HMSO.
FINEGOLD, D., KEEP, E., MILIBAND, D., RAFFE, D., SPOURS, K. and YOUNG, M. (1990) *A British Baccalauréat: Ending the Division between Education and Training*, London, Institute for Public Policy Research.
FOGELMAN, K. (1996) 'Citizenship education and education for adult life', SCAA National Symposium: Spiritual, and Moral Aspects of the Curriculum, London, School Curriculum Assessment Authority.
FULLAN, M.G. (1991) *The New Meaning of Educational Change*, New York, Teachers College Press.
HIGGINSON, G. (1988) *Advancing 'A' Levels*, London, HMSO.
HODKINSON, S. and THOMAS, L. (1991) 'Economics education for all' in WHITEHEAD, D. and DYER, D. (Eds) *New Developments in Economics and Business Education*, London, Kogan Page.
LAWSON, N. (1992) *The View from No. 11: Memoirs of a Tory Radical*, London, Corgi.

LAWTON, D. (1989) *Education, Culture and the National Curriculum*, London, Hodder & Stoughton.
LAWTON, D. (1992) *Education and Politics in the 1990s*, London, Falmer Press.
LAWTON, D. (1994) *The Tory Mind on Education 1979–94*, London, Falmer Press.
NATIONAL COMMISSION ON EDUCATION (1993) *Learning to Succeed*, London, Heinemann.
NCC (1989) *Circular No. 6. The National Curriculum and Whole Curriculum Planning*, London, HMSO.
NCC (1990) *Curriculum Guidance 8: Education for Citizenship*, London, HMSO.
OATES, T. (1992) 'Core skills and transfer: aiming high', *Journal of Educational and Training Technology International*, **29**, 3, pp. 227–39.
PRING, R. (1995) *Closing the Gap*, London, Hodder and Stoughton.
REICH, R. (1991) *The Work of Nations*, London, Simon & Schuster.
RICHARDSON, W. *et al.* (1995) *Learning for the Future*, London, University of London Institute of Education.
SCOTTISH OFFICE (1994) *Higher Still: Opportunity for All*, Edinburgh, Scottish Office.
SPENCER, H. (1878) *Education: Intellectual, Moral and Physical*, London, Williams & Norgate.
TASK GROUP ON ASSESSMENT AND TESTING (1988) *A Report*, London, DES.
TATE, N. (1996) Speech on 'Education for adult life: Spiritual and Moral aspects of the curriculum' at conference organized by the School Curriculum and Assessment Authority, Queen Elizabeth II Conference Centre, London, 15 January.
WILKINSON, H. and MULGAN, G. (1995) *Freedom's Children*, London, DEMOS.

8   A Comprehensive Curriculum 14–19

Sally Tomlinson

A major challenge for the comprehensive education system is to overcome the deep and damaging divisions which we have built into education and training for 14–19-year-old young people, and to have some vision about the sort of education these young adults will need in the twenty-first century. Until the 1970s, even into the 1980s, the division between those who were academically successful and moved into higher education and professional jobs, and those who entered vocational training or unskilled employment at 16, still made economic sense. Only a minority of young people were considered to need professional, scientific, technological and executive expertise (Crombie-White, Pring, Brockington, 1995). All this is now changing — the education of all young people aged 14–19 is beginning to be regarded as a crucial phase that needs considerable rethinking, although political, and some educational, thinking currently ensures that the structures and content of schooling for 11–16s and 16–19s are regarded as separate and distinct. Education 14–19 is not yet a cohesive system for the majority. It is fragmented in institutional, curricula, assessment and organizational terms. It is still dogged by a leaving age at 16, by early selection, by an academic-vocational divide, and by competing qualifications offered by organizations with strong vested interests. The academic route is still highly specialized and narrow and the vocational route is incoherent and confused. Successful comprehensive education must address the issue of a comprehensive 14–19 curriculum if it aims to produce what Stenhouse in 1967 called a 'community of educated people' (noted in Pring, 1995, p. 125). These are autonomous educated young adults able to create and perpetuate a fair, just, democratic and economically viable society.

I want to look briefly at the history of the 14–19 curriculum, note the plethora of calls for reform over the past few years — including the government response via Ron Dearing's reports (1994, 1995 and 1996), present some teachers' views of the 14–19 curriculum from a small pilot project I conducted last year for the National Union of Teachers, and offer you a view, perhaps a simplistic one, of a unified comprehensive curriculum 14–19. To link to a previous lecture given by Halpin in February 1996 (chapter 3 in this volume) I would like to see this offered in comprehensive community colleges open to all from the age of 14.

A Brief History

Concern with post-14 education for the majority is relatively recent. Until 1939, 88 per cent of young people had left school by 14. Post-war, an entitlement to secondary education for all was agreed by all political parties, although it was not until 1974 that the first generation of pupils who had experienced a full primary and secondary education (5–16) completed their compulsory schooling (Simon, 1992, p. 422).

Twenty-three years later, 16 is still the statutory leaving age, although a majority of young people now stay on in some form of education until at least 17. We do have a history of concern with the fortunate few who were educated to 18–19 in private or grammar schools. In 1892 the Rev J.W. Colenso, a public school head, was worried about low standards of numeracy in his school:

> Many persons who are supposed to have received the best education which the country affords, are in matters of numerical calculation ignorant and helpless, in a manner which places them in this respect, far below members of the middle classes.

He rectified this situation by producing a textbook of problems which included the following:

> A gentleman's income is £896.13s.4d per annum. If he gives £13.10s quarterly to the poor and lays up 200 guineas at the year's end, how much does he spend in 6 days? (answer: £10.8s)

For gentlemen forced to take employment, there was an empire to run and some very practical multicultural sums were required:

> A rupee contains 16 annas 12 pice. Find, in French money, the annual interest at 3.5 per cent on 5217 rupees, 3 annas, 6 pice if the exchange rate is 2.3 francs per rupee (answer: 480 francs 24.5 centimes). (Colenso, 1892)

Despite this, the elite curriculum at the high point of empire was generally imperialistic and anglocentric (McKenzie, 1986) and of a classical-liberal nature. There was, however, a stark academic-vocational divide. A 14-year-old girl leaving one of the newer classes for defective children in 1892 would have experienced a vocational curriculum of the 3 Ms — manual, mechanical, and moral (Hurt, 1987). Her manual training included cookery and laundry-work and one hopes her moral training equipped her to deal with any of her 'gentlemen' suddenly taking a passionate interest in the state of his smalls!

A unified curriculum is still hindered by the tradition of a liberal academic education for the upper and middle classes (with examinations validated by university-influenced boards), by trade certificates of the kind developed by City & Guilds and the RSA for the skilled working classes, and a practical education for the rest. The invention of mental measurement dating from the French scholar Binet's work in

1905 further reinforced the notion that only tested 'high IQs' or 'high ability' allowed entry to professions or business, low IQs and low ability being linked with manual jobs and manual workers. The Second World War, as Simon (1992) has pointed out, did throw new light on the educability of the supposed low IQ of the lower classes as they were rapidly trained as skilled engineers and electronics experts. It was a retrogressive step when the Labour government in 1946 endorsed a divided curriculum in grammar and secondary modern schools — the latter for children whose 'future employment will not demand any measure of technical skill or knowledge' (*The Nations' Schools*, 1946, p. 105). From the 1940s to the 1960s, selection at 11+, the 'grammar-school curriculum', narrow and early specialization, an arts-science divide, characterized the education of the supposed middle class elite, and a practical and vocational curriculum was considered adequate for the rest, with secondary modern schools initially prevented from entering pupils for public examinations.

The Curriculum into the 1980s

The development of the curriculum in comprehensive schools, which by 1979 were educating 88 per cent of pupils, has been well documented (Simon, 1992; Lawton, 1983 and 1989). Suffice to say that most comprehensive schools incorporated academic and practical courses into their curriculum and from the mid-60s to the 80s largely sorted pupils into 'O' level, CSE, or 'non-exam' with different curricula. Option choice at 13+ became crucial for future employment. Not surprisingly, academic courses were dominated by middle class pupils, working class and minority students were mainly directed towards technical, practical, creative, physical and remedial courses (Smith and Tomlinson, 1989). Many of these courses were interesting and useful but there was never any parity of esteem. The GCSE was an attempt to overcome the early division into the liberal versus the relevant, as was the Technical and Vocational Education Initiative, one of the criteria for funding of TVEI being the design of a four-year curriculum which stressed problem solving, individual initiative and personal development. Pring has raised the question as to whether TVEI and other pre-vocational developments contain the seeds of an educational philosophy which bridges the academic-vocational divide (Pring, 1995, p. 65).

The secondary curriculum became an arena for more acute political conflict in the 1980s. The HMI view of a common curriculum (HMI, 1981) based on 'areas of experience' received much teacher support. Despite this, it was modified by Keith Joseph in *Better Schools* (DES, 1985) and by 1988 the Baker National Curriculum had returned schools to a traditional-subject based agenda, plus 'new' technology. Crucial areas of political, social, and economic understanding, education for an ethnically diverse society, moral education, and other important areas were relegated to the margins of school experience.

By the end of the 1980s, post-16 education and training was still incoherent and confused, with competing courses and, qualifications, exacerbated in the 1980s by competition between schools, sixth form and further education colleges. 'A' levels, with added 'A/S' levels, dominated the academic route, despite a 20 per cent failure rate in some subject areas, and the Higginson report which suggested a modest broadening of 'A' levels (1988) was rejected by the government as compromising the 'gold standard'. The National Council for Vocational Qualifications (NCVQ) had been created in 1986 to develop NVQs, originally work-based qualifications based on competences culled from behaviouristic psychology, and in 1991 the White Paper *Education and Training for the Twenty-first Century* (DES, 1991) established the GNVQ, General National Vocational Qualifications, as a half-way house between the academic and the vocational.

> We aim to establish three broad qualification pathways for our young people — the 'A' level system, NVQs, and the new GNVQs — which will stand alongside academic qualifications on their own merit.

The 1990s have seen the development of GNVQ in what will ultimately be fourteen vocational areas studied at three levels. Figure 8.1 illustrates the three-track system which is now in place from 14–19, a more elaborate version can be found in Pring (1995, p. 71) together with a critique of lack of coherence, problems of programming, the nonsense of talk of parity or equivalence between tracks and qualifications, and the fragmented nature of a divided, competitive system which discourages co-operation between institutions.

Dearing

By 1993 the National Curriculum was in sufficient disarray for Sir Ron Dearing to be invited to 'slim down' the subjects and simplify testing. Incorporated into his final report (Dearing, 1994) was an acceptance of the three-track post-16 system:

- the craft or occupational — NVQ;
- the 'vocational' — a midway path between academic and vocational leading to GNVQ;
- the 'academic' leading to A and A/S levels. (p. 19)

His report suggested extending a vocational/occupational element post-14 as an option to 'better develop some young people into capable and sensible men and women' (*ibid.*, p. 20). This is the mixture as before — post-14 vocational courses are not likely to be followed by the children of Cabinet Ministers — or Shadow Cabinet Ministers for that matter.

Dearing's success at slimming the National Curriculum led to an invitation in 1995 to 'find ways to strengthen, consolidate and improve the framework for 16–19 qualifications' while maintaining the rigour of 'A' levels, improving participation in education and training and reducing wastage. His interim report (Dearing, 1995) indicated some amazement at the complexity of a world of education and

Figure 8.1:   The relationshiips between NVQ and GNVQ levels and academic qualifications.

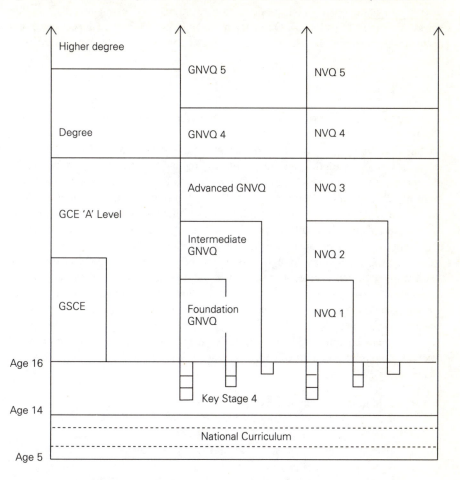

Based on *NVQ Monitor*, 1994, p. 19

training which remains 'intelligible only to specialists'. Despite an attempt to eschew jargon, his report included a page explaining forty-six acronyms.

His final report, (Dearing, 1996) appears to tinker with, rather than reform, the three-track system which will stay in place. GNVQs will be renamed Applied 'A' levels; there will be a continuation of experimental collaborative schemes offering common modules between 'A' levels and GNVQ (as for example, the scheme currently in progress between the RSA and the Cambridge University Examination Syndicate); there will be new 'A/S' levels; a revival of a 'S' level; and possibly a freeze on the number of pupils taking 'A' levels. What does appear to be new is a proposal for a new framework of national awards — an Advanced National Diploma (two 'A' levels or a GNVQ); an Intermediate Diploma; and a Baccalaureate-style National General Diploma. There is also a proposal to allow

14-year-olds who have been unsuccessful at school to leave and attend courses at further education colleges — particularly 'vocationally relevant activity' in 'the world of applied knowledge'. Once again students from lower socioeconomic and disadvantaged groups, are recruited as candidates for training rather than education.

Teachers' Views

Since the late 1980s there has been a plethora of calls for reform of the education of 14–19-year-olds. A divided and divisive system with a statutory curriculum pre-16 and an array of 'pick n' mix' courses and qualifications offered post-16 in different institutions with different levels of funding and resourcing, is clearly no way to approach the twenty-first century. One obvious answer seems to be the development of a broad, unified curriculum to 18–19, with an overarching qualification.

Since teachers' views have seldom been solicited on 14–19 education, the NUT commissioned a small pilot project in a geographically representative group of schools to discover what they consider a coherent 14–19 curriculum should be, what assessment they thought most appropriate and how they perceived the academic-vocational divide. The project worked with six comprehensive schools (one GM) — two in the North, two in the South, one Midlands and one Welsh school. Forty-eight teachers were interviewed, the majority with over nineteen years teaching experience.

You may be interested initially to learn that in the project 98 per cent of teachers supported a system of comprehensive schools which they characterized as places where:

- all abilities are catered for;
- there is a broad curriculum with a range of specializations;
- there is equal opportunity for all students to succeed;
- all students can share facilities and resources equally;
- the local community is served;
- social integration is facilitated. (Tomlinson for the NUT, 1994)

The kind of broad flexible 14–19 curriculum favoured by the teachers encompassed:

- a range of subjects and experiences;
- a breadth of knowledge and skills;
- the development of critical abilities;
- scope for independent learning;
- equal opportunities for all students;
- no early specialization;
- no arts-science divide;
- no academic-vocational divide. (*ibid.*)

The majority of teachers would opt for a broader curriculum to 18–19 with all students studying both academic and vocational courses and having work experience or work-related courses. In their view a National Curriculum 14–19 should include the humanities, science/maths, technology, aesthetic areas, physical areas, and practical areas. They were aware of an academic-vocational divide in their schools but did not think vocational courses should be solely for the 'less academic' despite some students post-16 being motivated by narrow job-specific courses. Those working with GNVQ students were trying hard to make the courses work, but were not happy with the speed of introduction, the underresourcing and the increased divisiveness.

Teachers had begun to question the necessity for a break and a 'final' exam at 16, particularly as a majority now continue in education post-16. The implications of this are that the time may now be right to question a legal education-leaving age at 16 and the necessity for a GCSE-type examination. They also questioned how long a separation of 'A' level and GNVQs could continue, were supportive of modular courses and pointed to the many possibilities for modularizing existing and new courses and creating new forms of assessment. They were opposed to selection for different schools at 11 and 14, but supported selection for different courses at 14 — done in a variety of ways — notably student choice, student choice guided by parents and teachers, an individual curriculum selected from a range of choices, and any testing to include continuous assessment. They also supported courses for special talents or skills. It was interesting that they did not want to segregate or exclude the 'special' or the 'difficult' but were not impressed by Codes of Practice that came without resources. They thought schools would continue to exclude some students until a broad, modular curriculum with access for all, but possibly at different levels, was developed.

Having completed the questionnaire, the teachers were invited to make further comments which proved to be remarkably good humoured and restrained! Overall, they thought the pace of change in the introduction of the National Curriculum and GNVQs, and the lack of real consultation had been detrimental to students' education and teacher morale. They did not however, wish to act as a professional interest group imposing their views on others. In matters of the curriculum and assessment reform, they thought that partnerships should be created and that central and local government, parents, employers, governors, students and local communities should all influence the education and training of 14–19-year-olds.

Calls for Reform

If put into practice, the teachers' ideas would obviously change the nature of the 14–19 curriculum and teachers are not the only people questioning the current situation and government-sponsored alternatives.

Since 1990, other calls for reform have come from sources as diverse as the CBI, the Institute of Directors, the TUC, the Royal Society, the Royal Society of Arts, the Advisory Council on Science and Mathematics, the National Commission on Education, the IPPR, the Labour Party, the CVCP, the Association of Sixth Form Principals, and (jointly) the Association for Colleges, Girls Schools Association,

Headmasters' Conference, Sixth Form College Association, and the Society of Heads in Independent Schools.

I will elaborate briefly on some of the suggestions.

Proposals for a unified system were put forward in 1990 by the IPPR in *A British Baccalaureate* (Finegold *et al.*, 1990). This proposed a three-stage system leading to an Advanced Diploma which would replace 'A' levels and all vocational qualifications. The curriculum would be organized into 'domains' of social and human sciences, arts, languages and literature, and natural sciences and technology including skill-based modules. Students would complete, at their own pace, core, specialist and work/community-based modules. The IPPR report also envisaged an eventual merging of FE and technical colleges, and sixth form and colleges into tertiary colleges, and close links with employers but discouragement of employers taking on 16-year-olds.

In the run-up to the 1992 General Election the (old!) Labour party committed itself to the introduction of a unified system leading to a unified Advanced General Certificate of Education. Derek Fatchett was a particular enthusiast for 14–19 education. In an article in *The Guardian* entitled 'Count on the comprehensive' (10 June 1992) he praised the success of comprehensive schools in helping more and more students to pass examinations and increase staying-on rates, but argued for a rethinking of routes from 14. He suggested the abolition of the GCSE, and a unified 14–19 curriculum with a unified qualification:

> If we are to offer greater flexibility and therefore the potential for special-isation, should we not open up our institutions post-14 so that the distinc-tion between school and college blurs, and the opportunity exists to develop non-selective community colleges, catering for all over 14, and possessing strength in particular aspects of the curriculum. (*ibid.*, p. 25)

The National Commission for Education (1993) also proposed a new General Education Diploma at ordinary and advanced levels, the latter replacing all other qualifications, the curriculum being modular and geared to individual needs. The Commission also envisaged some students leaving education at 16 and entering a new form of traineeship and the 1996 Dearing Report has proposals to expand youth traineeship.

One of the most surprising calls for reform came in 1994 when the Head-masters' Conference issued its joint statement on *Post-compulsory Education and Training* suggesting that academic and vocational pathways and qualifications should be brought within a single national framework, that a modular framework for curriculum delivery be developed but that academic and vocational units be separately and progressively assessed. Students could choose to build their own programmes of study to ensure a combination of breadth and depth appropriate to them. Their working party was 'convinced of the need for an overarching qualifi-cation, supported by a record of attainment' (p. 2) and questioned the need for the GCSE to continue.

In March 1996 the House of Commons Education Committee produced a report *Education and Training 14–19* which also suggested a new award, possibly including academic and vocational courses, and advising that students should study a broader range of courses post-16. The Committee was 'cautious' as to whether post-16 courses should be modularized and 'rejected suggestions' that school sixth forms should phased out (House of Commons Education Committee, 1996).

Conclusion

In the short term, despite the undoubted groundswell of support for a unified 14–19 curriculum there is to be no radical change. The Dearing interim report rejected any 'fundamental change to the present structure of qualifications' (Dearing, 1995, p. 12) and is defending the 'value that comes from having distinctive approaches to education'. These are weasel words defending an existing and intensifying academic-vocational divide. A change of government is unlikely to initiate immediate change. The new Labour party is retreating from the comprehensive ideal and has no new policies for 14–19, although two documents, *Aiming Higher* (Labour Party, 1995) and *Lifelong Learning* (Labour Party, 1996) criticize the incoherence of competitive institutions receiving different kinds of funding and the absence of a coherent 14–19 curriculum framework.

David Blunkett, Shadow Education Secretary, also outlined plans for 'families' or consortia of local comprehensive schools sharing expertise and resources. With a little imagination these could become the non-selective post-14 community colleges envisaged by Fatchett in 1992. However, no party is currently committed to breaking down barriers between institutions, reducing wasteful competition or seriously rethinking the principles or the content of a 14–19 curriculum that would move us away from our seemingly immovable obsession with an elite academic education which runs from 14–18 for the middle and aspirant middle classes and vocational and practical education for the rest.

John Dewey wrote in 1916 in his famous *Democracy and Education* that:

> there is a danger that education will perpetuate the older traditions of liberal education for a select few . . . and vocational education interpreted as trade education. Education thus becomes an instrument of perpetuating the existing order of society instead of acting as a means of its transformation. (p. 316)

We appear to be wedded to an old order rather than a transformation. A unified comprehensive 14–19 curriculum would be a tool for transformation.

References

COLENSO, J.W. (1892) *Arithmetic*, London, Longmans, Green and Co.
CROMBIE-WHITE, R., PRING, R. and BROCKINGTON, D. (1995) *14–19 Education and Training: Implementing a Unified System of Learning*, London, RSA.

DEARING, R. (1994) *The National Curriculum and its Assessment. Final Report*, London, School Curriculum and Assessment Authority.

DEARING, R. (1995) *Review of 16–19 Qualifications. Interim Report*, London, HMSO.

DEARING, R. (1996) *Review of 16–19 Qualifications. Final Report*, London, HMSO.

DEPARTMENT FOR EDUCATION AND SCIENCE (DES) (1981) *The School Curriculum*, London, HMSO.

DEPARTMENT OF EDUCATION AND SCIENCE (DES) (1985) *Better Schools*, London, HMSO.

DEPARTMENT OF EDUCATION AND SCIENCE (DES) (1991) *Education and Training for the Twenty First Century*, London, HMSO.

DEWEY, J. (1916) *Democracy and Education*, New York, Free Press.

FINEGOLD, D., KEEP, E., MILIBAND, D., RAFFE, D., SPOURS, K. and YOUNG, M. (1990) *A British Baccalaureate*, London, Institute for Public Policy Research.

JOINT STATEMENT BY HEADMASTERS' CONFERENCE (1994) *Post-Compulsory Education and Training*, London, HMC.

HIGGINSON REPORT (1988) *Advancing 'A' Levels*, London, HMSO.

HOUSE OF COMMONS EDUCATION COMMITTEE (1996) *Education and Training for 14 to 19 Year Olds*, Vol 1, London, HMSO.

HURT, J. (1987) *Outside the Mainstream*, London, Routledge.

LABOUR PARTY (1946) *The Nation's Schools*, London, Labour Party.

LABOUR PARTY (1995) *Aiming Higher*, London, Labour Party.

LABOUR PARTY (1996) *Lifelong Learning*, London, Labour Party.

LAWTON, D. (1980) *The Politics of the School Curriculum*, London, Routledge.

LAWTON, D. (1983) *Curriculum Studies and Educational Planning*, London, Routledge.

LAWTON, D. (1989) *Education, Culture and the National Curriculum*, London, Hodder and Stoughton.

MCKENZIE, J.M. (Ed) (1986) *Imperialism and Popular Culture*, Manchester, Manchester University Press.

NATIONAL COMMISSION ON EDUCATION (1993) *Learning to Succeed*, London, Heinemann.

PRING, R. (1995) *Closing the Gap: Liberal Education and Vocational Preparation*, London, Hodder and Stoughton.

SIMON, B. (1992) *Education and the Social Order 1940–1990*, London, Lawrence and Wishart.

SMITH, D. and TOMLINSON, S. (1989) *The School Effect*, London, Policy Studies Institute.

TOMLINSON, S. (1994) *Teachers' Views of the 14–19 Curriculum*, London, National Union of Teachers.

Effective Schools and Effective Teachers

9   Effective Comprehensive Education

Caroline Benn

Introduction

Originally I was assigned 'Effective comprehensive schools' as the title, but I asked if I could change it to 'Effective comprehensive education' taking the long view of the development of common education over several centuries. The reason was that, in discussion in recent decades in Britain of the 'ideals' of comprehensive education has been stunted by being confined to a single institutional model at secondary stage rather than being seen as a principle applicable to a multiplicity of institutional forms, as well as to learning at all stages of life.

Comprehensive education today is the culmination of that drive for secondary education for all — that has occupied the whole of the twentieth century in the same way elementary education for all occupied the nineteenth. In 1965 its leading edge reached the age of 11, while today it is passing through the 16–19 age range, drawing in to its orbit a whole array of work-related learning, both traditional and new. It is no longer confined to the academic elite gathered in sixth forms and upper standards but includes an increasing variety of venues, including the whole of the further education sector.

As the twenty-first century develops, comprehensive education will focus increasingly on adult learners and on learners before the age of 5. In both cases this means having to adjust comprehensive ideals to the principles of voluntary participation. Thus to limit comprehensive education to institutions in a compulsory system, as so many still do, is to discourage exploration of its full nature as well as its most important future development.

A second reason I asked for a change concerns the limitations of school effectiveness work itself. It was such a breath of fresh air when it started in the 1970s that maybe we have been slow to realize it had limitations. But what is increasingly in question is whether improvements made, which we know increase effectiveness in the short-term, will survive the long-term, as recent American research has started to question (Gray and Wilcox, 1995). So too, whether in individual schools or colleges, improvements do not have a very definite ceiling — even in the short run.

Effectiveness techniques will help some schools to improve performance over others with similar characteristics but do little to reduce inequalities in the system as a whole — that is, they make little difference to overall patterns of educational equality. Based as they are on correlation studies, effectiveness studies tend to ignore 'family background, social class, any notion of context' (Angus, 1993, p. 34). The domain of 'school functions' predominates and leaves little room for the 'culture of pupils, nature of the community, wider nature of society or the economy' (p. 341). In particular, it ignores local, regional and national democratic accountability as well as much of the self-directed activity of individuals and groups within communities.

In short, studying comprehensive education school by school, but excluding the education system in which schools and colleges are embedded (and ultimately the social and political system in which education itself functions), severely limits access to strategies for improvement. These limitations in turn eventually affect the way democracy itself functions.

New Research and the Resistance of Pernicious Myths

One of the advantages of the recent research I carried out with Clyde Chitty (Benn and Chitty, 1996) is that its scope allowed both school-by-school and system analysis to take place within one and the same project, and to look at the ways in which dozens of factors interact within a comprehensive education system in relation to various outcomes and measures of 'success'. Depending upon what your measures are, the relative importance of associated factors in achieving success is made more obvious.

But none of this can be seen without keeping up a full analysis of comprehensive education as a distinct system — rather than as one among many 'choices' in a basically selective system. One of the drawbacks attached to the development of comprehensive education in Britain since the 1970s is that in order to preserve it as 'just another choice', no government has charted its unique development in any large (or even medium-scale) way. As a result, we have lost track of what is actually happening in schools that claim to be comprehensive, and thus the capacity to be sure any longer that when we talk of practice in comprehensive schools that the practices we mention are in any way universal or representative.

One recent example has been the debate about returning to 'streaming' — defined as initiating a 'new' policy of setting by subjects — as opposed to mixed ability teaching, assumed not only to be universal but unique to comprehensive schools. In fact, neither assumption is true. Our research found that streaming (so widely used at the start of the comprehensive secondary reform) is rarely used any longer; and equally, that mixed ability teaching, certainly not confined to comprehensive contexts, is rare as a universal mode. The usual practice is to begin with mixed ability in the earlier years and thereafter set those subjects which staff within any one school believe to be best taught in this way (*ibid.*, chapter 6). The 'revolution' in practice, that political leaders insisted would soon be enforced, had already taken place.

Equally unrelated to real practice is the assumption that better results overall within a system flow from educating an academic elite separately, whether in their 'own' schools or by streaming inside comprehensive schools, when previous research showed that overall results are better in comprehensive systems (McPherson and Willms, 1987) and also showed that there was little difference in terms of academic attainment between the two grouping practices (Postlethwaite and Denton, 1978). In our own research, when schools with a majority of subjects set were compared to those with only a minority set, again it was found that there was no difference in academic results, using among other criteria, the five GCSE subjects A–C which are so widely used to determine 'league table' standing in the new competitive market (Benn and Chitty, 1996, pp. 286–7).

But still the myths will continue, for comprehensive education in its post-twentieth century form has been surrounded by myths which long ago should have been laid to rest but are kept alive by prevailing ideologies that continue to resist the reform. Another myth is that there is some deathly contest between the meritocratic and egalitarian school or system when it comes to the future of comprehensive education. At one time it was the latter that some espoused; today it is the former. But neither exists nor ever has, since the origin of this false debate (made so much of by almost all researchers in comprehensive education in the 1970s and 1980s) can be traced back to the late 1960s when some insisted that there was such a choice to be made (Marsden, 1969).

To show what was meant at that time, two long lists of what characterized practice in a meritocratic and, by contrast, an egalitarian school were set out. To those of us who opposed this division then, it was an attempt to categorize schools in ways that bore no relation to practice on the ground. Meritocratic schools, it was said, for example, did not allow extra-curricular activity, while egalitarian ones took no account of science — both propositions that were manifestly able to be contradicted in practice.

Sensible observers (of whatever ideological persuasion) could see at that time (as they can today when it comes to the new mythology of class teaching styles or reading methods) that schools never follow one course exclusively in these matters, but use a wide variety of practices, drawn from both sides of any supposed divide according to a combination of expertise, experience and enthusiasm of those working together. None sets out to be 'one type' and none is.

Dealing with these myths is important when it comes to comprehensive ideals. For until they are cleared away, the larger philosophical arguments cannot come to light. One that needs discussing all the time is that comprehensive education is very much centred on social justice, and involves engineering with an ideal of making society more cohesive in some way. Others, however, while not denying that comprehensive education might well produce a greater social cohesion (and it would be no bad thing if it did), nor denying that social factors are all important in education, nevertheless do not see comprehensive education as a social experiment. We see it, rather, as an educational reform.

We see its justification in educational and psychological terms, through the removal of barriers to effective education that have been imposed at successive stages of history for children, and also adults, allocating them to differential educational pathways, levels of resources, attention, prestige, without good educational reason — in fact, usually for reasons that were indeed socially or economically determined.

Caroline Benn

The Paradoxical Ideal

Comprehensive ideals are to be defined educationally, starting with the acknow-
ledgment of a common system and common learning, while at the same time
acknowledging the need to debate when that system should differentiate. That is,
what shall be learned in common in the curriculum or any core and what shall be
left open for individual decision according to preference? Each age group and each
generation will have its own view about the best balance in these respects. In a
democratic society this best balance should be a matter of common decision, where
the institutions themselves and those who work in them play a leading part in
setting the consensus at each stage and age.

It is this democratic process that is being transgressed today as, increasingly,
central government dictates what shall be learned, and when, and how — a form
of decision-making we have dropped in to accepting as the norm, when it need not
be. Just as we also seem to have dropped into accepting that education should be
driven by the commercial market, with institution pitted against institution, even
when it is clear that the negative effects of competition are outweighing any effects
that might be beneficial if the system were organized more democratically and
more cooperatively.

Comprehensive education has to enable the capabilities of the whole of each
age group to show themselves, be tested, engage in a full range of learning activity, and be encouraged to do their best — though none will succeed in everything
and some might only succeed in a little. For the ideal is that all learning and each
learner and each learner's path is of inherently equal value and is treated as such
within the system.

Equal valuing has been there before. Pat Daunt, an early comprehensive
headteacher, first suggested it is the 1970s (Daunt, 1975). But 'treated as such' is
new, born out of the experience of implementing comprehensive education since
that time. For 'treated as such' goes beyond merely affirming an intention. Parity
of esteem means nothing unless you demonstrate how parity works out in practice
in ways that provide the esteem in practice — that is, to the satisfaction of those
who are teaching and learning. It is *their* opinion that matters, not ours. The same
is true of 'equal opportunity'; it means little unless those who are teaching and
learning experience their valuing as equals — whether in terms of facilities, courses,
choice, quality of teaching, access to qualifications, knowledge that helps them to
advance their own lives, and honour and reasonable freedom accorded to them as
professionals.

This is a much more exacting ideal than the 'parity of esteem' so widely used
over the years, which is very hard to achieve in education when outside the system
certain types of intelligence or certain types of learning or institutions carry such
different ratings and status, and where society looks upon certain pupils and students and communities as inherently worthier than others.

But just because it is difficult does not excuse us from the obligation of
attempting to build into the education system practices that support different types
of learning as well as all learners in ways that demonstrate to them that they have

equal value. For it is their opinion that matters. When we do attempt this, it means that the least we can do is start with an education system that does not have attainment selection that decides ahead of time who will be successful; a system that does insist on the greatest possible degree of democracy in making the decisions about equal value, and about the way resources are distributed, learning conducted, and that balance struck between what everyone ought to be learning at any stage for the greater community good, and the freedom for teachers and learners to choose their own areas of interest. That is, striking a balance between the same for all on the one hand, and different for each on the other — the paradox of the comprehensive approach.

We have to acknowledge the paradox at the heart of our ideals: the same, yet different. It occurs over and over. We have to accept that society will always be involved in deciding anew where the same is needed and where the differences should start. It is a continual obligation in comprehensive systems to keep our eye on this balance, as society's own needs and goals change. And the only way it can be done is by democratic organization, consultation, and decision-making. Imposing from above never achieves lasting consensus.

Polarization

Since there is this need to continually adjust the balance anew at each age range and in each new stage of development, no system can possibly work until there is a commitment to a comprehensive principle to start with. Here lies the secret of Britain's educational malaise over so many recent decades, as we discovered from the last question in our research project which asked what each school and college would nominate as the one factor that would most improve prospects for each school or college.

There was a wide range of answers, but when they were analyzed in any depth — though one might have said 'more value added' and another might have said 'a new government, please — what was really there was a request for the unequivocal commitment of society, and that includes government and political parties, to the system which is responsible for the education of 90 per cent in state-supported education and which, it is now evident, commands the support of the vast majority of institutions as well as the general public.

The percentage of the population favouring grammar education will always be there, but it has not risen much for the thirty years from its support around the 25 per cent to 30 per cent mark, while those favouring a comprehensive system has gone up steadily over thirty years from about 10 per cent to 65 per cent in the latest polling (ICM, reported The Guardian, 7 February 1996).

It should by now be obvious that the majority, regardless of how they feel personally about being educated in the company of certain social groups (a special British hang-up), do not want a system where previous attainment will determine future achievement in any public education service being carried out in their name and with their funding.

What weakens the UK in terms of doing anything about the problems and promoting the positive developments so many want to see, are not hordes of misfit teachers or disruptive pupils or failure to have selection or failure to have streaming or mixed ability — although these are all important issues — it is the failure of those officially in charge to commit the national community and the national culture to the comprehensive principle by acknowledging the system that is there already.

It is this great contradiction running throughout policy at all stages that is damaging: on the one hand, ostensible support for a comprehensive system by all in official places combined with, at the same time, systematic support for policies that are obviously designed to undermine the system — intentionally and unintentionally.

And it is easy to see why. Practically no other country has tried to introduce comprehensive change as Britain has; that is, without changing the system. In the UK there was no similar historical moment of change, merely a process of introducing more and more schools named comprehensive into a system that continued to accept selection and still does, and which continued to accept that it is natural for the wealthy and influential to be educated entirely apart from everyone else, as it still does. We have tried in the past to examine that balance between what some call freedom of choice and others call provision of privilege that detracts from majority rights, as is reasonable in a democratic system, but even this basic right is no longer permitted; we act nationally as if the issue has been settled. Yet we know it is not. We act nationally as if the issue of selection has been settled, yet we know it is not.

Not ending this great contradiction that runs right through the system in the UK — the non-commitment going on for thirty years, and lately the undermining — not only holds up the reform (relative to other countries in the world) but it has resulted in considerable repolarization of schools and colleges along selective lines, and the erosion of democratic accountability to the community. Of the two, though selection often seems the most urgent to us in education, it is the erosion of democratic accountability that is the most serious threat in the long run.

These two matters of reducing selection and ensuring democratic accountability are quite impossible to tackle when comprehensive education effectiveness is viewed in terms of individual schools, especially when run entirely on market lines. The importance of the issues can only be seen when one looks at the system as a whole, where patterns of change affecting the system as a whole can be viewed in a way that is impossible when one looks at the system only institution by institution.

Our recently conducted research provided us with a chance to see a bridge between institutional effectiveness and the comprehensive education system — for it enabled us to look at comprehensive schools broken down into an almost indefinite combination of different groups and analyzed by different indicators of operation and factors relating to comprehensive type, social context, and academic practice. And thus it enabled us to see at a glance which combinations made for specific outcomes.

Although it is by no means necessary to have exactly the same balance of attainment in each school or college, it is fairly necessary to ensure that each school or college has a reasonable balance of attainment that each area contains. Back in

1968 in both the NFER (National Foundation for Educational Research), research and our own independent inquiry (Benn and Simon, 1970), overall some 5 per cent (Monks, 1968; see also Ross *et al.*, 1972) of the top attainment was found to be missing from comprehensive schools nationally. Thirty years later the same question was asked again and this time it was 2 per cent — an improvement of 1 per cent a decade, which may not sound like much, but in terms of capturing those percentage heights that account for so many of the qualifications in the UK, especially at higher levels it is (Benn and Chitty, 1996, chapter 4).

The bad news, however, is that in 1968 comprehensive schools were fairly uniform in their intakes, while today the picture is alarmingly polarized — with only about a quarter of all schools now in the comfortable comprehensive bracket of having intakes that run between 15 per cent and 25 per cent of the top 20 per cent (Benn and Chitty, 1996, table 4.3). The vast majority had them in 1968. What we have now is overall improvement, but in terms of spread within the system, a whittling away of the centre by growth at the two ends.

For there was a significant group in 1994, not present earlier, of 15 per cent of schools and colleges with intakes of the top 20 per cent that amounted to 50 per cent of their intake, sometimes over 75 per cent. Their definition of comprehensive was thus very different from that usually accepted: an intake roughly reflecting the ability range in the general area. Instead theirs is a definition that includes most in the grammar range but with a few in the middle ranks and a few who are slow learners, possibly the siblings of those accepted earlier. Such schools are comprehensive in a sense of having represented 'all' abilities, but not in any way in proportion to the way attainment is distributed naturally in their local areas. And possibly they are not even aware of this distorted intake at all.

And certainly they are not aware that in many areas their practices were resulting in distorted intakes in other comprehensive schools in their vicinities, leading to a reverse situation where one in ten schools had below 5 per cent of the top 20 per cent in their intakes. The point is that this latter group of schools and colleges was three times as numerous as those with an excess of grammar pupils. So that overall this showed a three-tier position of a large layer of schools lacking the top attainment, a middle group with a balance, and a smaller layer with over-representation of the top attainment — yet calling themselves 'comprehensive' schools or colleges.

The effects of these schools one upon the other when they occur in the same area, as they do, will be very much like the effect we can calculate already of what happens to comprehensive schools' achievement overall when legal grammar schools are retained in the area. There may be only some 160 but each will affect three or four other schools locally and thus some 500 schools in the UK are affected.

Table 9.1 below compares comprehensive schools, where there are grammar schools in the area, with comprehensive schools operating in areas where no grammar schools exist. Individually, school by school, this stark contrast could not be made — but when the system is viewed as a whole, we can see at once the way grammar schools in practice severely depress the capacity of comprehensive schools to do well.

Table 9.1: Comprehensive schools with/without grammar schools, 1994 (based on question 14A and question 17A)

	Grammar schools present in the area	Grammar schools absent from the area
Average size	801	1052
Percentage:		
In top 20 per cent of attainment	12	24
Going on in 11–16 schools	57	69
Staying on in 11–18 schools	49	60
Gaining five GCSE A–C	29	48
'A' level point score average	10.6	13.4

As we can see, there are great differences. Those not competing have better results all around, and those that had grammar schools in their areas have severely depressed academic results, skewed intakes, low staying on rates, and smaller size.

The thing to remember, however, is that in 1994 only 11 per cent of all comprehensives were in this category of competing against grammar schools as against 50 per cent at the end of the 1960s. But that 11 per cent is still a large number of schools and if the survey is representative, as we believe it is, it is 500 or so in the system as a whole. To this should be added comprehensive schools that are competing with the 'hidden selection' of some grant-maintained schools and some 'selective' comprehensives and some private schools with places paid for by public funds in the form of assisted places.

Social Mix

As well as showing that some 'balance' of intakes is required in an effective comprehensive system, our research of the picture as a whole also showed the importance of having a social mix. We asked schools and colleges to put themselves in one of five categories: mostly working class entry, mostly middle class (the one-class schools), and three others which were various degrees of social mix, namely more middle class than working, more working class than middle, and lastly, an equal mix. Two-thirds of comprehensives are socially mixed — the last three groups. Only one in three is one class and of those that are, one in five of these is mostly middle class, a category that did not exist thirty years ago.

We found evidence over and over again that having a mix — both in terms of attainment and social intake — made a big difference to schools, whether you looked at academic results, or whether you looked at figures relating to attendance or indicators like staying on. Again and again having a mix did not mean ending up halfway between the best and the worst results or highest and lowest scores of whatever was being measured, as might be assumed, but always towards the higher end.

Take attendance, for example, where schools gave figures that put them in one of three categories of attendance: good (over 95 per cent), average (over 90 per cent), and below average (less than 90 per cent). Below-average attendance applied to only 1 per cent of schools which were one class and that class was middle class, while where it was working class, the figure was nearly 50 per cent below 90 per cent (49.8 per cent Benn and Chitty, 1966, table 4.6, p. 188). However, when schools were mixed in terms of class, whether the mix was exactly equal (9.5 per cent) or mixed but more middle than working class (5.1 per cent) or mixed but more working class than middle (14.5 per cent) we see at once that poor attendance rates were all quite low, much nearer the 1 per cent middle class-only score than the 50 per cent working class only score.

In fact, differences in attendance rates relative to social mix gave us some of the starkest evidence for the thesis that mixing of itself creates its own positive effect. The same phenomenon applied in other types of mixing as well — like that of housing. Results for schools and colleges with intakes drawn from mixed private and council housing were very much nearer the results of intakes from private housing than they were from schools drawing only from substantial housing or council housing.

These results give us clues about the way housing patterns might be planned in future, ignoring great swathes of monochrome housing, and even more clues about the importance that should be attached to having admissions systems to all schools organized on the same principle and overseen in every case by the same democratic process for all schools alike, accountable to the community as a whole. Accountability to each school's governors individually as applies now to schools like grant-maintained or voluntary or partially-selective — without consideration of the needs of other schools in the area — is the route to polarization.

The information the survey gathered about grant-maintained schools showed evidence of growing polarization of these schools in this respect, but sadly, much of it could well be wholly inadvertent (as it has been in voluntary schools in the past), where the schools and colleges in question had no idea their intakes exerted such polarizing effects on other schools locally. Quite clearly, the ideal of locally (or regionally) accountable democratic control is the only way to guard against this particularly obvious phenomenon of unequal valuing: different admissions rules for different comprehensive school types.

This is another function of the accountable democratic process: to keep an eye on mixes, as it has to keep one on balances. Uniformity is not the comprehensive ideal. There will always be some differences owing to the nature of any individual area, but just because there will be natural differences, is no reason to build in the *un*natural division of selections, open or hidden, academic or social.

Parity in these respects can only be achieved by all schools and colleges cooperating together in making admissions decisions jointly among themselves, for it is they who have to live with them and account to their neighbours for their own actions. Once schools and colleges — and parents and students — are confident that polarization *is* being checked and that equity in operations can be demonstrated in them in practice, they will gain that confidence that comes from the assurance that they have the best there is, and can look upon their area and its intake as being just as capable of doing well as any other. But it has to be demonstrated to those in these situations that they are being valued equally in practice as well as in theory.

Neighbourhood

But will this not then lead to the neighbourhood condition, bringing us up against one of the biggest myths in the comprehensive system? It goes right back to Eric James of Manchester Grammar School and to teachers like Rhodes Boyson who saw 'neighbourhood' as an idea 'dreadful to contemplate' (Boyson, 1969). To have a connection with your own area was somehow inimical to good education!

Ironically, much of the early evidence was supposed to come from America, but conservative advocates forgot that in the USA, unlike the UK, the idea of neighbourhood was prized by conservatives. It was a positive word, whereas in the UK it was a negative word. Over time the UK has come to realize what the USA already knew: that most people like their own neighbourhoods and identify with them. Only specific (possibly 'inner city') areas are negative in the USA as, indeed, is the case now in Britain, for in both countries problems (involving race, poverty, class) relate to only a minority of schools.

Our research shows a move in the UK to the American point of view, as comprehensive education has taken hold. Despite extensive legislation in the Thatcher years to discourage neighbourhood (and legal judgments like that in Greenwich forbidding LEAs to reserve their own schools for their own pupils), in 1994 nearly 80 per cent of all comprehensive schools drew from their own neighbourhoods or from inside their own LEA as against drawing substantially from outside both or even half of their intake from outside (Benn and Chitty, 1996, table 4.11).

Neighbourhood was popular and this went for all types of schools. Contrary to myth that the most neighbourhood-based schools would be in big cities, this same research found just the reverse. Big city comprehensive schools were the least neighbourhood, the most polarized by class, even though in cities people live closer and have better transport. It also found that most schools were happy to organize their admissions systems in cooperation with their local education authorities.

A Unified System Post–16

After nearly fifteen years of attempts to downgrade and dispose of local education authorities, the research of 1994 gave ample evidence in this way, as in others, that their role was as important as ever. It was changing, of course, but that was because schools and colleges were taking on functions LEAs used to manage, leaving LEAs to take on a host of new responsibilities, particularly in relation to the provision of services.

What the overall examination of the system also showed is how important it is going to be in future to have local education authorities — and, possibly, regional ones as well — to undertake certain key tasks that are at present unable to be performed. One is the organization of the system at 16–19 so that schools and colleges cooperate together in the provision of education and training for the age group, pooling their premises, facilities and course offering. Table 9.2, showing the size of the 12th year in education throughout the UK, gives some interesting evidence of why this will be necessary.

At the start of the reorganization the large size of comprehensive schools was held against them — but, like neighbourhood, this is not so much heard these days. In fact, we found tentative evidence that the larger the school the better the academic results (*ibid.*, table 9.5, p. 414). Even so, the size of the problem that has plagued comprehensive education from the start is, if anything, becoming more acute in the 1990s: not overall size, but post-16 size.

By the start of the 1980s there was much accumulated evidence that many sixth forms were uneconomic in size. In many areas, therefore, there was steady progress towards recasting of schools with 11–16 age ranges, and the concentration of education after 16 in colleges — either sixth form colleges, tertiary colleges, or general further education colleges. There was also evidence that had been there since the early 1970s, that schools very often became sixth form colleges but very soon merged with FE colleges to become tertiary colleges. It was the tertiary college that was growing.

But from the middle of the 1980s — particularly from Keith Joseph's period onwards — there was a decision to refuse tertiary college planning. There was a further decision to increase sixth forms by giving short course comprehensive schools permission to start new sixth forms and by allowing schools, whose sixth forms were so small they were about to be closed, to become grant-maintained schools. Proliferation of smaller sixths began to take place.

The sixth does its best to have a full spread of 'A' level and, except for music and second languages, most have a good standard fare, but today the sixth should also be providing a good range of GNVQs. Already by 1994 a quarter of comprehensive sixths had GNVQs and the FE colleges were adding 'A' level courses at a rapid rate, to match those offered in sixth form colleges and tertiary colleges.

If anyone expected to find a picture in 1994 of colleges agreeing to do the vocational courses, while schools did academic, or a division where some schools were academic and others vocational, they would have been disappointed. It was clear, as befits a system that regards itself as comprehensive, and pays attention to one of the cardinal principles of comprehensive education which so many have forgotten (namely, the need to be sure that each institution in the system is able to provide for all its students all that is normally provided for the age group as a whole), each school or college was attempting to do just this.

The problem is, it cannot be done. The size range in too many schools is too small. From our survey figures we can see just which schools types and in which fields in the colleges these will be. So the answer will have to be some form of pooling of provision to meet that comprehensive commitment of providing the full range normally available for the age group: within an area rather than from within each institutions individually.

Table 9.2 shows how necessary it will be to pool. For it shows that for a

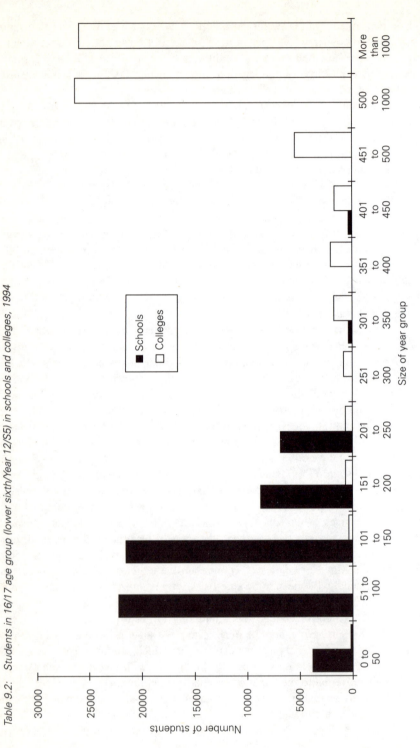

Table 9.2: Students in 16/17 age group (lower sixth/Year 12/S5) in schools and colleges, 1994

student population divided in half at aged 16 (an equal number in schools and colleges) that most of the schools' 12th years (shown in black) are below what OFSTED and others regard as an economic size. It means they are costing three or four times as much to teach as the same students in the same subjects as are the colleges at the other end of the table (outlined in white). They are doing it by repermutating — leaching — resources from lower down the school system, as expert witnesses from the DFE made clear to the House of Commons Select Committee on Education (1993, p. 27).

The obvious answer has already been discovered by schools and colleges themselves, in full defiance of an individualist market-lead competitive system: Cooperative working between institutions throughout the secondary years. We had expected to find no more than about a quarter cooperating, but in fact it was two-thirds of all comprehensive schools and colleges in the UK: some collaborating extensively, some in a small way. But all informally. That is to say, none had been asked for by any government or local authority initiative.

The experiments are legion. Yet none has the benefit of official government recognition or investigation or guidance or support or official circular — or even of much research. Some have LEA backing; some do not. Some have governors' support; in other cases governors were not even aware such experiments were taking place. All are entirely unofficial, flying in the face of considerable pressure from the market system to treat any nearby school or college as a mortal enemy.

Market forces have no power to promote such cooperatives or to rationalize such provision or to oversee its development. That is why democratic oversight, involving accountability to all the citizens in a given area, is so crucial to the future of comprehensive education — especially as the reform moves up the years to the age of 18, and then beyond. It is interesting that the directors of industry were already postulating institutional changes that grouped FE colleges around universities to make post-18 education clusters for each region, when the same change, grouping sixth forms around FE earlier down the system, has not even been discussed (see Council for Industry and Higher Education, 1995).

Only some democratically-elected body can oversee the tertiary pooling which is urgently required in each region, complete with government guidelines and support, so that each institution will be able to offer a varied array of work, with funding by the courses offered rather than by the number of bodies captured. It will be a big change, but from what we could see, it is already starting to take place in practice — like schemes and experiments of the early 1960s that heralded the comprehensive reform around the 11+.

A Democratically Accountable System

Changes like those are already taking place because those who seriously support a non-selective education system find themselves with the in-built criteria needed to judge the efficacy of policies and proposals related to grouping policy, curriculum, assessment and course development of comprehensive education as well as for judging the basic requirements of national policy to develop the system in the community. An integrated vocational and academic curriculum organized along modular lines within the same assessment system after 16, for example, may be delayed — but in time it will develop. So too will national proposals for achieving non-selective intakes to all schools, to take another example.

How long it takes depends somewhat on how quickly we can redress the harmful slide away from democratic accountability which recent years have allowed to develop. The incapacity of our normal democratic modes of implementing policy or translating it in to active practice, have been curtailed progressively. One by one the usual democratic channels have been rendered ineffective by a host of small, interlocking changes that have transferred power and decision-making steadily away from both learners and teachers in classrooms and lecture halls — as well as from the generality of the population who pay for our education services and facilities at every level, those normally represented through democratic elections.

A great deal of power is now centred in appointed self-perpetuating oligarchies of many kinds strategically placed throughout the educational and training system, ruling over individuated institutions that have been discouraged from acting collectively and forced into competition through ranking by a 'market' process over which neither they nor anyone else had any real control. At all levels this is why renewing democratic activity, leading to democratic decision-making and oversight, and involving all partners in the enterprise of education, is the first requirement.

Meanwhile, we can make it our business to devise better ways to assess existing comprehensive education by means that our compatible with comprehensive principles.

At present our judgments — through such devices as 'league tables' — are based on selective principles, in particular, the five GCSE A–C pass rate which is a direct descendant of the nineteenth century matriculation examination. We line up all our schools, for example, from best to worst in terms of this one score — even though research on the system (including that which Clyde Chitty and I have reported) shows fairly conclusively that when institutions are judged excellent it is often their degree of middle class intake or their degree of academic selectivity that is being recorded, not anything special about their own teaching or learning. Similarly, when a school is judged to be 'failing' it is almost always a school in an insalubrious area with working class intake missing a large share of 'high attaining' pupils owing to the overt or hidden selection of independent, grammar, voluntary controlled, or specialized grant-maintained schools drawing from the same area. Polarization increases as democratic accountability wanes.

Hidden Success as well as Hidden Selection

The expectation that failure must attend a school with certain characteristics can be confounded. Our research gave us one interesting example in the figures for university entrance among comprehensive schools which run to the age of 18.

Table 9.3: *All-through and upper comprehensive schools (UK) with other 75 per cent of year 13 (upper sixth) students gaining university entrance, 1994**

	Number of schools	Percentage staying on to 18	Percentage 5 GCSE (A–C) (O grade 1–3)	'A' level point score (Scotland omitted)
Schools with predominately middle class intakes	78	61	52	14.4
Schools with predominately working class intakes	63	53	32	11.5

* Academic year 1992/93, figures drawn from research database used in Benn and Chitty (1996) and based on questions 36 Band D, 36A and C, 115, 112–3, 140a Av.

Overall comprehensive education has a good record of university entrance and it is remarkable how few complaints have been recorded relating to students whose sights have been set on entry to higher education. One interesting finding from our research confirms why this may be so. Table 9.3 sets out statistics relating to those comprehensive schools with the most successful record for university entrance, over 75 per cent of their 13th-year students (upper sixth) obtaining university entrance in 1993.

What it shows is that high standing in the league tables is not required for a school to achieve this degree of success, for the schools are divided between those with predominantly middle class intakes and those with predominantly working class intakes. The seventy-eight middle-class schools have by far the 'better' results, for example, their percentage of five GCSE-C is 52 per cent (far above our survey average); while that same figure for the sixty-three working-class schools was well below average at 32 per cent (with the same difference for 'A' level point scores as well). Yet the two sets of schools are equally successful on the criteria being measured.

What it shows is that 'league tables' are not a reliable measure of success because they fail to show the high degree of hidden success of which many comprehensive schools are capable, not just in 'academic' terms like university entrance, but even more so in terms of vocational attainment and in a host of other ways related to a wide variety of achievements, and above all, in terms of the development of a wide range of different types of intelligence. Such findings as these show we have not even begun to map — and report — the true learning achievements of people, whether they are infants, school-age or adult. Successful comprehensive systems must always allow for the possibility of success in every context. We have 'miles to go' in developing ways to reveal — and encourage — achievement that is based on comprehensive-compatible criteria than on narrow selective measures which presently condition our judgments.

Caroline Benn

Conclusion

Reading through the research on comprehensive education over thirty years, time and time again, where the comments are critical, and they often are, the gist of the criticism is hardly ever that comprehensive education has moved too quickly or rushed its way into being — as populist and media comment so often imply. It has almost always been the conclusion that inappropriate ways of the past have been held on to for far too long, with chances to change repeatedly postponed. With 16–19 change now going on, again there is a chance for Britain to move quickly and to leap two historic stages at once, and so bring itself level with the rest of the world before the twenty-first century starts. It would be a great pity to have another century where Britain was always lagging behind. But that is what is destined to happen unless that full commitment to comprehensive education is finally made.

References

ANGUS, L. (1993) 'The sociology of school effectiveness', *British Journal of Sociology and Education*, **14**, 3.
BENN, C. and CHITTY, C. (1996) *Thirty Years On*, London, David Fulton.
BENN, C. and SIMON, B. (1970) *Half Way There*, London, McGraw Hill.
BOYSON, R. (1969) 'The right to choose', *Education*, 18 July and 29 August.
COUNCIL FOR INDUSTRY AND HIGHER EDUCATION (1995) *A Wider Spectrum of Opportunity*, London, CIHE.
DAUNT, P. (1975) *Comprehensive Values*, London, Heinemann.
GRAY, J. and WILCOX, B. (1995) *Good School, Bad School: Evaluating Performance and Encouraging Improvement*, Milton Keyres, Open University Press.
HOUSE OF COMMONS SELECT COMMITTEE ON EDUCATION (1993) *Minutes of Evidence*, 24 November.
McPHERSON, A. and WILLMS, J.D. (1987) *Equalization and Improvement: The Effect of Comprehensive Education in Scotland*, Edinburgh, Centre for Educational Sociology, University of Edinburgh.
MARSDEN, D. (1969) 'Which comprehensive principle?', *Comprehensive Education*, **13**, autumn.
MONKS, T.G. (1968) *Comprehensive Education in Action*, Slough, NFER.
POSTLETHWAITE, K. and DENTON, C. (1978) *Streams for No Future? The Long-Term Effect of Streaming and Non-Streaming*, The Final Report of the Banbury Enquiry, Banbury, Pubansco Publication.
ROSS, J.M., BUNTON, W.J., EVISON, P. and ROBERTSON, T.S. (1972) *A Critical Appraisal of Comprehensive Education*, Slough, NFER.

10   Teachers for the Comprehensive Idea

Ted Wragg

Teachers in comprehensive schools are asked to play many roles in our society. Not the least of these is the traditional one as 'keeper of the runes', bearer of what our civilization knows and has acquired over countless generations. Were that the only assignment teachers had to fulfil, then life would be more straightforward, but there are many others as well. In this contribution to the debate about the comprehensive secondary school I want to analyze some of these roles. I shall do that, however, in the context of looking at the future, for without a vision of the future, as well as an awareness of the past, education would be unfounded, detached from the sub- and superstructures that hold it in place. Some of the ideas put forward in the first part of this analysis are described in greater detail elsewhere (Wragg, 1997).

As medical treatments improve it becomes highly likely that children born in the late twentieth and early twenty-first century will live to be 90, 100 or more. The term 'future' can mean a very long time indeed. Some pupils may even survive until the twenty-second century. There can be a very long 'lead time' in education, and some payoffs many not occur for decades. If education is society's investment in its own posterity, then a long rather than a short term strategy is essential.

There have been numerous predictions about life in the twenty-first century, some gloomy, others more hopeful. Indeed, the same data can be quoted to support either a pessimistic or optimistic vision of what is to come. Forecasts that job opportunities may diminish can be used to predict boredom and street riots, or to welcome the release of people from dangerous and demeaning employment. The benevolence or malevolence of those in positions of power can determine the climate within which education flourishes or languishes. The support, or lack of it, from ordinary citizens and their children can be greatly influential on the success of schools. In the end the quality and character of the teachers in any comprehensive school will exert a critical effect, even against the odds.

Even intelligent guesswork about present and past trends and where they might eventually lead can go disastrously astray, so it would be a mistake to base a whole education system entirely on a single conjecture. It is hazardous enough predicting next year's events on the basis of what is happening this year, let alone what will happen in the next millennium. Small wonder that the great oracles have often spoken in ambiguous terms. I propose to deal here, therefore, with a range of possibilities that seem to be worth considering, and see what the implications would be were they to materialize, though none of the following messages is offered with any certainty.

Ted Wragg

Education for an Uncertain Future

Will pupils who leave comprehensive schools find employment in future? The jobs that people hold do not consume the whole of their life, but they are an important part of it. Until fairly recently many men, if they lived long enough, worked for some fifty or so years before entering retirement, while women tended to work in paid employment for fewer years, or did not return to their previous career after giving birth to children. Changes in work patterns have been dramatic in the last third of the twentieth century, but it is not entirely clear where these changes are leading.

A series of industrial revolutions in the nineteenth century saw masses of people move out of rural areas and into cities, as they left agriculture to seek work in factories. In early Victorian Britain about a third of the population worked on the land. Today about 2 per cent of the workforce is employed in agriculture, a remarkable transformation in the landscape of working life. Several significant changes have taken place during the last three decades of the twentieth century, but the eventual outcome of these post-industrial revolutions remains clouded. The disappearance of millions of jobs in the manufacturing industry has not led to a single type of employer emerging to absorb those displaced during the labour-shedding process.

What was notable about these huge losses of traditional forms of employment was that the vast majority of posts that disappeared were unskilled, semi-skilled or barely skilled. Graduate employment also suffered, but the biggest decline was in areas where machines were brought in to perform the numerous tasks that had previously been carried out by armies of worker ants. Firms that used to employ dozens of girl school leavers to fill cardboard boxes with their products, and dozens of boy school leavers to load them on to lorries, replaced the girls with automated packing machines and the boys with a couple of fork lift truck operators. As in other countries our society began to put an enormous premium on skill, and for those without it the prospects became bleak.

Unemployment gradually appeared to be endemic rather than cyclical. Recessions earlier in the century had been followed by boom times. Workers dropped to a three day week, or lost their jobs, only to regain exactly the same posts later, often with bonus and overtime payments, as the economy moved into a higher gear. When the cycle stopped it was partly because, in the new automated economy, no employer was going to get rid of two fork lift trucks and two drivers in order to employ twenty people with large biceps. Yet even in areas of high unemployment, there were vacancies. Unfortunately the vacancies did not always match the talents and skills of the jobless. It was of little consolation to the dispossessed coal miner or steel worker to see a job advert asking for someone to repair video recorders or computers.

Retraining became an important matter. Those who had no skills to sell, or whose skills had become outmoded, needed to acquire fresh human capital in order to become employable. There were even examples of people who did retrain and obtain another post, only to experience redundancy in their newly found career.

Serial retraining became a significant feature of their lives. It was not confined to the unskilled or those who worked in traditional craft trades in manufacturing industry.

In the case of office work, secretaries had to acquire the skills of word processing and other forms of information technology. Surgeons had to learn transplant surgery, the use of immuno-suppressive drugs, laser technology. Headteachers were pressed to turn into financial, marketing and resource management experts. Trade union officials, previously regarded as wage negotiators, found themselves increasingly involved in advising their workmates about compensation for accidents, or the workings of an industrial tribunal for those who had lost their jobs, so they needed higher reading competence in order to cope with the literature on health and safety at work, or employment protection. Some forms of knowledge and skill seemed to have a very short life before becoming obsolete. Few employees escaped the remorseless march of novelty and innovation.

There were other significant changes. New technology meant that certain kinds of activity could be done in the home, or in a remote satellite location at a distance from the main centre of production. Publishing, journalism, garment manufacture, design work, telephone sales, consultancy, all of these could, given the right equipment, be carried out as easily in someone's attic, as in a noisy and crowded office or factory. The shift to much more part-time employment, meant that women in particular often took jobs that required part of the day, rather than the whole of it. Many people moved to part-time employment as an element of an early retirement package. Hutton (1995) estimated the number of British part-time workers in the late twentieth century to be in excess of five million, of whom 80 per cent were women.

Part-time working and phased retirement liberated parts of the day and week for recreation or leisure, or for more time with family and friends. At its worst, however, part-timers and home workers were exploited, paid how wages, denied the same safety and employment protection rights as full-timers. Since some 70 per cent of all new part-time jobs were for sixteen hours a week or less (*ibid.*), this meant that the holders of them had no right to appeal against unfair dismissal or to redundancy payments. Much time had to be expended, by those who would have preferred a full-time post, trying to stitch together several part-time jobs, a practice which became known as 'portfolio' employment. Numerous families dropped to a lower standard of living, because the male adult had lost his full-time job and the female adult had only been able to obtain a part-time post.

The new opportunities for employment that did emerge were often in service and support industries. Alongside smaller numbers of the big employers of labour, there sprang up numerous small and medium-sized businesses. Unfortunately a number of these did not succeed and bankruptcies increased as several small concerns ceased training. This added to the problems of those seeking work, as small firms closed and some failed entrepreneurs returned to being employees of someone else.

There are several important messages for comprehensive schools from this analysis of work trends. They include the following: (a) as the numbers of unskilled and semi-skilled jobs decline, a much higher level of knowledge and skill will be necessary from those wishing to enter, or remain in employment; (b) if there are to be more jobs in service and support, leisure and recreation, rather than in factories, then social skills may become more valued; (c) people may have to retrain significantly several times in their adult lives, perhaps every five to seven years, so flexibility and willingness to continue learning are important; (d) as more people take part-time jobs, or work from their own home or in a place remote from their employer's headquarters, qualities such as independence, resourcefulness and adaptability may be highly valued; (e) people will need to know their rights and entitlements, as well as their obligations to others, if they are to play a full part in society and not be exploited by the unscrupulous.

Home and family life may also continue to change. Those that have full-time jobs often worker longer hours than they did in earlier times. Others are frustrated that their talents and aspirations cannot find expression. Some people have too little to do, while others have too much. The increase in working hours is explained by a number of factors. It is partly because of what Handy (1994) called the '$^{1}/_{2} \times 2 \times 3$' formula. Productivity and profit are increased if half the previous workforce are paid twice their salary to obtain three times as much output. The unemployed or under-occupied may pursue income-generating 'hobbies', like vegetable growing, collecting (buying and selling artefacts), decorating, or car repair.

Home and family life now require greater knowledge and skill than in former times. Families run into debt if they are unable to manage their own finances. Some fall victim to 'loan sharks' and others who prey on the ill-educated, paying vast amounts of interest on small loans which leave them in thrall for years. The predators in society exploit those whose rudimentary levels of numeracy, literacy or oral competence mean they are unable to calculate percentages, read legalistic agreements, or argue with articulate and persuasive usurers. Citizens unable to compose a letter, attend and speak at a public meeting, or combine with others to lobby decision makers, may find their child is unable to obtain the school place of their choice. All of these combine to exert considerable pressure on both primary and secondary schools to extract the maximum benefit from the eleven years of compulsory schooling.

The Four Ages

There have been and continue to be significant changes during what are sometimes called the four ages. The first age is the age of full-time education and training, the second age the period of working life, the third age the years of healthy retirement, and the fourth age represents the time of infirmity. Since the nineteenth century, when large numbers of people never even reached the later ages, the transformation has been dramatic. Children in school today, for example, may find that it is their third, rather than their second age, which occupies the greatest number of years.

These four ages have transformed dramatically. The first age has become longer. For much of the nineteenth century children were not required to attend school at all, and in many cases commenced employment at the age of ten or earlier. The twentieth century saw a significant lengthening of the first age as, in the United Kingdom, the school leaving age was fixed at 14 following the First World War, at 15 after the Second World War, and at 16 in the 1970s. Subsequently the advent of higher unemployment produced a variety of youth training schemes, first of a few months and later lasting one and eventually two years. This effectively lengthened the first age from less than a decade in the nineteenth century, to more like 18 years for the majority by the late twentieth century.

Evidence from earlier in the nineteenth century shows that girls, on average, entered the age of menarche, that is, started their periods, at about the age of 17. By the late twentieth century the average age of menarche was down to about $12^{1}/_{2}$. In the nineteenth century children left the first age physically immature and were still children for the first few years of their second age, when they commenced work. By the late twentieth century it was the exact opposite. They reached physical maturity, only to find that they had to spend at least four, and possibly up to ten more years in the first age, unable to start in a job. Boys in particular often go through a period of aggression on reaching physical maturity, so teachers in comprehensive schools have had to contain and educate potentially aggressive young adults who, 100 years previously, would have been well into their second age and off school premises. What had been a external social problem in Victorian times, had now become an internal school problem.

The second age has shortened at both ends. Children enter work later, and adults begin to leave it earlier. For many in Victorian times the second age was virtually their whole life, as killer diseases like typhoid and tuberculosis, the ravages of war, and deaths in childbirth robbed millions of their third and fourth age. It is difficult to say what the second age will become in future for those currently in school, as it may be that improved health in later years might lead to it lengthening once more, if people choose and have opportunities to work into their seventies. Present indications are that for many people it may not last more than thirty-five years.

By contrast the third age, the period of healthy retirement that was non-existent for most in the nineteenth century, when a mere 6 or so per cent of the population was over 60, is becoming dramatically longer, as the 60+ age group swells to a quarter or more of the population. Handy (1994) cites surveys showing that only a third of British adults over the age of 55 are still in paid employment, and in France and Italy the figures are 27 per cent and 11 per cent respectively. Many children currently in school may experience twenty, thirty or even forty years in the third age.

This particular social change has considerable implications for teachers in comprehensive schools, since children who are disenchanted with their schooling may be reluctant to take on fresh intellectual challenges in their third age. The evidence suggests that older people are perfectly capable of learning new knowledge and skills. Although they may need a little more time and slightly longer intervals between 'lessons', they can often draw on a wider range of strategies than are available to younger people with more limited experience. The Open University has thousands of students who graduate in their seventies and eighties.

Even during the fourth age, the time of infirmity, when the elderly may be confined indoors, most will be perfectly capable of continuing to learn something new, and continued mental activity in old age is often closely associated with better general health. According to 1990 census data, there are over 36,000 centenarians living in the United States. Hence the importance for the highly significant third age, and the not insignificant fourth age, of effective groundwork, particularly during the first age.

The Many Roles of the Comprehensive School Teacher

Traditionally teachers are *transmitters of knowledge*. They introduce their pupils to the knowledge, skills, values, attitudes and forms of behaviour that civilized societies have accumulated over several centuries. Millions of years passed before intelligent life worked out that water molecules consist of two atoms of hydrogen and one of oxygen. Teachers can transmit that information in seconds. However, the sheer amount of knowledge now available is awesome. It was dubious whether anyone could really absorb all of what was known even during times when 'Universal Man' was supposed to exist. In the eighteenth century writers like Goethe, who composed poetry, novels, plays, historical and philosophical works, and even a scientific treatise, were admired as complete scholars, yet they only knew a fraction of what had been discovered.

The quest for universal knowledge would be an impossibility in the late twentieth and early twenty-first centuries, as millions of books, articles, films, radio and television programmes, as well as ideas expressed in electronic media, are produced every year. Even with access to international databases containing millions of research findings in every imaginable field, it is inconceivable that anyone will personally know more than the tiniest portion of all knowledge available in their discipline or area of interest. The gathering of knowledge seems to be an activity which will, if anything, continue to quicken in future.

The consequences for teachers of this remorseless addition to the store of human knowledge are of several kinds. First of all, though we cannot teach everything, we have to teach something. Hence the interminable debates and discussions about the *content* of various subject curricula. In a vast field like health education, for example, what should pupils study at the age of 11, 13 or 15? When can they best learn about the need for a healthy diet and exercise regime, or the effects on health of smoking, alcohol or drugs? Some may already have been exposed to these in their primary school. What information, skills, attitudes and forms of behaviour might pupils need to acquire? When might be too late and when too soon to study a particular topic?

The second consequence of the knowledge explosion is that if we cannot teach everything in school, and have to settle for a small proportion of what exists, then pupils have to know how to find out for themselves. The ability to track down vital information, abstract its essence, work out how to apply what we have learned, often without external help, is a key element of independence of mind and action.

Most adults have to make numerous decisions on their own during the day, some trivial, like where to shop, others more profound, like what actions to take in their working or home life. This ability to explore, discover and then act, often with tenacity and imagination, is particularly crucial given the points made earlier about the length of adult life and the importance of the third age. Pupils need to experience many forms of teaching and learning if they are to be both autonomous and good team members in adult life, and it is a pity that the public debate about teaching styles has concentrated on a stereotyped division between 'traditional' and 'progressive' approaches. In the twenty-first century major social, as well as technological and scientific problems, are likely to be resolved by small or large teams of resourceful and flexible adults.

We live in a society that is rich in information, but information is not the same as knowledge. Information is 'out there'; knowledge is what is inside the brain, digested and understood. Indeed, children in particular, unable to chart a path through the dense mass, might despair if left to explore unaided. What is essential in this burgeoning expanse of information is people who can structure and track what is going on, in other words, *teachers as annotators* who can help to unravel and explain what might otherwise be an enormous bewildering maze. Other annotators include writers, publishers, broadcasters. In the future, as in the present, numerous sources of information will be available to pupils other than what their teachers choose to bring before them, and it will be important for them to develop the skill and resourcefulness not only to act on advice and help, but also to pursue their own pathways through what they are studying.

Alongside the many demands on comprehensive school teachers as repositories of subject expertise are numerous others. Some of these are social roles. For example, there are pupils who fail to attend school. Teachers have to try and ensure that they are present, even if children's parents condone their absence. *Teacher as jailer* is an assignment that ought not to exist in an ideal world, but the reality is that schools are also judged partly by truancy tables, so failure to keep in those that would rather be absent is seen as a dereliction of duty.

One prime strategy is to make sure the work done is sufficiently interesting to ensure that pupils are keen to attend, but even the most dynamic and engaging of teachers may still find that some pupils are reluctant to come to school no matter what they do. Yet support services for teachers have been eroded as a consequence of large reductions in the budgets of local education authorities. In keeping with the 'tough talking' image that many politicians prefer, there are proposals for volunteers to report truants seen in shopping centres and elsewhere, rather than the hiring of more Education Welfare Officers, or home-school liaison teachers.

'I am a teacher, not a social worker' is a slogan that has been declaimed at teachers' conferences for many years. *Teacher as social worker* is a role that some teachers take on gladly, others reluctantly. Certainly few have been trained properly for it, even though they may teach children from families with severe problems. I asked one of my former students how she was enjoying her first year of teaching. It was fine in most respects, she explained, but she found the circumstances in which some pupils lived to be harrowing, and she regularly made breakfast in her laboratory for two pupils who never had much to eat at home. Running soup kitchens was something of which the Mafia proudly boasted, but the only decent meal that some children will get is their school lunch.

Indeed, *teacher as parent* is an interesting variant of this particular role. Teachers may find they are given confidential information by their pupils, or even asked for advice by those who have no-one else to turn to. Many senior women teachers have at some time had a private conversation with a girl who either was, or though she might be pregnant. Teachers' own role as a parent might also be called into question, particularly in lesson to do with pastoral care, the teaching of literature and the humanities. Where their own children attend school, their attitudes towards teenage behaviour in their own family, the career choices their children make, can all be given scrutiny. In small communities it is especially difficult to detach personal life from professional life.

There is another important aspect of teacher as parent. Good parents fight for their children's rights, stand up for them, support them when they are down, treat them fairly, give them every chance. It is more difficult for teachers to generate equivalent effort for every single child in a large secondary school, but many do put themselves out to ensure justice, fairness and fair opportunities. This is what comprehensive education is supposed to stand for.

Teacher as hero is an image that appeals to young people before they start their career, determined to shed light wherever there is darkness, but to their dismay they soon see their profession depicted in the popular press as the Anti-Christ. Heroes are of many kinds. Some, like Hercules, show great physical prowess, personal skill and ingenuity. Others heroes are more reflective, producing great works of art, music and literature, writing inspirational treatises or making important scientific discoveries. Teachers are often only labelled 'heroes' in the public mind if they display courage when their children are in danger.

The daily job of educating the next generation is seen as more mundane and routine, unglamorous to the outside world. Perhaps those who work in public service should be resigned to being categorized in this low-key way. On the other hand many teachers fill out the concept of 'hero', albeit in a modest way, and few adults would not acknowledge a lifelong debt to at least one of their mentors, no small contribution to society. I was once talking to James Stone, or 'Joe' as he was known, the imaginative Chief Education Officer of Nottinghamshire in the 1970s, about the frustrations of trying to cope with the many difficulties in education. Hercules, I pointed out, found a quick solution to the problem of clearing out years of accumulated dung in the Augean stables by knocking a hole in each end and diverting a river through them. Joe reflected for a moment. 'The trouble is', he mused, 'I'd never get planning permission'. It is increasingly difficult for teachers to be heroes amid shelves full of government regulations and syllabuses.

Just as pupils need to be able to work in teams as preparation for a complex future, so too do teachers. *Teachers as team players* is a vital part of comprehensive education, as most will belong to a subject team, a planning group, or an administrative unit. Harmonious rather than dissonant relationships are essential ingredients of successful teams. Learning to pool one's knowledge and skills as part of a greater whole is an important element of such spectacular global enterprises as the American space programme, which involves the world's leading authorities on a variety of scientific, technical and human matters combining their expertise to achieve what none of them could do individually. On a more modest scale team play is also a feature of the comprehensive school staffroom.

Teams need leadership, and it is not only the responsibility of the head to provide this. Many teachers will, at one time or another, offer leadership to their colleagues. The model I prefer is that of *teacher as Viennese orchestra conductor*. There is a tradition in Vienna, when playing Strauss in particular, for the conductor to join in, not merely wave a baton. Viennese conductors are themselves proficient musicians, usually violinists, so they often hold their instrument, wave their bow, and then, with evident enjoyment, play along with the orchestra during certain passages. Admittedly it must be difficult for double bass or tuba players, but leadership through participation and collaboration must be a better model than one based on conflict or a sense of superiority.

The formidable demands of these several roles mean that teachers need to rethink what they do. Skilful and sensitive appraisal can be an important part of this, but the Leverhulme Appraisal Project (Wragg *et al.*, 1996) found that only half of the teachers in the sample said that they changed what they did as a result of appraisal. Many found there was not enough time for a proper analysis, few had experience of studying classroom processes in a systematic way, and over a quarter of teachers were only observed once instead of the minimum of two sessions that was required.

Lack of time and the conflicting demands of other priorities means that professional development can, if we are not careful, become crude and pragmatic. I have written elsewhere (Wragg, 1994) about the need for dynamic practitioners in dynamic schools, reflecting judiciously and then improving what they do, and I reject entirely the mechanistic approach of some vocational qualifications which, at their worst, make for *teacher as YTS trainee*.

I was once served breakfast by a YTS trainee who had received what was known as 'training to standards'. Checklist duly completed he brought me a plate of bacon and eggs, cleared it away nicely when I had finished, and then served me the grapefruit. It reminded me of the television sketch in which Eric Morecambe is accused by Andre Previn of not playing the correct notes. 'I am playing the right notes', he replies indignantly, 'but not necessarily in the right order'. Teachers lay down deep structures over a professional lifetime which determine how they teach. The crude competency approach which dominates the thinking of the Teacher Training Agency is completely inadequate for the complexities I have described.

One role which has become increasingly important in education is that of public relations officer, *teacher as Kenneth Baker* as it should be known, in honour of a Secretary of State who set the standard for attaching more importance to form and tone than to substance. Glossy brochures, advertising, image making are all well established artefacts of the commercial world that have begun to intrude into education as part of the market model. Yet the commercial analogy hardly bears scrutiny. None of these things increases the numbers of pupils, in the way that advertising might increase sales. All of them sap teachers' time and energy away form their central purpose, and money is wasted on moving round a small number of pupils.

But the saddest role at present is that of *teacher as football manager*. This applies in particular to heads. Just as football managers are made to resign if their team has a bad run, irrespective of whether or not they have acted intelligently, so too teachers are scapegoated in the press and by politicians. Increasingly after an inspection by the Office for Standards in Education headteachers resign, not always justifiably. Many teachers now leave the profession early, some three-quarters quitting before they reach retirement age. Over 6000 teachers now retire each year on health grounds, a threefold increase in eight years. In many cases it is a scandalous waste.

Like karaoke singers teachers may now find that the music moves on relentlessly, whether or not they can mouth the words fast enough. If education is as important as society, press, politicians and others always say it is, then the least we should be doing is supporting teachers in comprehensive schools. In the world of business and commerce it is regarded as good practice to make demands on workers, set targets, but then to provide the means by which the targets can be met, a two-sided contract. It should not be too much to ask for teachers in comprehensive schools, especially those working in the most difficult circumstances, to be given the same opportunities.

References

HANDY, C. (1994) *The Empty Raincoat: Making Sense of the Future*, London, Hutchinson.
HUTTON, W. (1995) *The State We're In*, London, Jonathan Cape.
WRAGG, E.C. (1994) *An Introduction to Classroom Observation*, London, Routledge.
WRAGG, E.C. (1997) *The Cubic Curriculum*, London, Routledge.
WRAGG, E.C., WIKELEY, F.J., WRAGG, C.M. and HAYNES, G.S. (1996) *Teacher Appraisal Observed*, London, Routledge.

Effective Learning

11   What Comprehensives Schools do Better

Bernard Clarke

What I have to say is based on twenty-five years working in three schools, quite different and remarkable in their own ways, but all sharing a commitment to comprehensive education. The last eight of those years have been at Peers School in the historic city of Oxford where the word 'education' has a resonance and significance probably unequalled anywhere else in the world.

Another qualification, or prejudice, or both, derives from the unusual circumstance of being a former grammar school student whose two brothers attended respectively a boys' public school and the local secondary modern. Both of them have spent much of their adult lives coming to terms with the damage done to them by their secondary education — one trying to recover from the isolation and uncertainty of being a shy 11 year-old inexplicably sent away from home to an alien, all male world where warmth and love were significant by their absence; the other, by far the most innately creative of the three of us, seeking to overcome the stigma of failing the 11+ for which his solitary 'O' level (in woodwork) was no consolation.

In preparing this chapter I recalled my childhood in a small Midlands town with one grammar school and three secondary moderns. You will note the proportions. From the age of 11 we lost contact with close friends from primary school. Some of us at the grammar school would be taken thirty miles to play football or cricket against other grammar school teams, but we never played against any of the local secondary moderns. There was no contact with them whatsoever. They inhabited an entirely separate world. In fact, I remember being advised to avoid the children from those schools, including my brother! Not only were they rough and to be feared, but they had nothing in common with us, the chosen ones.

Many will share the anger one feels at the damage such arrangements have done to countless thousands of young people and the consequent waste of human potential. And there are those who would have us return to such waste, inefficiency and disruption to individuals, their families and communities.

Other chapters rehearse the arguments for comprehensive education using important research and statistical data. Is it not extraordinary that we need to justify the simple idea that all young people should attend their local school and receive as good an education as possible? On the contrary, it is an aim we should all be declaring with pride. I agree with Brian Simon (chapter 1) when he concludes that the comprehensive principle is now in place and 'as firm as a rock'. When you consider the alternatives, he must be right.

That is not to say that all is well in every comprehensive school. Obviously,

Bernard Clarke

it is not and there is not a school in the land that does not need to improve in important ways. Nor should we stick nostalgically to formulae which may have served quite well in even the recent past. As H.G. Wells said, we need fewer professors of history and more professors of foresight. The world in which our children become adult citizens will be unrecognizable from the one we inhabit.

In an earlier phase of a somewhat idiosyncratic career when I trained as a social worker, one of our required textbooks was The Faith of the Counsellors by Paul Halmos (1965). In a nutshell, his thesis was that, whilst they should and must involve the development and practice of skills and techniques, 'the helping professions' (social casework, counselling, psychotherapy etc.) cannot be reduced to technologies. In the last analysis, they are the expression of a set of values and the faith that what one is doing is right and will have some beneficial effect for the person one is seeking to help.

The same applies to teaching. Ultimately, most teachers in comprehensive schools, be they primary or secondary, are there because they *believe* that what they are doing is right, and also that it will do some good. We should not apologize for using the word 'believe'. Ultimately, our work with young people and their families is based on faith — the faith which has motivated and sustained schoolteachers here and elsewhere for hundreds of years.

In this temporary, brief period during which some would hold that effective education is summed up by the OFSTED number-crunching, bean-counting culture, there is a considerable danger that, under pressure to justify ourselves, we might lose sight of that faith and the values which are fundamental to comprehensive education and which most of us *know* to be right. It is interesting how proclaiming such values has come to be seen as 'old fashioned', nostalgic or irrelevant by some people.

In this chapter, which will rely quite heavily on the anecdotal experience of children and teachers, I will attempt to describe why thousands of people — teachers, parents, students and others who are directly involved with comprehensive education — believe it remains not only relevant, but fundamental to the very future of our society. As far as possible, what I have to say is rooted in practical experience in comprehensive schools.

I want to say something about Oxford and the context in which I work. Then consider what in my view comprehensive education is and should be about. In doing so, I will use some currently unfashionable phrases and dirty words — children and young people; the real curriculum including the hidden curriculum; good teachers; community education; success; and, the biggest 'bogey words' of all, social engineering.

The Context

Oxford, a city of around 132,000 people (including 25,000 students), is the hub of one of the most concentrated areas of world class research institutions and associated businesses in Europe. It also includes major industries such as publishing,

150

vehicle manufacture and tourism. It has world class medical institutions, is also a county town and much more.

There is another side to Oxford. The Department of the Environment's Index of Local Conditions shows that it is amongst the most deprived 20 per cent of English districts and suffers deprivation on a scale more than equal to the worst parts of the South East. Teresa Smith, Michael Noble and their colleagues at the University of Oxford Department of Social Administration have shown that in 1994, levels of poverty in Oxford were comparable with those in Oldham (Smith and Noble, 1995). Much of it is concentrated in what have become known as the ring road estates.

Peers is an upper school of about 670 13–18-year-old students which lies in the parish of Littlemore, just outside the ring road, and adjacent to the large council housing estates of Blackbird Leys and Rose Hill. Approximately 85 per cent of our students live in the immediate locality. Many are educationally disadvantaged and arrive at the school with low levels of basic skills and little personal confidence. A recent survey indicated that in the region of 90 per cent of students in the sixth form were among the first generation in their families to benefit from post-16 education.

The other five upper schools in Oxford all have more favoured natural catchment areas, and public transport across this small city is cheap and convenient.

For many years, Peers has endeavoured to provide as good an education as possible for its students. Since 1988 and the advent of formula-funding (based on the assumption that it costs the same to educate all young people regardless of their circumstances), open enrolment and league tables, our determination has been given added impetus!

Shortly after starting my present job eight-and-a-half years ago, I was asked to see Nicola, a bright student in year 11 who was rapidly losing her way with her GCSE work. When I asked her what was wrong, she explained that she was very tired. Like many young people in Oxford, she had a part-time job at one of the college kitchens. She served at table, cleared up and helped with the washing-up. Unlike many of her colleagues, though, Nicola was not working to earn pocket money. She was working because of family poverty. Her tiredness was the result of clearing tables for several hours every evening after school, with two shifts on Saturday and three on Sunday. For some reason, she felt it important to tell me that she received a bonus whenever she had to clear up vomit.

The story may appear exaggerated or sentimental, but, however offensive to the reader, it is perfectly true and by no means uncommon. The education of thousands of children up and down the country is blighted by their need to work part-time in order to supplement meagre family income. Although she had the ability to go into higher education, Nicola left school at 16 with one or two GCSEs. She lived within three miles of two universities but that kitchen is as close as she will ever get to either.

The point is obvious. If young people are to succeed, the conditions must be right. Fortunately, as we all know, some are able to triumph over the most appalling circumstances, but we should be in no doubt how great the odds are against such people succeeding nor what it costs them or their schools to do so. We may teach them until we are blue in the face, but hungry, tired and unloved children cannot learn . . . even in Oxford.

What Should They Learn?

With regard to the curriculum, I agree with Tom Sobol, formerly Director of Schools for the state of New York, when he said, 'if you always do what you always did, you always get what you always got' (Sobol, 1994).

What may have served in the past will no longer do. We need to think afresh about what young people should learn in school and how they should learn it. The National Curriculum has been a huge and wasteful distraction from that central point. Furthermore, after all the squabbling and changes of mind of the past few years (it would be nice to say debate, but real debate has not been a feature of the introduction of the National Curriculum) many of its prescriptions just will not achieve what we are told are their purposes, for instance, raising levels of attainment of all young people or making the country more competitive in the international market place.

On this point, there is real confusion in what we are constantly being told about the relationship between the educational attainment of our young people and the nation's economic performance. The argument seems to suggest that if we meet the National Targets for Education and Training with, for instance, 80 per cent of young people reaching NVQ level II or equivalent by 1997 our economic productivity will improve and will get ourselves out of the low skill, low wage cycle. One is tempted to respond by asking when! My knowledge of international economics is slight, but I believe it is the case that, whereas South Korea has high levels of education and high productivity, China has high productivity, but appallingly low education and Germany increasing educational levels but falling productivity. In other words, other economic and cultural factors would appear to be just as important for economic success as educational attainment however measured.

There can be no argument about the importance of raising levels of attainment for all our young people, and it is probably a necessary precondition for economic improvement. However, it is certainly not sufficient and all manner of other political, social and economic changes must occur if we are to become a more productive nation. In any case, there are times when it does feel as though the debate about the purposes of education has been hijacked and that the only role schools have is to prepare young people for the economy.

A couple of years ago a group of 14-year-old students from our school were randomly recruited to spend the day at a major, local, 'cutting edge' business. During their visit, they were invited to take part in a manufacturing simulation exercise the purpose of which was, as a team, to make small items from stickle bricks and by paying attention to quality, production levels, efficiency etc. to reduce the unit cost as low as they could. They were allowed five attempts. On their fifth, this group of young people who represented a very broad range of ability as measured by National Curriculum assessments, had reached the theoretical minimum and outperformed every group of workers, managers and directors who had been through the exercise. The organizers concluded that their success was the result of uncluttered minds, the ability to think creatively and, above all, the ability to cooperate. Perhaps we need to think some more about the nature of the so called skills crisis.

As Dennis Lawton earlier argued (chapter 7), in planning the curriculum, you do not start with ten subjects, you begin with the nature of society and the needs of young people within it. What can we possibly know about the world that children starting their education at the age of 5 next September will enter when they leave school at 16 in 2007? If it comes to that, what can we say about the world school leavers will enter in two years time?

Not very much, and it is with that reality in mind that we should be thinking about the curriculum. What do *all* young people need to know and be able to do to be effective citizens in a rapidly changing world? Competence with information technology will be fundamental. What else?

Anita Higham (1995), Principal of Banbury School, is absolutely right in suggesting that three fundamental areas of learning for all young people in their preparation for life as citizens, workers, lifelong learners and parents in an uncertain future are understanding about boundaries and relationships, values and personal responsibility. Such understanding is not best acquired by young people, or anybody else for that matter, via conventional, didactic teaching. One of the biggest mistakes some of us in schools have made in the past twenty-thirty years is believing that it is possible to *teach* young people how to have good relationships. Fundamentally, the only way we acquire and develop the ability to form relationships with other people is through the relationships we experience ourselves. What many of us were saying about the hidden curriculum in the 60s and 70s remains true. Do what I do, not what I say. This is fundamentally important, particularly with regard to adolescents who, in my experience, are fitted with highly sensitive bullshit detectors which can pick up the slightest whiff of hypocrisy. If young people experience mature, rational, sensitive relationships with their teachers, they are more likely to be able to form them with other people. Not for nothing did Douglas Hamblin write many years ago that it is the responsibility of the mature adult to adjust to the needs of the immature adolescent and not vice versa.

Incidentally, why as a nation do we dislike children so much? Friends from France, Italy, Scandinavia, the USA confirm that it really does appear that we do. By the time they reach adolescence our feelings towards them have developed into a form of paranoia dominated by fantasies about all the terrible things they might do. Consequently, one of our first impulses in relation to adolescents en masse is to try to control them. The quasi-military or monastic overtones of much of our schooling and the fact that they remain popular with so many parents and other adults does seem to support this view. As teacher, headteacher and parent of four children, there has been ample opportunity for me to learn about the importance of a framework of discipline and order for young people growing. But does it need to be separate and different from the framework of discipline and order in which we as professional adults operate?

My experience is that it does not and, furthermore, that adolescents are much more likely to accept a framework which they see being applied to adults as well as themselves. It is for such reasons that Peers does not have a set of rules. So often, school rules seem to assume the worst of young people. 'Don't do this. If you do, this is what will happen to you.' Teacher is always right.

Some years ago, having taken issue with a teacher (male) for shouting at a student (female), I was invited at a staff meeting (under any other business!) to outline my 'policy on shouting'. Three points occurred to me:

(i)   if mature adults disagree, they generally don't shout at each other;
(ii)   it is hard to ask students to keep their voices down if the teachers shout;
(iii) it is impossible to say, hand on heart, that we do not have bullying if big, powerful men verbally assault small, powerless young women.

There followed a long period of discussion and consultation between all the staff, students, parents and governors which started with the notion that Peers is a place of work where everybody has a job to do and the right to get on with it without hindrance from anybody else. Given that and in the spirit of what is sauce for the goose is sauce for the gander, the question boiled down to 'what do we all have the right to expect of each other?' The result was a statement of rights and responsibilities which embodies two principles which, given the unequal distribution of power, are fundamentally important. First, staff will not ask students to do anything they are not prepared to do themselves. Secondly, all the adults at Peers understand that they provide constant models of work and behaviour for young people growing up.

We should never underestimate the extent to which adolescents observe adults. I recall reading, many years ago, an American study which analyzed teenage gang behaviour and came to the conclusion that a high proportion of their time 'hanging about' on street corners etc. was devoted to watching adults and learning about what adults do. Anybody who works in a school knows this goes on all the time. If you think back to what you remember most clearly about your own schooling it will probably be the teachers.

Read in isolation, Peers School's 'Rights and Responsibilities' is unremarkable stuff. The significant thing about it and the reason it works effectively is the process by which we arrived as it. Treating all the students as equal participants in its production communicated a very strong message. This is not something that is done to or applies only to them. It is a statement of the expectations of *everybody* at Peers.

A word about teachers and, particularly, good teachers in comprehensive schools who, in my experience, represent the large majority. There are many reasons why they are good, but, for me, three stand out. First, the 'faith', referred to earlier, which brings them into the profession. Secondly, good teachers know that learning takes place most effectively when the context of relationships and ethos is right.

Thirdly, and of profound importance in the context of the current debate about comprehensive education, because they work in comprehensive schools and teach some students for whom learning does not always come easily, they have to work particularly hard to make what they teach stimulating and accessible for everybody. As a result all the students, including the 'most able' benefit.

What Else Should Our Young People Learn?

For me, one answer lies in the National Curriculum of which I carry a copy in my briefcase all the time. The Norwegian National Curriculum (Royal Ministry of Church, Education and Research, 1994), all forty pages of it, was introduced to me by a friend who has just taken early retirement from HMI. It is a pleasure to read, the text being supplemented with a large number of colour photographs of works of art and scenes from Norwegian life. The opening sentence of the introduction sets the tone:

> The aim of education is to furnish children, young people and adults with the tools they need to face the tasks of life and surmount its challenges together with others. Education shall provide learners with the capability to take charge of themselves and their lives, as well as the vigour and will to stand by others.

Thereafter, each of the seven chapters is devoted to one quality of the educated human being — spiritual, creative, working, liberally-educated, social, environmentally aware and, finally, the integrated human being.

What a great day it will be when our policy makers produce phrases like this:

> Education must be based on the view that all persons are created equal and that human dignity is inviolable. It should confirm the belief that everyone is unique; that each can nourish his own growth and that individual distinctions enrich and enliven our world.

Or this:

> Education shall impart in the learner a zest for life, the courage to tackle it, and a desire to use and extend what they learn.

Or, above all, this:

> The most important of all pedagogical tasks is to convey to children and the young that they are continuously making headway so that they gain trust in their own abilities.

The vehicle for giving practical expression to such principles may well be academic subjects. The Norwegian's National Curriculum does not say and it certainly does not make them the raison d'etre as in our present, temporary National Curriculum.

Is it too much to hope that those with national responsibility for the education service should provide just a little real leadership by setting out the aims and purposes of the enterprise in which we are engaged. It could be said that this has been done for us in the 'Aims of the School Curriculum' which formed part of the 1988 Education Reform Act, but thirty-one words does seem a bit brief when set alongside the volumes of National Curriculum verbiage which have been despatched to us in the intervening years.

'Vision' has become another dirty word in some quarters of the education world. It is interesting that many of the business gurus held up to us as models of leadership do not seem to have a difficulty with it. Indeed, years before New Labour coined the term, a highly successful local business was devoting much of its energy to developing a culture in which everybody with any involvement in the company became a 'stakeholder'. That business leader, at least, recognized the psychological importance of vision as a motivator. How sad that our political leaders do not seem to understand. A depressed, alienated teaching force is scarcely likely to produce the results we all want.

Almost as inspiring as the Norwegian national curriculum, because we have made it ourselves, is the curriculum statement agreed recently by the headteachers of every LEA primary, secondary and special school in Oxfordshire (Oxfordshire County Council, 1995). This is an important statement for a number of reasons. Only one small primary school in Oxfordshire has opted for GM status. All the others, primary, secondary and special, remain committed to working in partnership with the LEA for the benefit of all the children and young people in the county. In producing it, we, the educational professionals, wanted to reassert our proper role as leaders, managers and developers of the curriculum. The introduction begins:

> A comprehensive curriculum is the entitlement of all pupils and should provide access to all the relevant areas of experience: expressive and aesthetic; linguistic and literary; physical and recreational; scientific and mathematical; social and environmental; spiritual, moral and cultural; technological; vocational.

No head or governing body can be bound by it, but it serves as a touchstone for us all. There is little doubt that we would not have been able to produce such a powerful, unanimous statement had we not all represented LEA maintained comprehensive schools.

Community Education

Many comprehensive schools regard themselves as resources for all the people in their locality. At Peers we have, amongst other features, a public library, sports centre, nursery, further education centre, commercial business employing fifty people, a 10-year-old link with a school in Tanzania, and an annual tea dance for 200 elderly people from all over Oxford. Saturday Plus is a programme of educational activities for local families. Next year a school for young people with profound learning difficulties and the headquarters of PEEP (Peers Early Education Partnership), a family-based project designed to raise levels of literacy and numeracy in the area, will join us on the campus.

This is not serendipity, but the result of thought and planning. If lifelong learning and genuinely comprehensive education are to mean anything, the local schools have an essential role to play. Furthermore, how does any of us acquire (not learn about, but really acquire) understanding and tolerance unless we encounter at close quarters people from different backgrounds, cultures, generations and circumstances? And what value would any of it have for our students if the school excluded some local young people from attending it because they were different in some way? Comprehensive education must be inclusive education.

Success

Another anecdote. Recently, during our OFSTED inspection, Nicholas, the hitherto shy and anxious 15-year-old son of professional parents, was referred to me for being rude to a teacher. And he had. Not the least of his offences was telling her that he was going to get her sacked by the inspectors! When I asked him what had made him be so rude, he shouted through his tears, 'I hate Gs'. He eventually explained that he had worked for hours on an assignment, gone to the library and even missed Oxford United's promotion match against Crewe in order to produce ten sides. For his efforts he had been given a G. His friend had done one side and got an A.

We very nearly had a disaffected student on our hands. Why? Lazy? Violent? Delinquent? Not a bit of it. We had told him he was a failure. We do it all the time and the National Curriculum assessment arrangements are demanding that we do it more and more. Is this really the way to raise national standards?

Think about anything you are good at and ask yourself why. In most cases, the reason will be that you were told you were good at it and encouraged to continue and get better. Now think about anything you cannot do and ask yourself the same question. Usually, if we are bad at something it is because we have failed at it and not been helped to overcome that failure. For those of us who are regarded as generally 'successful', the odd area of weakness does not matter a great deal, at least publicly, and can, indeed, be used as the butt of jokes against ourselves without seriously damaging our self-esteem. But, what about those countless people who believe they are no good at anything (or 'anything that matters')?

Social Engineering

Finally, to the real bogey words of the conspiracy theorists — 'social engineering'.

Yes, those of us involved in comprehensive education should proclaim proudly that we are social engineers. How else are we to play our part in achieving 'a society at ease with itself'? And what a marvellous goal John Major set out for us in a moment of political vision.

As Hawkes (1995) has reminded us, 'Schools cannot afford to be ethically neutral nor allow the important task of educating our children to be subverted by those enslaved to numbers.' We are told that there are currently 30,000 'gated communities' in the USA providing enclaved security and privatised protection from the 'have-nots' (Clark, 1994).

All the signs are that Britain is moving in the same direction.

How at ease with itself is Oxford?

Bertrand Russell described the natural human impulse 'to view with horror and disgust all manners and customs different from those to which we are used' and saw it as 'one of the gravest dangers to which our overcrowded world is exposed' (quoted in Hawkes, 1995).

Sophies' parents were threatening to remove her from the school because Tracey was threatening her. When I sat down with them, Tracey, in her blue jeans and black leather jacket said she did not like Sophie's clothes. Sophie was wearing a Laura Ashley floral dress and a straw hat. 'Anything else?', I asked. 'Yes. She talks funny. She uses stupid words.' Sophie: 'Oh, don't be so preposterous'. Tracey: 'There. See what I mean?'

Two worlds existing within two miles of each other had collided. One 'solution' would have been to insist both young women, and all the others, wear identical clothing. Another would have been not to resist Sophie's parents' impulse to remove her somewhere 'safer' where she would be surrounded by other girls with similar home backgrounds, attitudes, clothes and ways of speaking.

We worked with Sophie and Tracey so that, even if they did not become best friends, they could, at least coexist and respect each other's right to be themselves.

My wife and I have four children who have all chosen to attend the schools I was working at. As we expected, they have all been successful (largely because of wonderful teaching) and, in addition, have had the incalculable advantage of working and playing alongside young people from very different backgrounds.

Julius Nyerere, the inspiration for the Peers link with Katumba School in Tanzania, described our obligation as educators in the following words:

> . . . to prepare our young people to play a dynamic and constructive part in the development of a society . . . in which progress is measured in terms of human well-being. The children must learn from the beginning to the end of their school life that education does not set them apart, but is designed to make them effective members of the community — for their own benefit as well as that of their country and their neighbours. (quoted in Hawkes, 1995)

Are there many better cases for comprehensive education?

All very well, you might say. A bit of a dream. What about the realities?

Langston Hughes (1991), the black American poet, knew all about the realities when he wrote *Harlem*:

What happens to a dream deferred?
Does it dry up
like a raisin in the sun?
Or fester like a sore —
And then run?
Does it stink like rotten meat?
Or crust and sugar over —
like a syrupy sweet?

Maybe it just sags
like a heavy load.

Or does it explode?

References

CLARK, P. (1994) 'Fortress America', *Sydney Morning Herald*, 30 April.

HALMOS, P. (1965) *The Faith of the Counsellors*, London, Constable.

HAWKES, T.F. (1995) 'Teaching social responsibility', *World Principal*, autumn.

HIGHAM, A. (1995) *Tomorrow's School*, Leicester, Secondary Heads Association.

HUGHES, L. (1991) 'Harlem' in *The Norton Introduction to Poetry*, New York, Norton.

OXFORDSHIRE COUNTY COUNCIL (1995) *Statement on the School Curriculum*, in association with OSSHTA, OPHTA and OASSH.

ROYAL MINISTRY OF CHURCH, EDUCATION AND RESEARCH (1994) *Core Curriculum for Primary, Secondary and Adult Education in Norway*, Oslo, RMCER.

SMITH, T. and NOBLE, M. (1995) *Education Divides*, London, Child Poverty Action Group.

SOBOL, T. (1994) lecture given at the North of England Education Conference, Chester, January.

12 Information Technology and the Comprehensive Ideal

John Abbott

In *Affirming the Comprehensive Ideal* let me start by reminding you of an obvious statement:

> The 'human race' is the planet's pre-eminent learning species; it is our brains that give us our superiority, not our muscles.

. . . and that includes even the most difficult, obstructive young adolescent you ever met last period on a wet and windy Friday afternoon!

It has taken humanity a long, long, time to get where we are now. Some evolutionists would limit this to a couple of million years. Others to five million years or more. It makes little difference. In either instance that is an almost incomprehensible array of ancestors. Slowly — by processes we are only just beginning to glimpse — each of these generations has helped to develop in each of us a unique set of 'predispositions' (ways of thinking and processing that help us make sense of our environment), which open up the possibility that each of us can be just a little smarter than our predecessors.

I believe passionately that it is the first duty of every society to prepare its young in ways which will enable them to be wiser than their parents. Simply to know more is not enough; it is to be wiser and more adaptable that matters. This leads to my own definition of learning.

> Learning is that reflective activity which enables the learner to draw upon previous experience to understand and evaluate the present, so as to shape future action and formulate new knowledge.

Learning is an active, reflective, constructive activity. As we learn so we change . . . at least, if we don't then we don't grow. If we don't grow we just won't survive. As an extremely egocentric generation, concerned with the needs of here and now rather than the Hereafter, I believe we are in danger of forgetting the message contained within that Native-American proverb:

> We have not *inherited* this world from our parents, we have been loaned it by our children.

Education should truly be the first call on our investments for the future. It is the 'wits' of our children which will be more significant than roads, airports or electronic superhighways. My definition of 'our' is highly inclusive, as was the American Indians. It covers every child. The childless adult has a responsibility, as well as the parent. After all, we all depend on the next generation to create the money to pay our pensions!

For the greater proportion of my professional life I was Head of a Comprehensive School. I chose this after having taught geography at Manchester Grammar School, and having some prior experience teaching in both preparatory schools and a secondary modern school, because I believed that until England decides to take the education of all its children seriously, we have no chance of creating either a civilized or a productive society.

It was a truism in the Second World War that the speed of the convoy was the speed of the slowest ship. To war-starved Britain every cargo of grain, tanks or of aircraft parts mattered, and so ships struggled to stay together for mutual protection. It was an expensive strategy, but Britain won the Battle of the Atlantic. It may not make for a politically popular analogy today to liken comprehensive schools to convoys — even less to liken an LEA trying to balance the needs of different schools where some have obvious advantages over others. But to many of us the principle is the same. The child whose potential is not realized is a loss to our society. Good as I believe the analogy is, there is one key difference. A ship once torpedoed was lost forever; an unfulfilled, frustrated and disaffected child lives to become an unproductive and uncooperative adult who has no loyalty to the convoy that left him or her behind. So all children matter, whatever their size, shape and temperament. That is why I believe in comprehensive schools, and that is why I believe in community. As Benjamin Franklin said as he signed the Declaration of Independence, 'We all have to hang together, or else we will each surely hang.'

I have three sons, each of whom went to the local primary school and to (someone else's) comprehensive school. Living as we do now in the United States I have suddenly become in practice the father of three American high school students. So, I do have a certain width of experience of what is happening both to schools and young people!

Through this I have come to realize that, in our zeal to give young people the very best start to life we can, teachers have taken onto their own shoulders too heavy a load. Society, at large, has been happy to let us do this, but in the process has forgotten its own responsibility for the young. Let me quantify a simple aspect of this.

No child in Western society spends more than 20 per cent of its waking hours in a classroom. Several surveys show that the greatest proportion of a child's waking hours are actually spent on their own — and feeling bored. One recent survey showed that just over half the fathers of sons under the age of 15 admitted to spending less than five minutes each day with their sons (Bernardo's, 1995; Csikszentmihalyi, 1984). So much for adult society developing the concept of learning as an active, reflective collaborative activity!

Learning and schooling are not synonymous. And they never have been. Think of your own experience. What experience gave you so much to think about that it literally changed the course of your life? Was this experience strictly 'formal', and came as the result of a logical progression of a curriculum, or was it a result of being in the right place at the right time — in other words 'informal'?

Mine was a combination. As a very young child I was taught to wood carve by a very old sailor. I simply knew him as 'Old MacFadgan'. He had served his apprenticeship in the Royal Navy in the 1880s. From his example I learned how to sharpen my chisels correctly, how to understand the subtle differences in the grain of a piece of wood, and how to see the relevance of basic skills to the creation of a job well-done. On Friday evenings, in my parent's kitchen, I was treated as a young apprentice.

Years later at a public school I passed all the exams that I needed for university entry except 'O' level Latin. The reason was simple. I was bored. I could not connect the exercises in Hillard and Botting with what I later came to realize was the immense vitality of Roman society. Latin, in all senses, was dead. Tragically, I think it was dead also to my teacher who, as a distraction, spent every lesson telling us how he had won the war single-handedly in his tank in the North African desert. I failed Latin not once, but twice, and I was within six weeks of taking it for the third and final time, when the school carpenter — a man so menial that he was not even allowed in the staff room — took me to one side and said, 'Congratulations, you have been chosen to represent the United Kingdom as a school boy woodcarver at an International Exhibition at Olympia. I am immensely proud of you!'

I was delighted, and very excited. Three hours later I crashed. This was not a result the school would recognize. It was neither a rugby result, nor a debating result, nor even was it to do with Shakespearean drama, so it would therefore go unnoticed. But its effect on me was dramatic. 'If I can beat everybody else at woodcarving why can't I pass Latin?' Now I knew the answer. It was because I was not in charge. So that afternoon I went to see my teacher — 'As I have to pass Latin in six weeks time, I will not be coming to any more of your lessons. I think it better if I spent the time teaching myself.' The walls of that school shook! It was me against the staff. For six weeks I sweated. It paid off. I passed the exam, I got to university, and I forgot almost all my Latin (which I now regret). But I still woodcarve!

It has left me with a deep belief in the power of children to sort matters out for themselves, and a deep love-hate relationship with teachers! And a commitment not to dismiss people too quickly. Late-developers often outrun the early stars.

Of course it is not only the schools that matter. As another Native-American proverb makes clear:

It takes a whole village to raise a child.

Too often we forget the significance of modern-day 'Old MacFadgans', and the enormous significance they can have on young people. These, in truth, are a community's most precious commodity.

Let me raise a note of caution. Schools must not develop such an inclusive view of their own community that they effectively remove the child from the greater community outside. After all, that is where they will live for the greater proportion of their lives. That is where they most need to feel a sense of 'belonging'. How many of you have had heard that proverb reversed? 'It takes a child to *save* a village.'

Those of you who already think like this will have long speculated on just what a traumatic effect the institutionalization of learning had on late-nineteenth century life, and will know how this still influences our thinking to this day. Once the responsibility for learning was taken out of the home and the community, both lost that essential activity, which since the beginning of time, had given each their essential 'reason to be'. That critical link between learning, working and living was broken. Home and community are still paying the price.

So, you have probably read my agenda. Dedicated as I am to the full development of young people, I am as concerned about their experience in the community, as I am in the school. To me it is as shocking an indictment of our society that parents are often too frightened to let their children walk to school, as it is that classrooms are drab and too many teachers have lost their passion for teaching. Learning is driven by passion; so too is teaching.

I fear for our children when the pressures in our schools become so great that *doing* takes over from *thinking*. Not because education is simply concerned with the mind — far from it — but because doing without thinking does not extend a child's mental faculties in ways which could help them shape the future.

I cannot visit Oxford without paying tribute to the writings of the late Sir Richard Livingstone, one-time President of Corpus Christi College who, in a little book published in the darkest years of World War II said:

> The test of a successful education is not the amount of knowledge that a pupil takes away from school, but his appetite to know and his capacity to learn. If the school sends out children with the desire for knowledge and some idea of how to acquire and use it, it will have done its work. Too many leave school with the appetite killed and the mind loaded with undigested lumps of information. The good school master is known by the number of valuable subjects he declines to teach. (Livingstone, 1941)

I tried sharing that thought with a latter-day Oxford don who was, at the time, Secretary for Education, but I am afraid he failed to see the point! As learning is more a matter of knowledge construction, than it is of knowledge transfer, that was essentially tragic.

* * * * * *

To 'think about thinking' is to be consciously aware of yourself as a problem-solver, and to monitor and control one's own mental processing. How this is done has been engaging the attention of cognitive scientists since the early 1980s, and the neurologists for the past five or so years. But I think 'Old MacFadgan' understood it all right. The skills of metacognition incorporate, but go further than, the ability to perform routine tasks or to demonstrate effective memory, or to use weak or strong methods. It is essentially the ability to see oneself, and others, as problem-solvers.

One method of instruction — probably the oldest known to humans — is that of apprenticeship ('learning the ropes'). The cognitive processes involved in apprenticeship should be reconsidered in our own times (Collins *et al.*, 1991). There are four components:

- Modelling
- Scaffolding
- Discussion
- Fading

The key difference between apprenticeship and modern teaching lay in the fact that the young apprentice was always aware of the overall task in which the master craftsperson was also involved. This is best illustrated by the story of a visitor to Italy who saw two men working in a quarry. He approached the first and asked him what he was doing. Pulling a cigarette from his mouth the man said 'I am squaring this damn piece of rock'. He looked at the second who smiled and said 'I am building a cathedral'.

Apprenticeship (at its purest) always emphasized the significance of learning basic skills in terms of the cumulative ability to construct a masterpiece. Every task poised a challenge 'to do things just a little better'. The apprentice understood the model towards which he/she was working.

Scaffolding was the provision of just enough essential support to assist young apprentices as they began to master the essential skills of the trade, and left the craftsperson time to be profitable.

Discussion was actively encouraged amongst the apprentices, and with the craftsperson. Continuous discussion about processes, application, and self-assessment, was critical to becoming 'good enough' to be able to sell your product.

Fading was the final component. The whole intention of the craftsperson was to get the apprentice to the craftsperson's stage of ability. While scaffolding was important in the initial stages it was steadily reduced until the point at which the apprentice was able to deliver 'the masterpiece' without any extraneous support. This is in stark contrast to our present practice in which, with our largest class sizes in the primary schools and the smallest in the last year of the sixth form, pupils tend to see themselves as becoming ever more dependent on the teacher.

Apprenticeship was therefore a way of 'going beyond what comes naturally'. A form of intellectual weaning that balanced the rate of physical maturation.

*　*　*　*　*　*

This brings me comfortably to the study of the potential of the new technologies of information and communication. Let me start with one of the simplest, but one which undoubtedly has the power to transform formal schooling: word processing.

Many people at my age became expert, when in school, at writing essays sufficiently good to keep us out of trouble, but never going much beyond this! Take me for example: to get 7 out of 10, or 14 or 15 out of 20 was not difficult. Frankly I never even bothered to read many of the comments written by my teachers because I was never going to incorporate these into a redraft. I just hate writing things out time and time again! Consequently, I never really went out of my way to incorporate such suggestions and I always wrote 'moderate essays'.

Young people living with word processors are growing up in a very different age. To them writing is not strictly a linear activity. They put down thoughts as they occur, move them around and add to them, change the shape and gradually fill out the detail. Writing becomes more a work of art, than an exercise in moving from first proposition to final conclusion. They can write without the inhibition of the physical labour of pen on paper — what bliss! Many of them write two or three times as fast using the keyboard as ever they can using a pen. To them writing is interesting, and as they master their own thoughts they are not adverse to talking about them with their friends and colleagues. Writing becomes a collaborative activity.

I once enthused about this to the Chair of a University Examinations Board. He became progressively quieter and quieter, and more withdrawn. Eventually he looked at me and said 'do you realize that we have been making a good living by examining people's first drafts for more than 200 years!' He continued 'I really don't think that word processors should be used in exams. It is a form of intellectual cheating really, isn't it? It doesn't really show what is there in the mind by itself, rather it extends the mind through the technology and doesn't give us a true picture of that person's actual skills and limitations.'

If that frightens you, let me go further. My eldest son took GCSE in the summer of last year. He was projected to get good grades, but twelve months beforehand his (very caring) form teacher suggested that he should give up using a word processor at home, and get used to writing out all his essays freehand. 'You must learn to get it right the first time.' That evening a confused young man said to me, 'But Dad, I just don't think like that any more. I am constantly trying to rework my ideas. Working with a pen stops me doing that, and writing by hand slows me up. But, don't worry, I'll just work that much harder to make sure I can do as well using a method of writing which I don't find particularly effective.' He was lucky. He could do that. Vast numbers can't.

The introduction of new technologies is always difficult in any profession. Theory challenges the nature of earlier jobs, and theory probably upsets the accepted way of allocating resources. This will be as true for educational establishments as it was for banking or telecommunications. But we — by this I have to start with the Department for Education and Employment — have delayed on this too long. I believe in the critical importance of good teachers — let me make that quite clear. But I am convinced that the benefit to children of being able to use word-processors to escape from many of the limitations of working at the speed of paper and pencil, is such that we cannot afford not to use this widely. If that means that expenditures on IT and associated facilities has to double from its present 0.7 per cent to something like 1.5 per cent of total school budgets, then so be it. Where

John Abbott

does this money come from? Perhaps by having slightly larger classes with the role
of the teacher being progressively different, but more interesting, and more rewarding. I find our reluctance to move on this deeply disturbing. I believe it is leading
people to question our professional competence. We need young people with the
highest level of communications skills, and we should encourage them in all possible ways. Talking this through with businesspeople they look aghast.

This is surely absurd. After years of talking about partnership and collaboration — with education and business partnerships set up all around the country —
we seem to be just not bold enough to look into the core of the problem. And what
do we see in that core? Muddled thinking. Muddled thinking by parents, administrators, teachers and politicians. We are still committed to a chalk and talk, show
and tell technology in which teacher time (rather than pupil opportunity to learn)
is seen as the main variable. We just don't realize that times have changed. We are
spending our money in the wrong places.

Technology has been struggling to make its impact on education for a long
time. It was almost exactly thirty years ago that I started teaching geography in the
sixth form. In my first term I had three classes for geomorphology, and it was my
task to go through a six week unit on plate tectonics — the building of mountains.
Personally I found this fascinating, and I had little difficulty in constructing diagram after diagram on the blackboard, showing the movement of mountains, the
sub-duction of geothermal currents and the nature of eventual erosion. My students
had to spend hours copying all this down. To my amazement at the end of that
term, BBC2 produced a two hour documentary program entitled *The Restless Earth*.
I was spellbound. Here, within a mere two hours, was everything that I had struggled with for six weeks — everything that is, and much more. It was more interesting than anything I could have ever produced.

The next morning I visited the Head of Department and I asked if he could
buy a copy. He frowned and explained that it would be far too expensive. I remonstrated and suggested that as I had three classes and he had another one, in future
years we could put the four classes together and the one person could use the film
and in a fraction of time cover the whole subject. He looked me up and down as
if I were a creature from another planet. 'My word' he said, 'you really are one of
the angry young men, aren't you? Don't you realize that this will just not fit into
the system!'

Professor Christopher Dede (1995) at George Mason University in Washington says,

> We have found that learner investigation and collaboration and construc-
> tion of knowledge are vital, and these things don't follow teaching by
> telling and learning by listening. It isn't that assimilation of knowledge
> isn't a good place to start, because it is hard to investigate something
> unless you know a bit about it. But assimilation is a terrible place to stop.
> The excitement about the access to information is that it is the first step
> in access to expertise, to investigations, to knowledge construction. Only

if access to data is seen as a first step — rather than as an end in itself will it be useful.

* * * * * *

Two years ago we put in a CD ROM system at home. It has been fascinating. Watching the children use this night after night I have learnt a lot. One evening on the Encarta CD I noticed that there was a section on geology. I encouraged my 11-year-old to explore what was there. Suddenly I saw a heading on plate tectonics. 'Let's take a look at that' I said. There, to my utter amazement, were three ninety second video clips showing the whole process of the evolution of mountain building with graphic/diagrammatic form. I was so fascinated Tom looked at me and said 'Daddy, if you are that interested all you have to do is stop it every ten seconds and then I could give you a colour print out of the diagrams. In that way you would have twenty-seven different diagrams to look at as much as you like!'

Did I really need six weeks to teach that particular piece of geomorphology? Was it a good use of the pupils' time to do all those diagrams? Was it a good way of developing the pupil/teacher relationship, which is such a fundamental part of a young person's social development? All of these are, I believe, quite fundamental but nevertheless still open questions.

* * * * * *

As a headteacher I always argued most piously that one of the most important aspects of schooling was the way that pupils learnt how to do homework. They were often pretty empty words, because homework badly delivered can be a pretty awful waste of time! However, to argue for homework was not to commit oneself to any resource implications — children simply borrowed a textbook, an exercise book and a pencil, and went home and got on the best they could. But now we have technology in the home, something very different is happening.

Listening to others talking about this, as well as watching my own children, I am quite amazed how suddenly homework takes on a totally different dimension when children have access to a whole range of technology and genuinely enjoy finding out about things and, even more, enjoy putting them together through a desktop publishing unit with all the professionalism normally associated with adult graphic designers. In our home, homework now takes time from my wife and myself, as well as extending most significantly the amount of time the children themselves spend working.

Always trust a child to come up with a profound observation! Last year Tom, then aged 11, and just starting secondary school said to me in all seriousness one evening, 'Daddy it isn't fair is it? Three of my friends, as well as me, have this technology at home and now we are getting the best marks for our homework. What we can do is much more than anybody else. But surely that's not really fair is it?'

No, it is indeed not fair. At this point technology is leaping out of the classroom and it is going to change the nature of schooling forever. Will this be good, or bad? What does all this mean for the future? Does this give us any clue as to how we should restructure education? I believe it does.

It starts with the need to be far clearer as to what I believe has now to be the key aim of formal schooling — the need to ensure that every child so understands how he or she learns that, before the age of 18, each has become *weaned* of their dependence on a teacher, and no longer thinks of learning as tied to a classroom. A quite specific aim — the mastery of technique through multiple demonstrations of proficiency in content (not the other way around).

To achieve this the educational system as we currently know it has effectively to be turned upside down and inside out. Instead of having the smallest class sizes in the last year of the sixth form, and the largest sizes in the first year of primary school, we have to restructure progressively this so that, over time, we can institutionalize the cognitive processes of apprenticeship into the whole way in which we think about the organization of schooling. We have to use all the community's resources to help the youngest child not just to learn something, but to learn how to learn something. Those with experience in primary schools know just how enthusiastic are young children to do this. Helping the child to understand how they do this, and how 'they go beyond what comes naturally' is a most expert and rewarding task.

Lifelong learning will depend not just on understanding your own learning processes, but being able to work as a team and to use a variety of information and communication technologies. I propose that, for a whole new generation of pupils coming up through the new kind of primary schools that could so easily be within our reach, it would be a natural progression for at least 20 per cent of the curriculum to be delivered 'off-site' at the age of 14. This could well rise to as much as 40 per cent by the age of 18. I propose this not as a method of saving money (which it might or might not do), but because I believe that young people are ready for this kind of responsibility by this age, and that it is the absence of such a challenging set of tasks that leads too many to approach adult life thinking that 'someone else will tell them what to do'.

There will be a problem of equity for those children who have not got the technology in the home. It would seem to make eminent sense if primary schools became 'the local area learning node' with at least one room open for 17 or 18 hours a day, seven days a week, not providing any form of formal instruction, but giving those children who live in that neighbourhood open access to the technology which they need to support their own study. I think, incidentally, that this would be of immense good, not only for the children, but for the communities as well. Suddenly children would see that they could achieve within the community that which previously they had to go a great distance to find.

This is where the community comes in. The crisis in education is not so much the failure of teachers in the classroom, but the failure of the community at large to capture the imagination, involvement and active enthusiasm of young people. Modern society has inflicted a terrible toll on community. But people are starting to fight back. 'People have a great hunger to belong', say the management consultants, we all need to feel useful. Young people can be and should be the heart of the community.

Let me close with a plea that we take a longer perspective on the whole issue. We must go beyond the four or five years which seems to dictate political policy. Children entering primary school this year will be in their mid-50s in the middle of the next century. By that time it is suggested that the world will be facing at least a double crunch — the population will have more than doubled and, according to the influential American economist Neil Heilbroner, capitalism as a system may well have exhausted itself.

I doubt if any of us has any serious proposals as how to deal with either of these challenges. The least we can do is to ensure that the children whose education we are now responsible for will be able to do so. Otherwise they will, quite rightly, hold us responsible.

Yes, I am impatient. Too often we go for things urgent, rather than things important — which we then forget about.

The story is told of Napoleon who, in his last years of exile on the island of Elba, was supervising the design of a beautiful garden. He was getting impatient with the gardener who remonstrated 'What is the hurry? This tree will take 200 years to reach maturity!'

'Yes', said Napoleon, 'that is why it has to be planted this afternoon!'

References

BERNARDO's (1995) *A Survey of Young People's Attitudes and Behaviour*, London, Bernado's.

COLLINS, A., SEELY BROWN, J. and HOLUM, A. (1991) 'Cognitive apprenticeship: making thinking visible', *The American Educator*, **15**, 3, p. 6.

CSIKSZENTMIHALYI, M. (1984) *Being Adolescent*, New York, Basic Books.

DEDE, C. (1995) 'Technology schools'. A conversation with Chris Dede, by John O'Neil *Educational Leadership*, ASDC, October, pp. 7–12.

LIVINGSTONE, R. (1941) *The Future of Education*, Cambridge, Cambridge University Press.

The Organization of Comprehensive Education in the Future

13   A Local Democratic Framework

Tim Brighouse

This chapter is an administrator's account of some of the organizational issues arising from the introduction of comprehensive secondary education. It attempts also to reflect briefly on the negative impact of parental choice on the comprehensive ideal, especially in urban areas, where it will be argued that there has been, and will continue to be, a different and much more difficult comprehensive tradition than has been the case in rural areas. Finally, it speculates on how the comprehensive principle in urban settings may be strengthened over the next ten years.

Others will have dealt with definitions of what is meant by comprehensive education. They will have assumed it is an issue related to secondary not primary schooling: yet, as I shall briefly explain, that may be an over-simplification.

Of course, the social composition of the pupil population of any comprehensive school will inevitably be governed by the locality it serves: in that sense, at least for me, the word comprehensive applied to the composition of its pupils equals a school which is the common experience of all who happen to live in a particular place. In the end any attempt to achieve a truly representative social mix will be defeated: for the unwary the need to be reminded that their espousal of social mix should not stop at the level of definitions which incorporate middle or affluent and working/under or impoverished classes, but might for example embrace ethnicity — at least in a large city. 'Bussing' provides us with some sobering transatlantic lessons. I shall in consequence be driven to argue strongly for an extension of parental rights beyond the present ones, which in relation to choice of school include the right to express a preference for a secondary school and to complain or appeal when it is not granted. For me the key to an extension of the comprehensive principle must reach as far as an entitlement in an urban area to send their child to the school that is closest to where they live and for the child to be offered the opportunity, in association with attending that school, of participation in a wider educational experience than that at present associated with the school curriculum.

Nor in respect of the composition of a school's pupils am I to be tempted, after my experience in the Inner London Education Authority, to notions of defining comprehensive in terms of ability, for then as I shall explain, I get myself trapped in the spider's web of Burtian influenced notions of ability. It is important to remember that the terms of this particular aspect of the comprehensive debate have shifted since the argument began. We all recall Wilson's phrase 'grammar schools for everybody' but we should remind ourselves that we have travelled to a better understanding of the nature and complexity of intelligence. We are all Gardnerians now. In consequence for me a comprehensive schooling system will be so arranged to have a greater rather than a lesser chance of unlocking Howard Gardner's (1983) range of intelligences. It will be mindful of different learning styles and organize its curriculum and teaching and learning opportunities accordingly. Very few schools do that at present. To these matters I shall return: for the moment a glimpse of the recent organizational story seen through the eyes of what has, in the main, been an administrator's career.

'The future lies in the comprehensive school. Apply for a job in one'. Thirty-five years ago Harry Davies, later to be the Director of the Institute of Education at the University of Nottingham, but then Headteacher of the city's High Pavement Grammar School, acted as local mentor to my initial teacher training school placement from the Oxford Delegacy, which in those days had the habit of abandoning students for half the year in far flung parts of the United Kingdom. The Delegacy had told me nothing of the comprehensive story and assumed, wrongly, that I would find a place in one of the many prestigious independent or grammar schools with Oxbridge connections.

I did not know then that my working life would be dominated one way or another by the comprehensive idea. At that moment I had neither thought nor ambition to pursue a managerial and administrative career pathway which, apart from a decade in Oxfordshire, has turned out to be preoccupied by the injustice which seems to be exacerbated in the absence of a comprehensive system. So there were periods in what was Monmouthshire where the Welsh Labour Party accepted the comprehensive imperative reluctantly. 'We are not bloody communists here' is how one of the councillors defending Tredegar Grammar School put it. The biggest obstacle in realizing the ideal in that particular historic Monmouthshire town was not to make the councillor toe the party line but to find a site unthreatened by tip or mine-shaft, yet large enough to house a comprehensive school. Perhaps it was a comment on the enthusiasm for the comprehensive ideal that they settled eventually for the Ty Tryst site. (The English translation is 'House of Sorrow'.)

Buckinghamshire was another story. It was a county as naturally conservative as Monmouthshire had been loyally radical. There, contiguous with Oxfordshire, where I was later to work, I saw how close was the difference between an uncontentious comprehensively reorganized county and one that was not. It lay in the quality, imagination and willingness of a core of grammar school heads — usually male — to make a confident leap of faith. So while Oxfordshire at that time was quietly completing its comprehensive reorganization, Buckinghamshire lacked that elusive something that enabled more than one of the heads at any one time to go out on a limb. The county wobbled. In Bletchley the citadel was breached. In Marlow, however, at Sir William Borlase's under the Headteacher Hazelton and in Buckingham at the Royal Grammar School under Embleton there were finely poised moments. But the combination of a failure of nerve and the conservatism of Sir Aubrey Ward, then Chair of the County Council, and of the Verney family, combined with the golfing habits of the Amersham Divisional Education Officer was sufficient to preserve the status quo. It was in Buckinghamshire too that I encountered the first primary school in a remote hamlet, Chenies, which recruited and coached pupils intensively for the 11+. I did not see that phenomenon again until 1993 when I took up my present appointment in Birmingham. Secondary grammar schools I realize beget primary crammer schools.

Now in Birmingham in the twilight of my career I can see the full impact of an unrestructured selective system. Five King Edward grammar schools, the Sutton Coldfield Grammar Schools, Bishop Vesey's and Sutton Girls, all are sound schools. So too are some of the so-called comprehensive schools whether mixed, single-sex, church, aided, GM or county in status and character. But there is a pecking order and there are many young people out of school. It is tackling the consequence of that which will be the subject of a later and major part of this particular contribution to the series.

It is worth remarking, however, that it has never seemed to me that the comprehensive argument lies in securing the best education for what I shall for the moment call the most able children. In my judgment comprehensives are slightly better at doing this, but grammar schools do reasonably well. It lies in the consequences of the selective system for those who do least well out of our schooling system.

One of the purposes of education is presumably to enable each of society's children to become a participating citizen in a democracy. That purpose presumes a bias towards equality of opportunity. In other words, participating citizens in a democracy will have been educated in a way which is designed to give each of them an equal chance, to enjoy both activities relating to crafts, the arts, sports, humanities and scholarship and the dignity and differential wealth which comes from choosing to spend the fruits of remunerated work which one way or another may also contribute to the common wealth and health of society as a whole. On arrival in Birmingham I drew heavily on the well of our American cousins' experiences when I expressed our collective determination to make this world worthy of its children. 'They are 100 per cent of its future. Let this be the beginning of a wish for every Birmingham child that we would want them to be people with a strong sense of themselves and their own humanity, with an awareness of their thoughts and feelings with a capacity to feel and express love and joy and to recognise tragedy and feel deep grief. . . . Above all, we would want Birmingham children to cherish the vision of the person they are capable of becoming.'

There seems to me to be no logical reason why that small percentage of a child's life which is spent in school — it is after all less than 15 per cent of their life from birth to age 16 — should be so arranged that some of our future citizens should be selected and schooled away from others. Although it is a small percentage of their overall time it is a high percentage of the time they will spend in their life with large groups of people of the same age. It is important that they live with the range of citizens who will with them shape the society they occupy as adults. Certainly in a democracy, consideration of conferring privilege or preserving advantages of class and wealth would be no justification for such action. Nevertheless, some may argue that from a certain age children with different aptitudes — and of course all of us have certain aptitudes — will flourish the better when they learn for part of the time in the company of others with similar interests and aptitudes.

Personally I accept that argument, but as I shall explain later, that does not lead me to argue for the creation of separate schools. Rather it argues for creating different specialized learning opportunities in different places within one single organizational structure.

The school curriculum carries the heavy burden of the nationally prescribed element occupying 15 per cent and the home and community components occupying the balance of the environmental experiences which shape a child's values and attitudes and influence their knowledge, skills and understanding. I shall in the end therefore argue for the comprehensive ideal to be realized not within a narrow school focus, but within a broader picture and by simple gradual steps not by the major reorganizations thought necessary during my career. The need for these reorganizations in any case stemmed from assumptions about school size related to Burtian views of ability which are outdated.

That brings me back to the beginning of my personal story. The Oxford Delegacy brought me up on Cyril Burt and Eysenck. So for a long time, I thought, intelligence, general, inherited and arguably fixed. They cast a long shadow. When I planned comprehensive schools in Monmouthshire, after *Circular 10/65*, we thought we needed eight forms of entry for a viable comprehensive school because anything less than a two-form-entry grammar school was unviable and the 11+ had served more of less successfully to select the top 25 per cent of the ability range — ability that is by Burtian definitions — to attend the shortly to be replaced grammar schools. Moreover, even eight forms of entry was regarded as doubtfully small if one were to have a sixth form that could generate sufficient 'A' levels — note 'A' levels! Later Burt still stalked the corridors of County Hall when I joined the ILEA in the mid-1970s, even though Peter Newsam had daringly challenged the conventional wisdom for the massive urban comprehensive school — the bigger the better in the 1960s — and had finally taken London down a comprehensive path.

Burt misinforms our language even today. When we talk loosely — as I did earlier — of mixed ability teaching, it is a Burtian assessment of ability or intelligence we refer to. Even though we have understood Gardner's theories of multiple intelligence we are still Burtian thinkers in our behaviour and language.

As I implied earlier, interlaced with this ability viewpoint of the comprehensive school has been a social one. So administrators have argued that in some areas such and such a school is not truly a comprehensive one because it lies in and serves a predominantly single class area.

These underlying and limited assumptions — a mixture of social composition and Burtian influenced views of intelligence — about the nature of comprehensives have led to two distinct historical developments of the comprehensive school: one in comparatively stable rural and suburban estates and the other in metropolitan areas.

Oxfordshire was typical of the county scene. It went all comprehensive without fuss and in a non-political way in the 1950s and 1960s. It combined the necessary replacement of all-age schools with a population expansion by focusing on market town grammar schools which were turned into comprehensive schools. It recruited distinguished headteachers, Geoffrey Goodall, Harry Judge and Bill Percival, for example, to Thame, Banbury and Bicester at old and established grammar schools.

These heads were then encouraged to create federal comprehensive schools: this they did with great success. Gloucestershire, Buckinghamshire, Essex, Kent and the North Riding were exceptions to the steady and uncontentious advance of the comprehensive ideal. Wherever one looks in Surrey, East and West Sussex, Hampshire, Somerset, Devon, Cornwall, Hertfordshire, Bedfordshire, Northamptonshire, Suffolk, Leicestershire, Nottinghamshire, Staffordshire, Oxfordshire, Hereford & Worcester, Wiltshire, Shropshire, Cheshire, Derbyshire, Cumbria, Northumberland, Durham, Cleveland, Avon, Humberside, in Wales and, of course, in Scotland, there is very little contention. Yet within these individual stories we glimpse a slightly different element: it is the metropolitan tradition. Oxford City, Nottingham and Leicester, for example, came painfully late and with a rush just prior to local government reorganization in 1974 — fitting-in reluctantly with the counties which surrounded them. For all large inner-city areas, not just London, comprehensive reorganization has been a more hard won and contentious story and the benefits have been by no means unmixed.

Why should this be? Are the communities more consciously heterogeneous in a social sense in the counties than they are in cities? Do the rich and the poor realize that they live in each other's lap in a way that cities, fashioned on the sharp disparities and competitiveness that was involved in the successive wakes of the industrial revolutions and acting as magnets to thousands of economic migrants attracted to the chimera of affluence surrounding industrial employment, do not? Certainly in urban areas the contrast is stark — even in matters of school design-between those which future leaders might be expected to attend, namely the grammar schools, and those for the rest who attended the all-age or pre-war secondary schools. Whatever the reason, the transition to comprehensive education in metropolitan areas has been sometimes reluctant and not wholly successful. As Sir Rhodes Boyson (1996) said recently on a radio programme 'We have never really tried comprehensive education in this country. If we had it may have worked.' He was surely thinking of the urban areas he had taught in as he spoke. The survival of Manchester Grammar School, or the King Edward Foundation Schools and of the Great London day schools, and the transformation, for example, of Clifton College in Bristol from a mainly boarding to a mainly day school, is testimony to a different and less than full-hearted commitment to the comprehensive ideal in the great conurbations.

In these metropolitan areas there is likely to be a long pecking order of schools, each with a fairly clearly defined allocated social position for the mobile members of the communities they serve.

One more point demands notice. So far the urban rural distinction I have made around comprehensive education has been illustrated at the secondary level. Yet in these heavily metropolitan areas the same social selection informs the provision of primary education. Some primary schools are covertly socially selective, or they suffer from a growing habit of parents' misregistering' the home addresses of some of their pupils.

Nor does it necessarily begin even at the primary level. Admission to LEA self-standing nursery schools has always been left to the individual school (and usually to the headteacher) to administer and manage. Whatever the policy guidelines — and often these have been few — the practice in the most deprived urban areas where the nursery schools have been situated has meant that the least well off and least socially attractive parents have often mysteriously not found a place in a nursery class or school, even though parents having businesses in the city, but living outside, have dropped off their children for the huge advantage that the nursery gives.

So the most well off find their inner-city nursery school, play the address game for their primary school and find a more or less selective haven in the storm of the secondary years, unless by that time they have decided to develop the notion of the colonial plantation owner by ceasing to live in the plantation in which they work and have taken off each evening after work to more pleasant homes in the surrounding hills where their children attend comprehensive schools and they can feel comfortable with their consciences.

The issue therefore of comprehensive schooling, where it remains contentious, is inextricably bound up with the challenge of urban living. Those few areas of North Yorkshire, Lincolnshire and so on represent the exception not the rule of rural suburban living. Nobody wants to go back to selection in the counties.

Let us therefore consider the reality of secondary schooling in heavily urbanized areas. In these settings it can be seriously argued selection has never disappeared: certainly the last sixteen years have witnessed a worsening of the prospects for future citizens as a consequence, principally, of the 1980 and 1981 Education Acts. This legislation when considered as a whole elevated for the first time to a matter of principle what was erroneously called 'parental choice' — a good that no-one dared challenge. Initially it had a seductive attraction for administrators faced with the unpalatable decisions over school closures as school rolls fell during the decade that followed. But it is a 'good' which is, as we all know, illusory and has set in play a virus which even now has not run its course and for which we know no antidote. Let me explain.

Rapidly falling rolls as a result of a decline in the birth-rate first affected primary schools in the mid-1970s. Separate junior and infant schools on the same site combined to form one primary school. The management of the school was therefore relatively uncomplicated. By the late 1970s, however, the same phenomenon affected the secondary sector where simple solutions were not so readily at hand. Shirley Williams first considered a device called 'planned admission limits' which were intended to allow an orderly and moderately uncontentious management of declining rolls among groups of secondary schools, especially in areas where numbers were expected subsequently to rise again. Many of us took advantage of that in the market towns where two or three schools might otherwise have embarked on unhealthy competition. The 1980 and 1981 Acts were passed by a Conservative government which was not yet in the thrall of Friedman/Hayeckian economics. Nevertheless, in granting the administrators' request for planned admission limits, the government decided that administrators' powers needed to be moderated by making it plain that parents had the right to express a preference in a way that was popularly called parental choice. Schools for the first time were asked to produce brochures or prospectuses. Before 1980 no school prospectuses were in evidence in the maintained sector of schooling in this country.

At first administrators, especially in large urban areas, decided that the simplest thing to do was to allow the market to decide rather than tackle the issue head on. So they left the admission limits high and allowed schools thereby to prosper or wither on the vine. In the main, in the most socio-economically deprived quarters of the large cities, they withered. In consequence children, some of whom were from the least motivated and supportive backgrounds, suddenly found they had a dauntingly greater distance to travel to school. The rest is well known. Successive Acts of Parliament extended the exercise of parental preference and diminished the power of the LEA, at first to plan the system, and then to administer the admission arrangements — all within the context of a government programme by that time heavily influenced by the socio-economic theories and policies of economic liberalism. By then, too, individual schools, often operating their own admission arrangements, could see the value of each individual pupil to their budget through the age weighted pupil unit and to their reputation through the league tables. The vestiges of control over the market place of schooling are now loose and few.

From this largely unhelpful and equality damaging model there emerges one interesting phenomenon, namely that what will matter in any future drive towards a more comprehensive system of schooling will be control not over the ownership of the schools but over access to them. We have lived for years with the fact that aided schools are the legal owners of their school buildings in any case, so the continuation of ownership of the property and assets of a school and its site, whether aided, GM, foundation, even private, is of no consequence given three provisos. First, some agency accountable both to all the schools and to local democracy should be charged by society with guaranteeing equality of access. Secondly, and contentiously, the experience of what happens beyond the individual school needs to be changed so that there is an additional range of comprehensive experiences. (In this last respect I shall be arguing for an encroachment, however modest, on the 85 per cent of time pupils at present spend engaged in the curriculum of the home or of the community.) Thirdly, each secondary school needs to be challenged to provide success for everyone of its pupils rather than for some of them.

Let me deal with each of these provisos in turn. First, we need a single admission agency — at least for secondary schools. I can think of no better agency than the local education authority, but I would listen to the arguments presented for a regional rather than a more local body. I have set out the arguments elsewhere (Birghouse, 1996a) for the democratic element in such a body whether local or regional. What will matter are the criteria for admission and the reward we should offer as a bonus to schools who manage successfully to serve all their local pupil population. Within the criteria for admissions, therefore, absolute priority needs to be given to those applicants for whom the school in question is closest to the child's home. Naturally this may require some extra school building in some areas: indeed, the planned capacity for a school would be governed by the number of children for whom that school is the closest, with due extra allowance in space for the percentage for whom children in the community might be expected to have special educational needs. Over a period — say seven years — the school would set out to persuade parents to exercise their right of selecting that school. If schools were successful the school would be rewarded with a 10 per cent bonus in funding. It should be noted that I am not arguing against the exercise of parental preference for a school other than the school closest to the home, simply that priority should be given to that criterion. In the case of oversubscription, once the first criterion has been met, I favour the drawing of lots.

My second proviso relates to transforming what goes on in secondary school by adding to the 15 per cent which the individual school will already provide as curriculum experience. In Birmingham we are moving to what may turn out to be the next stage in the development of the comprehensive ideal. It is important to remember that the context is a heavily urbanized setting. It happens to be additionally a multiethnic and multifaith and faithless combination of communities. In short, it presents urban challenges which are at least as great as in any other setting.

The University of the First Age bids fair to transform the nature of secondary school experience in the city: it will extend pupil and parental choice, provide curriculum and learning diversity, contribute to matters of equality and promote teachers' professional development. By adding a consistent and distinctive experience to the sum of the individually different offerings of the city's mix of independent, grammar, secondary modern, single-sex, Catholic church aided, grant maintained and local authority secondary schools, the University of the First Age will of course extend beyond the school curriculum into the 85 per cent of community curriculum. It will also affect, in due course, the nature of what goes on in the secondary school each pupil attends. Thirty-eight weeks schooling for youngsters in years 7, 8 and 9 will extend to forty. Part of the nature of that extension in curricular experience will be interest-led, mixed-age and intensive. So youngsters in years 7, 8 and 9, for example, will get together because they are interested in, and have an inclination to want to extend, their skills, knowledge and understanding in, for example, a language, some aspects of science or the arts, or sport, or maths, or technology, or the humanities. They will pursue that interest in a week or a fortnight on courses organized at the end of the spring and the summer terms in the city's network of schools, universities, colleges, sports centres and arts provisions, each of which will be a magnet for those drawn to the offer from the various schools of the city. The curriculum experience will in consequence be a 'setted' one, which offers considerable pace and progression. Accelerated learning is on offer here without all the normal social disadvantages either to the individual or others which would be inevitable in the normal school timetable. The courses in these spring and summer weeks will be planned and provided by groups of volunteer teachers drawn from the city's schools. Mindful of the various intelligences of the students and of their different preferred learning styles, the teachers will design high quality learning experiences across the familiar disciplines. Common to all pupils' experiences, irrespective of the interest they have expressed for their preferred intensive learning programme, will be citizenship and an introduction to, and development of, thinking skills. At their home schools will also be tutors in the University of the First Age. Not only will they offer counselling at an appropriate time of the year to students who are selecting their prospective choices in spring or summer courses, these tutors will also be at hand to help in the second element of the University of the First Age, which will make a distinctive contribution to realizing a totally comprehensive secondary experience. This will lie in distance-supplied courses which will take advantage of the latest advances in IT. All pupils in years 7, 8 and 9 will be able to consolidate and extend their learning on return from their spring and summer vacation courses through this device, which will also contribute to the homework timetable of youngsters and provide a context for the network of study support centres available to students both in the schools and the libraries and in other modes of access to a cat's cradle of learning opportunities. The University of the First Age will be staffed by professors, assistant professors and lecturers all jointly appointed with, and from, the secondary schools which will therefore provide a timely boost to the secondary teaching profession as well as providing curriculum enrichment and extension. Consider how progress in community languages could be accelerated and how particular cultural studies could be brought into focus through the extension of time and learning patterns that would be offered. Fundamental to the success of the University of the First Age is, of course, the application of the principle of 'just in time examinations'. That is to say, youngsters will take accredited success whether in GCSE or other recognized examination when they are ready for examinations and not at a predetermined point.

Through the gradual development of the University of the First Age schools will increasingly become more interdependent and be affected by what will have been offered by the leaders of pedagogy in a particular city.

Finally, however, there is the need for schools to set out to provide success for all their pupils not merely some of them. This follows naturally from the first two provisos I have outlined. Schools will after all wish to provide for the totality of pupils in their local community and equip them through cooperation with the University of the First Age with a wider range of learning opportunities. Now it will be necessary to challenge the secondary school to provide success for everyone. There will be less excuse for them failing to do so. The scheme envisaged here is that schools will be invited to subscribe to something akin to, but different from, the chartermark movement. It would be similar in the sense that the scheme would be formal, voluntary and stipulate certain principles, interventions and standards. But it would be different from the chartermark in the sense that schools would never achieve but merely extend their record of success as they strive to come ever closer to the ideal that provides success for every youngster.

The scheme is described elsewhere (Brighouse, 1996b). Broadly speaking it involves schools which would expect to be comprehensively successful for all their pupils to sign up to certain principles. These include a commitment by staff example to being a place of life-long learning, to organizing their experiences on Gardnerian views of intelligence, to behaving inclusively not exclusively and to emphasizing competition against self — improving on previous best is what we call it — rather than against unequals. Schools will subscribe to certain specified processes of school improvement; they will guarantee to each child a set of experiences and they will strive to certain set but differentiated standards of provision in the arts, in sport, in science, in IT, in equal opportunities as well as in language and maths.

The purpose of the scheme is to set in place an administrative framework which will bring us closer to the comprehensive ideal.

The questions I asked myself at the beginning of my career were: How large does the school need to be to be comprehensive? Does that size vary if there is no sixth form? Is it the size of the staff that matters? How should we create catchment areas to ensure a truly fair social mix? — all seem to me less relevant now. The ready availability of IT with all that implies, the growth of social exclusion, especially in cities, the greater but still, of course, very limited knowledge we now have of human intelligence, suggest different answers.

Within the school I would ask myself more sharply focused questions.

- Does every child enjoy a residential educational experience?
- Do all the staff provide a role model of learning? If so, how?
- What opportunities are there for accelerated learning for each child? What does this profile/portfolio show?
- What would be the musical, motor, spatial range of intelligences and talents in each year? How are these talents stimulated?
- Which member of staff is in charge of learning styles and what is the learning style profile of each class?
- What is the distance learning assignment for each of our profiles?
- Who is in charge of research and innovation in my school?
- What is the 'one-to-one' tutoring profile of each member of the school?
- What does our citizenship programme look like and what is the intelligences profile of each pupil?
- What targets have we set year on year for pupil improvement; for staff improvement; for school improvement?
- Does our school cater for all the children for whom we are the closest? If not why? Do we reject any?

These are among the questions which may prompt a school towards being comprehensively successful. However, within the 'Success for Everyone' mark, linked to the University of the First Age and operated within a system of school choice I have outlined here, the comprehensive ideal could be closer to being realised than it is today or that it was five, ten, fifteen or twenty years ago. At least in urban areas.

References

BOYSON, R. (1996) Interview on the *Jimmy Young Show*, Radio 2.

BRIGHOUSE, T. (1996a) *A Question of Standards: The Need for a Local Democratic Voice*, London, Politeia.

BRIGHOUSE, T. (1996b) *In Press*, London, Institute for Public Policy Research.

GARDNER, H. (1983) *Frames of Mind: The Theory of Multiple Inteligences*, New York, Basic Books.

14   For Citizenship and the Remaking of Civil Society

Stewart Ranson

Introduction

The comprehensive school must continually review and refashion itself if it is to further the ideals, which inspired it, of creating a more equal and fairer society of opportunity for all to develop their powers and capacities. My arguments will be that at the centre of the new learning is the making and remaking of civil society. I want to develop an understanding of the values, purposes, tasks and conditions for the comprehensive school in support of a learning society as we approach the year 2000. The essence of a learning society is one which has to learn to remake itself.

   We cannot make sense of the comprehensive school for the future without an understanding of the changes of our time, and so clarifying in this context what values, purposes, dispositions of character we wish institutions to foster. The changes cause us to reflect deeply on what an education should be for, but also what an institution is for and what form it should take in this context to be appropriate for the time. One thing is clear — there is no return to the past. The task cannot merely be a recovery of the past, wishing away the intervening nightmare of a predatory market society which has destroyed the quality of life of so many. There is no escaping rethinking anew for our generation what the ideals of comprehensive should mean.

Living in a Different World: The Spectre of Uselessness

The social and economic changes which have been accelerating since the mid-1970s imply structural transformations for our society. The changes are not cyclical. Our world has become different in form and will not return to what it was before. The very language now being created to characterize these transformations — 'post-modern', 'post-industrial', 'post-fordist' — anticipates an historic juncture taking place. Understanding these changes is a pre-condition for interpreting educational purpose but more deeply what it is to live a life at the turn of the century.

   For, what makes the changes we are experiencing quite historic is that the restructuring of work, driven by what Edward Luttwak (1995) has called technology powered, deregulated, globalising 'turbo charged capitalism' will remove secure work or paid employment as the central experience from most citizen's lives leaving them to lead chronically insecure, vulnerable lives. Structural change accelerates the 'downsizing' of firms, flexible labour and declining income. The less skilled are condemned to a life-time of declining earnings. What (some) have failed to grasp is that the upheavals and disruptions condemn most first world working people of *all* skill levels to lives of chronic economic insecurity.

Exclusion from work and well-being leaves many living outside the routines and structures which the included take for granted. Disadvantage isolates individuals and communities and sets them apart. They feel themselves and are believed to live 'in a different world' — a world apart. The experience of alienation excludes. Living in poverty typically influences how young people think of themselves: with low self-esteem, eroded belief in what they can achieve and thus low expectations and withered motivation to learn. Individuals and their communities can feel beleaguered by their sense of 'otherness'.

Worlds of Difference

This material difference grows within a world typically characterized by clashes of cultural traditions whose values, histories and identities are said to be chronically agonistic and thus rival and incommensurable, compounded by a poverty of recognition and mutual understanding (MacIntyre, 1981; Gray, 1995). Many schools, in this context, are a microcosm of the predicament facing the post-modern polity. The challenge for an institution as for society is to discover processes which can reconcile the valuing of difference with the need for shared understanding and agreement about public purpose that dissolves prejudice and discrimination.

The experience of cultural difference can also be one of otherness and exclusion. Cultures codify the essential boundaries of social classification. To be placed in a different world is thus to experience the deepest codes of: who is to be included as members, who excluded as alien sets the boundaries of the social order; the identities of self and other, of sacred and profane are defined within the moral order; while the relations of power, of super and subordination, constitute the political order. Systems of social classification so embody the relations between communities that to be regarded as other, outside, profane, is to experience the greatest disadvantage — to be denied the dignity, and thus the sense of agency, that derive from being acknowledged as a fellow citizen with shared rights and responsibilities.

Collective Action Dilemmas

The trends towards fragmentation implied in the post-modern society threaten to undermine the cooperation and trust that define a community and thus the possibility of cooperative action upon which any society depends. The most serious 'collective action problem' is the predatory exploitation of the environment with its dramatic consequences. Mounting litter, traffic congestion and the prospect of global warming reveal the unintended collective consequences of our individual choices: self-interest can be self-defeating. The seductive, yet ultimately irrational compulsion of some to 'free-ride' presents perhaps the most significant challenge for future society. Parfit (1984) succinctly describes the dilemma: 'it can be better for each if he adds to pollution, uses more energy, jumps queues and breaks agreements; but if all do these things that can be worse off for each than if none do. It is very often true, that if each rather than none does what will be better for himself, this will be worse off for everyone' (p. 62).

Legitimacy

What will be the nature of work in the future and who will be required to work? Do individuals need to work to express their identities, develop their capacities, acquire status and contribute as citizens to the commonwealth of the community in which they live? Will those who remain outside work be regarded as 'members', as 'citizens' by others in the community? Will they be accorded equal rights and status and power in the community? Social, economic and political changes have, through the uncertainty they have generated, raised the most fundamental questions for a society to cohere during a period of transition: what is it to be a person? is there any such thing as society? what form should democracy take in the post-modern polity? The effect of these structural changes and the questions which they have given rise to has been to cause a fundamental reexamination of the social democratic polity and the management of the public sector. Has our society the political resources to create a new framework of justice about rights and duties which acquires legitimate authority across a fragmenting society?

What is to be Learned: Renewing the Public Domain

In periods of transition learning becomes central to our future well-being. Only if learning is placed at the centre of our experience will individuals continue to develop their capacities, institutions be enabled to respond openly and imaginatively to change, and the differences within and between communities become a source for reflective understanding (Ranson, 1992, 1994).

Yet the key issue is which learning do we have to learn. The predicaments of our time are public (collective) problems and require public solutions yet the public institutions required to support the resolutions have all but eroded: our society has developed institutions that are not constituted to encourage an active public domain. The characteristics of structural change in society (fragmentation, privatism and sectionalism) and the qualities of the neo-liberal polity (competitive individualism) mutually reinforce the erosion of public life and thus the conditions for personal autonomy as well as collective well-being. If the task for the time is to recreate a public domain that can support society through an historic transition then the challenge will be to learn, relearn two indispensable capacities: the capacity for cooperative action; the capacity for action, for agency.

Learning the Capacity for Cooperative Action

The predicaments of our time — whether in understanding how to sustain the environment or to reconcile the rights and well-being of diverse communities — cannot be determined by individuals or groups in isolation, nor by 'exit' because we cannot stand outside them. The predicaments of our time are faced by communities and societies as a whole:

> they are urgent problems for human beings together and in common.... If we are so much as to survive as a species ... we clearly need to think about well-being and justice internationally, and together. (Nussbaum, 1990)

What each individual or group experience as separate concerns, have actually to be faced together and can only be tackled through public institutions that enable us to share understanding and act together:

> facing the obscure and extravagantly complicated challenges of the human future our most urgent common need at present is to learn how to act together more effectively. (Dunn, 1992)

Learning as the Cultural Reconstruction of Agency

The post-war social democratic polity emphasized a passive public, taking its lead from professional experts and distant elected representatives. While much was achieved, excluding the public from participating in the development of society led in time to a withering of identification and support. The vacuum in the polity was the absence of public engagement. Public consent and legitimacy have atrophied as a result. Understanding of this predicament has been widespread but differences surround the appropriate response.

Learning requires individuals to progress from the post-war tradition of passivity, of the self as spectator to the action on a distant stage, to a conception of the self as agent both in personal development and active participation within the public domain. Such a transformation requires a new understanding from self-development for occupation to self-development for autonomy, choice and responsibility across all spheres of experience. The change also presupposes moving from our prevailing preoccupation with cognitive growth to a proper concern for development of the person as a whole — feeling, imagination and practical/social skills as much as the life of the mind. An empowering of the image of the self presupposes unfolding capacities over (a life) time. This implies something deeper than mere 'lifelong education or training' (referred to as access institutions). Rather it

suggests an essential belief that an individual is to develop comprehensively throughout his or her lifetime and that this should be accorded value and supported.

The Challenge of Remaking

Thus the challenge for our society at the turn of the century is to remake itself. It
is a task of cultural renewal, requiring a cultural of cooperative action we are to find
ourselves by remaking the communities in which we are to live. This makes the
central task of our time to transform the way people think of themselves and others
and what they are capable of. It is only by changing the sense students have of
themselves as learners that they will begin to develop their capacities and realize
their potential. This will depend upon the creation of a learning society which
nurtures the sense of agency amongst its citizens to enter into the remaking of the
communities in which they are to live. The values and conditions of this learning
society are: citizenship; democracy; justice.

Citizenship

Social and political theorists in search of perspectives which might illuminate and
resolve the puzzles presented by the post-modern politics of difference have drawn
upon theories of citizenship and civil society to offer interpretive analyses of a
changing democracy at the turn of the century. Traditional models of 'entitlement
citizenship', which emphasize membership of the nation state and formal legal
rights (Marshall, 1977; Plant, 1990) have been subjected to critical analysis because
they ignore the contemporary condition of plurality (Parekh, 1988) and neglect the
tradition of participation, exercise of agency and deliberation which also informed
classical traditions of citizenship (Barber, 1984). The task has been to reconstruct
a theory of citizenship which is grounded in the experience of heterogeneity and
elaborates the need for different groups to enter a discourse in which they voice
claims for their identities and interests to be recognized and accommodated in the
public space. Theorists (Young, 1990; Phillips, 1993 and 1995; Mouffe, 1992 and
1993) point to the mistaken illusion of a unified polity, of homogeneous communities which form a universal citizenry and civic public, which is required to leave
behind particularity and difference in the public domain. Traditional models of
citizenship imposed a univocal understanding of what should count as 'universal'
values that excluded and silenced the voices of 'other' traditions, whether they are
gendered, ethnic or class. A conception of citizenship is needed, Yeatman (1994)
argues, which acknowledges the contested nature of public purposes and enables
the different voices to represent their cultural traditions and material class interests
in the public space in conditions of unconstrained dialogue.

The motivation of members of society to acknowledge mutuality, to deliberate
with others and to search for shared understanding is more likely to succeed if they
regard each other as citizens with shared responsibility for making the communities

in which they are to live. This makes the agency of citizens central to personal and social development. Our active participation in creating the projects which are to shape our selves as well as the communities in which we live provides the sense of purpose to work together with others and to secure trusting relations with them. There is no solitary development or learning: we can only create our worlds together. The unfolding agency of the self always grows out of the interaction with others. It is inescapably a social and creative making. The self can only find its identity in and through others and membership of communities. The possibility of shared understanding requires individuals not only to value others but to create the communities in which mutuality and thus the conditions for learning can flourish.

A Participative Democracy for Communicative Action

We can only make ourselves and our communities when empowered by a public domain which recognizes the distinctive contributions each have to give. For Habermas (1984 and 1990), the processes of a discursive democracy provide the conditions for differences to be brought into the public sphere and negotiated through procedures of fair, equal and unconstrained discussion undistorted by power. Identities are respected and compromises if not consensus reached between rival traditions.

Such a view of democracy recognizes an understanding, effaced by rights based models, of the duality of citizenship: that citizens are both individuals and active members of the whole, the public as a political community. Citizenship in this view is not a passive status (Turner, 1993): membership brings with it a sense of responsibility, on the part of citizens, to become involved, and speak out in the public sphere exercising their agency to deliberate with other traditions in search of a good for the community as a whole. For Clark (1996) this deep 'democratic citizenship' requires for the recovery of collaborative participation, the establishing and strengthening of the spaces, the intermediary institutions of civil society, in which such active citizenship can be practised (Keane, 1988a and 1988b; Hirst, 1994; Cohen and Arato, 1992; Cohen and Rogers, 1995). A domain is formed in which private meets public, providing the conditions for what Mouffe (1993) argues strong democracy needs — an articulation between the particular and the universal. A sphere which recognizes and mediates, through the arts of association, a diversity of particular interests for the public good. By providing forums for participation the new polity can create the conditions for public discourse and for mutual accountability so that citizens can take each other's needs and claims into account will learn to create the conditions for each others development (c.f. Dunn, 1992).

Justice: A Contract for the Basic Structure

The conditions for agency of self and society depend upon agreement about its value as well as about allocating the means for private and public self-determination.

Freedom rests upon justice, as Rawls (1971) and Sen (1992) argue. But this makes the most rigorous demands upon the polity which has to determine the very conditions on which life can be lived at all: membership, the distribution of rights and duties, the allocation of scarce resources, the ends to be pursued. The good polity must strive to establish the conditions for virtue in all its citizens: the conditions — material (for example, clean public water); institutional (for example, education); and moral (a civic ethic). These issues are intrinsically political and will be intensely contested, especially in a period of transformation that disturbs traditions and conventions.

Renewing the Comprehensive Vision

Institutions matter! They are powerful human constructions. Their distinctiveness lies in the intensity of their function: they are constituted to shape human nature, to form the person — her dispositions, powers and capacities. An institution, in conception, leaves its mark on 'a life', in its identity, thinking, feeling of the person. Institutions frame: they shape horizons of their members and thus their sense of place. They mediate the relationship people have to their society through social time and space. At the same time what institutions become, the values and interests they embody, are shaped by the agency and power of those that come to control them.

Public institutions must embody, express these values and purposes historic role of institutions is to take up this challenge support the remaking of society by citizens. This will necessitate changes in the nature of the comprehensive school. The comprehensive school has typically been a creature of its time and needs reforming if it is to take up the new vision which is being proposed for it here.

Since the 1950s the predominant vision for the comprehensive school has varied but, throughout the development of comprehensives, there have been schools which have committed themselves to an ideal of community education: of the school as a resource of, and for, the community as a whole. This tradition has incorporated a number of practices: perceiving parents as complementary educators of their children, extending educational opportunities for all members of the community, making facilities and resources available to the community; involving parents and members of the community on governing bodies and community forums to participate in the decision making processes about the reciprocal contributions of the comprehensive school to and from the community; and seeing this process of community participation as enabling the purpose of empowering community development.

The community education tradition was never the dominant tradition within comprehensive education, and within that tradition those who went beyond extending educational opportunities to pursue a vision of community empowerment were rare. Yet it is this tradition and its practices which it is argued now need to inform a renewal of the comprehensive school for the twenty-first century to support the recreating of civil society. The purposes, form, pedagogy and style of the comprehensive school for the future are discussed in turn.

Comprehensive in Purpose

Early proponents of the comprehensive school often spoke of it as 'the common school' which would provide an education for all in the community who would have access to the same common curriculum. While the term 'common' communicates the strength of our shared humanity it can be interpreted to mean similarity, the same humanity, and as such presents only half of the duality which needs to be at the centre of public propose in our time: to recognize and celebrate what is different as well as what is the same in our shared humanity.

The constitutive condition of many urban schools reflects the cultural diversity of the wider society in which they are located. Schools are a microcosm of the predicament facing the post-modern polity. The challenge for an institution as for society is to discover processes which can reconcile the valuing of difference with the need for shared understanding and agreement about public purpose. The motivation to learn, to develop agency will grow out of recognition of different identities (Taylor, 1994). Processes, thus, which are central to pedagogy are those which also deepen and reconstitute institutional legitimacy.

The term comprehensive, given this understanding, provides the appropriate constitutive values and purposes for schools at the turn of the millennium. For comprehensive suggests comprehending while including, recognizing while incorporating, the differences of the communities which a school will serve and embody. The purpose of the comprehensive school is to develop the capacities of citizens to engage in the remaking of their societies in a post-modern world of difference.

Constituting Difference

The task for institutions is to develop educational values of citizenship which is grounded in the experience of heterogeneity and elaborates the need for different groups to learn together to shape a shared world which accommodates and values different cultural identities and traditions. Theorists (Young, 1990; Phillips, 1993 and 1995; Mouffe, 1992 and 1993) point to the mistaken illusion of a unified public space, of homogeneous communities which form a universal citizenry and civic public, which is required to leave behind particularity and difference in the public domain.

The challenge for the comprehensive school, where it does not already do so, is to reach out to constitute difference (social, cultural, ethnic, class, multiple (dis)abilities, ages etc) in the form of the institution. A number of strategies present themselves to enable the comprehensive school in the monocultural enclave to comprehend and embody difference in its very structure and working:

— the travelling school post 15: developing curricular programmes which bring together young people from different enclaves. This is the equivalent of Richard Sennett's 'active edge' planning of architects and geographers. To create zones of interaction which dissolve the boundaries between young people in different communities enabling them to interact and learn together. In the past schools have been good at interinstitutional curriculum planning to educational opportunities in the sixth form and students have grown used to travelling to learn, the hidden curriculum — of learning to engage with new people and environments being as important arguably as the formal curriculum of subject learning.

— forming partnerships with schools/colleges in very different settings presents similar opportunities for young people to encounter difference and learn together in unfamiliar but challenging contexts.

— multi-age schools: do schools have to be differentiated by age? The tradition of adults learning in schools has become firmly established in Scotland and in some schools in England, with young people benefitting from experiencing the serious commitment which adult return to education typically bring to their learning.

The challenge for the truly comprehensive school is be imaginative in recognizing and valuing difference in its constitutive form.

A Pedagogy of Cooperative Making

The central task for comprehensive schools is to develop pedagogies of active learning which support the reconstruction of agency. To learn is to develop understanding which leads into, and grows out of, action; to discover a sense of agency that enables us, not only to define and make ourselves, but to do so by actively participating in the creation of a world in which, inescapably, we live together. Realizing this will require schools to challenge the received cultural codes of classification within and beyond the institution. Their task is to dissolve the boundaries of otherness and to establish cultures of learning which value difference.

Learning itself begins with a sense of discovery of new knowledge or skills. But the deeper significance of learning lies, through its forming of our powers and capacities, in our unfolding agency, in our understanding of who we are and what we can do as a person. The purpose and outcome of active learning may be a particular 'competence' which alters our capacity to intervene in experience. But the central purpose of learning is to enable such skills to develop our distinctive agency as a human being. Learning involves becoming aware of our difference but also, significantly, how to enact its distinctiveness. Learning to develop the agency of the person is inescapably a temporal process: it takes time.

There is, however, no solitary learning: we can only create our worlds together. The unfolding agency of the self always grows out of the interaction with others. It is inescapably a social creation. We can only develop as persons with and through others; the conception of the self presupposes an understanding of what we are to become and this always unfolds through our relationship with others; the conditions in which the self develops and flourishes are social and political. The self can only find its identity in and through others and membership of communities.

The possibility of shared understanding requires individuals not only to value others but to create the communities in which mutuality and thus the conditions for learning can flourish. The telos of learning is to learn to make the communities without which individuals and others cannot grow and develop.

Such organizing principles for a pedagogy of active learning can be illustrated from the work of some schools.

Cases of Learning to Remake our World

(a)   Knowsley: learning, even in the traditional subject curriculum, can be given purpose by being oriented to serve the needs of, and taking responsibility for others in the community. A senior adviser in this borough described a physics lesson in which the students, to develop understanding of electrical circuitry were asked to design and test a mechanism to be used in sheltered accommodation for senior citizens to alert the warden if one of the residents needed help. For the adviser this project gave meaning to education. It illustrates that learning is about something useful. It shows an application of learning to help someone lead a better life. Right across the curriculum teachers should seek to relate what is happening in schools to what use can be made of it in the community.

(b)   Waltham Forest: community service encourages young people to take control of their learning and involves them in setting up projects which will be of benefit to the community. They set themselves up as a group, identify a need and organise how they will work. 'Ice-line' has been set up by students to help the aged during the winter — providing a telephone service, information and advice about conserving energy, blankets etc. Other initiatives include support for the disabled in the community.

(c)   Glasgow: a secondary school committed to the idea that the quality of learning and of life in the community must be perceived as mutually enriching. A whole school project focused upon recovering and remaking the 'waste' land around the school. The head argued that 'it is only by the school valuing a waste area that you encourage the children to see the possibility of a future that is different from the past. Enriching the curriculum with environmental studies and performance arts is building a new confidence, skills, social abilities and creative imagination. It is a mistake to see the practical and the academic as separate. They feed in to each other. The environmental work is providing the motivation for formal learning. It is also practically sustaining the local wood and in so doing showing them the possibility of acting upon and changing their environment. This is important for human survival.

(d)   A Birmingham primary school: a project was introduced with the story Nowhere to play by Karusa, about a group of children who have lost their play spaces through urbanization. It tells how they organize themselves, protest to the council, and eventually use a derelict piece of land with the help of adults to build a play area. Drama was used to start the class on designing an imaginary park, taking on the role of park keepers, dealing with litter, finding finance for the bins, charging entrance fees and working out the effect on the community. Photography and video were used by groups of the children to record the area. Each child made a plan of the area as they would like it to be. Visits were paid to other play areas such as Aston Park and South Aston play centre. Catalogues of play equipment were studied and safety surfaces were investigated. 'Experts' from the parks and planning department and play areas were interviewed and further contacts were made with people who offered support for the project. Local residents were consulted to gather opinions.

Each child designed a piece of play equipment for the park and models were then constructed from plans. Models for the whole park were subsequently built (design). In groups the children grew seeds of plants that could be planted in the park and also investigated suitable trees. They also studied different habitats and the ways in which these attracted different mini-beasts (science). The proposed plot was surveyed and calculations were made for instance how much turf was to be used. This was costed out, along with the pricing of trees, fences and so on at a garden centre, in order to arrive at an overall cost for the project (maths).

Learning to Learn in the Learning School

If the learning comprehensive school is to reconstruct the sense of agency amongst young people and their capacity to make the communities in which they are to live, then many schools will have some fundamental relearning to do. They must learn to value the capacity and celebrate the culturally diverse identities of all their young citizens as the precondition for creating the motivation to learn. If schools are to realize this ambition they will have to learn about how they work as an organization, bringing to the surface the deep categories which typically selectively differentiate what they expect different young people to achieve. Schools cannot transform the way disadvantaged young people think of themselves, support their unfolding sense of agency, unless they can surface, confront and resolve the different beliefs which teachers can hold of student powers and capacities. Schools must become learning organizations if they are to enable the necessary cultural renewal of active citizenship.

The 'learning school', which a number of our schools wish to recognize themselves as, places dialogue at the centre of its management strategy for change. Questioning and discussing the assumptions which underlie institutional practice can be a painful process, but it is the only way for organizations to address the inconsistencies in practice between colleagues in a way that enables them to unify around shared purposes. Without dialogue, struggles between internal groups continue and erode the institutions capacity for coherent purpose driven by strong values.

The most effective process of learning forms a further stage of complexity: learning how to learn. Organizations experiencing change need a general predisposition to learn if they are to succeed. The learning organization becomes self-aware about the cycles of learning and the conditions for learning. It becomes proficient at asking questions, developing ideas, testing them and reflecting on practice. In this way the learning process explores the structures of action: the values which underlie the perspectives, the forms of interaction and the nature and distribution of power that drives action. Learning about these systems of action within organisations is best nurtured within 'action learning sets' that enable the participants, through collaborative working and reflection, to open out to and accommodate the value in each perspective and to develop the predisposition to change practice. The capacity for learning is the capacity for dialectic in changing practice.

Unless schools develop the qualities of the learning organizational then their capacity to lead the reconstruction of agency and contribute to the learning society will be considerably reduced. A learning organization will be more likely to engage in an internal discourse — able to challenge its deep seated assumptions about 'ability' — if it is located within, and part of, an active, democratic public domain (Ranson and Stewart, 1994). The organizing principles of that domain are principles for learning that can challenge existing organizations and activities. That will be achieved by open public discourse which is not bounded by existing activities. The process of discourse in the public domain is the basis for learning to learn.

Governing with Consent

The conditions for young people taking themselves and thus their learning seriously depend upon the comprehensive school establishing a vision of achievement and practices of learning which are shared by teachers, the different parent communities and the young themselves. Schools can transform the way young people think of themselves and what they are capable of achieving when shared values — of the highest expectations of potential, belief in capacity, and value of cultural difference — are invested in agreed practices of learning and teaching.

The learning comprehensive school grasps that if the dialogue about expectations and capacity is to be effective it cannot be enclosed by the profession alone. The recognition that the motivation of young people to learn is enhanced with the support of parents has been accelerating across the country for some time and has led a wide variety of practices that involve parents individually in the life of the school. But in the enclaves of exclusion which constitute many disadvantaged communities the fundamental issues of what an education is — what is to be taught and how — cannot be taken for granted. Only by listening to the community and its different traditions can a school begin to develop agreement about its most basic purposes and policies.

The school learns that it can only dissolve the boundaries of social classification which stifle the aspirations and agency of young people by reaching out to, and seeking agreement with, the traditions which it serves. An institution needs to constitute within itself the differences which live within the wider community so that by recognizing and according them value a school celebrates the springs of identity and purpose of its young people.

For some schools the differences between traditions appear so significant that they are creating forums for parent groups to meet, and represent their educational traditions, in a discussion of the key issues facing the school that can allow shared purposes and policies to emerge for governing body decision-making. A school cannot proceed without the agreement of its parent community and some institutions are learning that because this can no longer be taken for granted new forms of governance must be constituted to allow democratic participation, agreement and consent. By providing forums for participation the new polity can create the conditions for public discourse and for mutual accountability so that citizens can take each other's needs and claims into account will learn to create the conditions for each others development. Learning as discourse must underpin the learning society as the defining condition of the public domain.

Conclusion

Learning requires motivation, self-worth, confidence and a sense of purpose which generates the energy for endless hard work. These are qualities which society expects of young people in the most difficult of circumstances. In some communities the scale of disadvantage is such that living itself is an arduous struggle. Many live in the shadow of enclaves of 'otherness'.

Despite the scale of such corrosive disadvantage comprehensive schools can and are succeeding in motivating young people to realize their potential. What we learn from them is that if they are to alter the way students think of themselves and what they are capable of, to transform hopelessness into purpose and kindle capacity, it requires a sharing of vision, an energy and cohesiveness of purpose amongst teachers, parents and community traditions.

Working together, comprehensive schools with their communities will generate the sense of purpose that can dissolve the boundaries that emphasise place above horizons and generate the agency necessary for the recreation of civil society.

References

Barber, B. (1984) *Strong Democracy: Participatory Politics for a New Age*, Berkeley, CA, University of California Press.
Clark, P. (1996) *Deep Citizenship*, London, Pluto.
Cohen, J. and Arato, A. (1992) *Civil Society and Political Theory*, Cambridge, MA MIT Press.
Cohen, J. and Rogers, J. (Eds) (1995) *Associations and Democracy*, London, Verso.
Dunn, J. (1992) *Democracy: The Unfinished Journey*, Oxford, Oxford University Press.
Gray, J. (1995) *Enlightenment's Wake*, London, Routledge.

HABERMAS, J. (1984) *The Theory of Communicative Action Vol 1*, London, Heinemann.

HIRST, P. (1994) *Associative Democracy*, Oxford, Polity Press.

KEANE, J. (1988a) *Democracy and Civil Society*, London, Verso.

KEANE, J. (1988b) *Civil Society and the State*, London, Verso.

LUTTWAK, E. (1995) 'Turbo-charged capitalism and its consequences', *London Review of Books*, **22**, November, pp. 6–7.

MACINTYRE, A. (1981) *After Virtue*, London, Duckworth.

MARSHALL, T. (1977) *Classes, Citizenship and Social Development*, Chicago, IL, Chicago University Press.

MOUFFE, C. (1992) *Dimensions of Radical Democracy*, London, Verso.

MOUFFE, C. (1993) *The Return of the Political*, London, Verso.

NUSSBAUM, M. (1990) 'Aristotelian social democracy' in MARA. G. and RICHARDSON, H. (Eds) *Liberalism and the Good*, New York, Routledge.

PAREKH, B. (1988) 'Good answers to bad questions' (review of R. Dahrendorf *The Modern Social Question*) *New Statesman and Society*, 28 October.

PARFIT, D. (1984) *Reasons and Persons*, Oxford, Oxford University Press.

PHILLIPS, A. (1993) *Democracy and Difference*, Cambridge, Polity Press.

PHILLIPS, A. (1995) *The Politics of Presence*, Oxford, Oxford University Press.

PLANT, R. (1990) 'Citizenship and rights' in PLANT, R. and BARRY, N. (Eds) *Citizenship and Rights in Thatchers Britain: Two Views*, London, Institute of Economic Affairs.

RANSON, S. (1992) 'Towards the learning society', *Educational Management and Administration*, **20**, 1, pp. 68–79.

RANSON, S. (1994) *Towards the Learning Society*, London, Cassell.

RANSON, S. and STEWART, J. (1994) *Management for the Public Domain: Enabling the Learning Society*, London, Macmillan.

RAWLS, J. (1971) *A Theory of Justice*, Oxford, Oxford University Press.

SEN, A. (1992) 'On the Darwinian view of social progress', *London Review of Books*, **5**, November.

SENNETT, R. (1995) 'Something in the city', *Times Literary Supplement*, 22 September, pp. 13–15.

TAYLOR, C. (1994) *Multiculturalism*, Princeton, NJ, Princeton University Press.

TURNER, B. (Ed) (1993) *Citizenship and Social Theory*, London, Sage.

YEATMAN, A. (1994) *Postmodern Revisionings of the Political*, London, Routledge.

YOUNG, I. (1990) *Justice and the Politics of Difference*, Princeton, NJ, Princeton University Press.

Afterword

Rt Hon John Prescott MP, Deputy Leader of the Labour Party

This is a slightly edited version of a speech given at Ruskin College Oxford on 13 June 1996. The speech was seen as a fitting conclusion to the series of lectures on Affirming the Comprehensive Ideal. John Prescott failed his 11+ examinations and attended a secondary modern school in Ellesmere Port. Leaving school at 15, he began working in hotel catering, then became a merchant seaman and later an official with the National Union of Seamen. For two years he was a mature student at Ruskin College where he studied for a diploma in economics and politics. Some time later, in 1976, Ruskin College provided the setting for James Callaghan's Ruskin College speech that launched the Great Debate on Education.

It's great to be back here at Ruskin, the College which opened a whole new world to me, for which I will be eternally grateful.

Let me say from the start, I do not intend to give you an exposition of Labour Party policy proposals. I will not attempt to give you a lecture on educational theory. What I will do instead is to draw on my own personal experience and explain why I so passionately oppose selection through the 11+ and so passionately support comprehensive education. It is based not on theory but on my practical experience — warts and all — as an 11+ failure, as a correspondence course freak with the WEA, as a mature student here at Ruskin, as a graduate of the University of Hull, as a parent of two children who attended comprehensive schools, and as an MP hearing the worries constituents feel about their children's education, and their worries about trying to get the best education for their children, or even the so called 'right school'.

I will speak not as an expert, but as someone who feels passionately about education and who has gained powerful impressions about our education system. So this not so much a lecture, more a John Prescott experience. Nevertheless, I hope you will see it as an appropriate follow-on from the series of lectures 'Affirming the Comprehensive Ideal' recently organised by the University of Oxford's Department of Educational Studies.

Many will remember Jim Callaghan coming here nearly twenty years ago. I was already an MP by then. Jim's speech made a big impact and was said by some to lay the foundation for a National Curriculum. But elsewhere in his speech he also spoke of how education was always right at the heart of the Labour movement's beliefs. Labour's pioneers fought long and hard for education to be free of charge, for comprehensive education and for lifelong learning. Education has a vital part to play in freeing human beings from the shackles of ignorance which locked people in poverty. He also reminded us of RH Tawney's phrase: 'What wise parents would wish for their children, so the state must wish for all children.' This country's comprehensive school system — despite all its ups and downs — has a thirty-year record of overall success.

But it is now under fundamental attack by the leaders of the Tory Party in a way not seen for many years. It is no good trying to pretend that every school has succeeded. They have not. It is no good pretending they couldn't do better. They could. But the task of government is to set a framework which encourages a system to meet the needs of all our children, not the chosen few.

A Labour government in which I serve will sing the praises of good comprehensive schools to the rafters. And we won't blame schools for the failings of government. But we will not flinch from criticizing those that let down our children. And we won't stop working until we have raised their standards to give our children the high quality education they deserve. That is Labour's crusade. And crusade is not too strong a word for the passion that we feel for education. For we have a fundamental belief in comprehensive education, and we want to cater for the needs of every single pupil not just the 20 per cent or so who used to be creamed off at the age of 11.

It is worth remembering that Mrs Thatcher presided over the conversion of hundreds of grammar schools into comprehensive schools. Kenneth Baker was recently quoted as saying that he had pointed out to Margaret that she had signed the closure of more grammar schools than any other Minister. He added: 'She glared at me and changed the subject'.

Now John Major wants to put the clock back decades and restore the 11+. The man who said he wanted to see a country at ease with itself, now wants to see a return to a system which divided the nation. He wants to divide our children and future generations into the 11+ successes and the 11+ failures. In contrast, I believe — and the Labour Party believes — that a genuine comprehensive system, with a full ability range of students, provides the best chance of developing the talents and catering for the interests of *all* the pupils.

A system which is based on deliberate rejection of 80 per cent of children cannot succeed for them or for the nation. And if we cannot get our children to get on in our schools, what chance is there of getting them as adults to get along in society as a whole? And let's not forget that support for comprehensive education is the majority view in this country. It is the view of Labour, of the Liberal Democrats, of the nationalist parties and, actually, of many Conservatives, up and down the country. But most important of all, the majority of parents of this country do not want to see their children divided at the age of 11.

But simply sticking up a 'comprehensive school' notice outside the gate did not solve all the problems in our schools, still less all the problems in our society. Far from it. It did not break all the barriers overnight for students who found learning difficult. Indeed, I believe that in the push for comprehensives politicians tended to give priority to the creation of large buildings rather than the teaching under the roof. The essential conditions for comprehensive education were left to the local education authorities and the headteachers. Obviously there was a variety in the end results — some were good, some were bad.

There was a huge variety within a supposedly common comprehensive system. No two comprehensives are exactly alike. My two sons had a comprehensive education in Hull with a three-tier system with three schools at ages 5–9, 9–13 and 13–16 designed to avoid the 11+ exam. Other authorities had 11–16-year-olds together. I was amazed there was no core curriculum in the feeder schools. To maintain a balanced intake at the schools, they bussed children around the city, a practice which has now ended. Some schools had streaming. Some had setting. Some had neither.

Securing a successful comprehensive system in practice depends on the full backing of local authorities and school governing bodies, parents and communities; a headteacher and senior staff who are capable of operating the system; and close cooperation among the staff — with weekly meetings if need be — to ensure our children are getting the best out of the system. Every school will partly stand or fall on the strength and quality of its headteacher, its teaching staff, and the resources it has. Each will have their own strengths and specialities. That is why Tony Blair has specifically endorsed the need to respect the professional judgment of teachers. And he has reaffirmed that we will not attempt to impose one rigid pattern on 25,000 schools. A comprehensive system is not about uniformity. A comprehensive system recognizes that children are different, their needs are different and over time their interests, abilities and needs can change. Like flowers, some bloom early, some bloom late.

Tony Blair has made it clear that education will be the passion of his government. I applaud his call to build an education and training system which provides real learning opportunities, for young and old, irrespective of birth or privilege — giving them the chance to achieve their true potential.

In contrast, John Major is now trying to impose his plan to raise the number of grammar schools from 153 to one in every town in England and Wales. If this happened, it would step up the pace of undermining the very fabric of the comprehensive education system. Let me repeat what ought to be obvious — even to John Major. You cannot have widespread selection and non-selection side by side. If we have a grammar school in every town, we cannot have genuine comprehensive schools as well.

While the Tory Party wants to see success for a minority only, it is a fundamental principle that we should challenge the notion that success is only possible for the minority. Underneath a national culture of elitism and snobbery, people have always been keen to learn when they are given the chance. That is how the Labour movement started — in study groups and meetings, and then in the WEA and in union branches. We achieved secondary education for all, we set up the Open University. Today, there are one million people in higher education and three million further education students. And when ordinary workers are given the chance to learn, for example by the Ford EDAP scheme or the Unipart University, and they snap it up.

It is the Tory lie to say that the British don't want to learn or cannot learn. It's our mission to help show what people can achieve. Labour's value is to include people, to do our very best for all, no matter who they are, where they come from or how rich or poor they are. We are the party of the many, not the few. Compare that to the Tories whose aim is to perpetuate an elite while excluding the majority. The return to the 11+ would be a mistake of monumental proportions. There is absolutely no sound argument whatsoever to bring it back. Let me tell you about my experience and the lessons I learned under the old grammar school-secondary modern system.

The first lesson I learned was this. I went to a secondary modern school. That meant I was an 11+ failure in the eyes of that system, a scarring experience that affected about 80 per cent of my generation who were designated as failures. It split me from my friends — it even split from a girl I carried a torch for. She passed. I failed. She went to grammar school. I sent her a love letter telling her how I'd miss her — she sent it back with my spelling mistakes corrected. I was promised a bike by my father if I passed. I didn't get it. Instead I was bussed out of my home town of Chester every school day to my secondary modern in Ellesmere Port fifteen miles away.

But that sense of failure didn't stop when I was 11. People like me were expected to be pigeonholed, branded — a ceiling put on our ambitions. It was like that old sketch with John Cleese and the Two Ronnies back in the 1960s. Little Ronnie Corbett in his cloth cap looking up to the other two and saying 'I'm working class — I know my place'. Well you know where I stand on that now, admitting to living a middle class lifestyle. Just don't tell my dad! I don't want another debate with him and John Humphries on the *Today* programme. Back then your future was mapped out for you — your career ring-fenced — because you failed an exam. Failing the 11+ helped to build an identity based on discrimination. Humiliation was always part of the old system. Yes it hurt. No, it didn't work.

Some people thought I had reached my educational peak by the time I was a waiter on the liners. 'Another gin and tonic, Giovanni', as one Tory MP bawled at me while I was speaking in the House. But in my twenties I arrived at Ruskin College — without an 'O' or 'A' level to my name. Mind you, I had organized a couple of strikes — an acceptable qualification for Ruskin. For, as Walter Vrooman, one this College's founders said: 'The purpose of Ruskin is to take windbags out of the movement, open them up, fill them full of sand and send them back'.

But in spite of studying hard, getting a degree at the University of Hull and twenty-six years service as an MP, I am still seen by some to be inadequate. Can you believe that forty years on from that corrected love letter I still get pulled up by the likes of Matthew Parris for bad grammar? As he said about my 'One Member One Vote' speech 'John Prescott went twelve rounds with the English language and left it slumped and bleeding over the ropes'. And by some I wasn't seen as leadership material because they thought I might fluff my lines at the despatch box.

I learned that the mark of your education marked you for life as either a first class or second class citizen. Grammar schools provided the classics like *Julius*

Caesar for their pupils. At secondary modern, I had to make do with *Dick Barton*. Grammar school kids had French and Latin — we just got basic English. This taught me that the privileged got knowledge and knowledge was a privilege.

But, as I said, I was lucky — Ruskin was my second chance. I still look back on that time with fond memories. It was a wonderful and exciting experience. For the first time in my life, people were open to my ideas. The teachers wanted to help, setting high standards and expectations. One lesson I learned from my time here is that you need self-belief and confidence to handle the great pressure of getting back into education. I remember my first day at Ruskin, we were given a 2000 word essay to complete by Friday. The title of the essay was 'Power corrupts. Absolute power corrupts absolutely. Discuss.' I didn't have a clue. Though some might say I have a better understanding now thanks to the people who sit on the benches opposite me at work. But at that stage of my life I can tell you a 2000 word essay was a very daunting prospect. There was one chap there in my class, a lorry driver. He seemed to be so confident. But when he was given that essay, he went back to his room, packed his bags and we never saw him again. He was scared. He felt he wasn't up to it. He lacked the confidence.

It was then that I realized that I wasn't the only one terrified about failing. I started talking to other people on my course and they felt the same as me. But quitting wasn't the answer. It was the same when I went to the University of Hull where I studied economic statistics as part of my degree course. I didn't know anything about logarithms. I spent a week in the library trying to understand the theory of logarithms. At last someone explained that you didn't really need the theory, just how to look them up in a book of tables. I learned that you should not be afraid to ask questions to the answers you seek. That's an essential requirement for the second chance student. If lifelong learning is to be a reality, mature students require the building blocks. To recognize that it's often not the concept that frustrates but the explanation. The language of books, lectures and grammar can become a barrier to educational advancement while intelligence and motivation are ignored. Learning is a two-way process. The student needs to be motivated and determined. But the teacher needs to explain things clearly, especially in our information rich society, where knowledge is the greatest asset a person can have.

This highly personal view comes from my experience of the 'secondary modern / grammar school' system which this government wants to return to. I believe the products of our comprehensive education system since the 1970s prove that students now have a better education and provision for lifelong learning. And let's not think that education ends when you leave school. The benefits of a learning society are being enjoyed by a narrow segment of the population. As the recent Competitiveness White Paper confirms, Britain lags behind our major competitors in skills and qualifications. And after seventeen years of Conservative government we are still slipping back. A recent report by the National Institute of Adult Continuing Education and Gallup stated: 'The UK is increasingly two nations — one convinced of the value of learning, participating regularly and planning to do more; the other so far choosing not to join the learning society.'

More people are taking part in post-16 education. But it is only among the under-25s that participation has increased significantly — and that's a good deal to do with lack of job opportunities. It all depends where you live, what skills you already have, what size of firm you work for, how secure your job is, and most of all what qualifications you left school with. In all these factors, it is a case of 'to those who hath, so shall they receive'. I don't need to remind a Ruskin audience about these facts. On average, the lower your qualifications, the higher your chance of being unemployed and the lower your wages. But the lack of lifelong learning is not only a barrier to individual development, it is not only a tragic waste of people's talents, it is a fundamental handicap to our country being economically competitive. That is recognized in the White Paper and is indeed becoming the consensus view in industry. Lifelong learning can help bring personal development, can help with job security and promotion, and is essential to our national economic success.

Motivation, the belief in the worth of every individual and the need to develop our talents are central to my beliefs and I hope to yours. That means we have to break down barriers not reinforce them. We need to reject a system which brands whole sections of the community with a sense of failure and an inability to learn more.

Under the Tories, we now see signs of the slippery return to the grammar school system in many areas under the guise of parental choice. With the advent of crude league tables and the proposal of increasing selection, this government is hellbent on bringing back the grammar and secondary modern system, not only through resurrecting separate schools, but this time by having both under the same roof. That means 20 per cent will excel, while 80 per cent will be classed as the old secondary modern failures. Success and failure decided by what stream you're in.

This is not the way to educate our children. If we exclude 80 per cent of the three-quarters of a million 11-year-olds — then every year we will be telling 600,000 children 'you are failures'. That would make six million failures every decade. Just think of the utter folly of having six million people in their teens, their twenties, their thirties, their forties, all believing they're stupid. All because their card was stamped at the age of 11. That's why I'm passionate about education and that's why I fervently want our comprehensive schools to work so we can take on the best in the world in an expanding global market. That's why I want an education and training system which provides genuine learning opportunities for all our people — young or old — throughout their lives. That's why I believe that people should be able to rise by their talents, not by their birth or the advantage of privilege. The government must challenge the deeply embedded and destructive British cultural attitude which holds that success, by definition, is only possible for a minority. We believe in the comprehensive school system.

The choice for the future is clear: we can go back to the old system of selection at age 11, with all the damage that did OR we can accept the principle of all-in schooling, the comprehensive principle, but modernize it. We believe by following the second course, we can raise standards in all comprehensive schools to that which the best grammar schools used to provide, and which the best comprehensives now provide. The key lesson is that we should never ration excellence. If excellence is rationed to the few, the talent of the many will eventually inevitably be excluded from the opportunity for excellence.

Labour thoroughly condemns the Tory blue-tinted glasses that view our school-children as commodities, parents as simply consumers, schools as rival businesses and teachers as technicians. A first-class education for all is not just a political slogan. It is a crusade and a crusade that must be won.

Index

teachers 137–46, 150, 153–5, 168
technology colleges 6, 61
Thomas, L. 103, 107
Thomas, H. 44, 53
Thomson, G. 14, 27
Thrupp, M. 71, 72, 82
Tomlinson, S. 7, 103, 109–18
Trade Union Congress 14
Trainor, D. 102
Turner, B. 188, 196
TVEI 58–9, 88, 105, 111

University of the First Age 180–1

Vernon, P.E. 2, 9, 23, 27, 54, 65

Wales 14, 17, 36
Walford, G. 1–9, 54–65
Wallis, J. 50, 53
Walsall 13
Waltham Forrest 192
Warnock Report 33
Waslander, S. 71, 72, 82

Webb, B. 13
Wells, H.G. 150
West Bridgford 34, 35
West Riding 13
White, P. 73, 82
Whitty, G. 46, 52, 58, 59, 65
Wikeley, F. 75, 82
Wilcox, B. 121, 136
Wilkinson, H. 102, 108
Williams, S. 178
Williams, W. 42, 52
Willms, J.D. 4, 8, 72, 81, 123, 136
Wilson, H. 173
Wiltshire 31
Windermere 13
Woodhead, C. 46
word-processing 164–6
Wragg, E.C. 7, 137–46

Yates, A. 1, 9, 22, 23, 27, 54, 65
Yeatman, A. 187, 196
Young, M. 105, 107, 116, 118
Young, I. 187, 190, 196